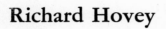

Richard Hovey

RICHARD HOVEY

Richard Hovey

Man & Craftsman

Allan Houston Macdonald

DUKE UNIVERSITY PRESS
1957

Cambridge University Press, London N. W. 1, England
Library of Congress Catalogue Card Number 57-7647

Printed in the United States of America
by the Seeman Printery, Inc., Durham, N. C.

This book is for Betty

Preface

Allan Macdonald was born May 20, 1901, in Lawrence, Massachusetts. He studied at Phillips (Andover) Academy, Princeton, and Harvard, afterwards joining the Department of English at Dartmouth, where he taught for twenty-five years. He died in Hanover, New Hampshire, November 8, 1951.

Both as a man and teacher he was erudite, excellent in workmanship, memorable in exposition. He aroused in his students allegiance to the values he expounded because in his own person he exemplified them so fully. Chief among his writings is this life of Richard Hovey, the manuscript of which was completed at the time of his death. Both for the soundness of its scholarship and its imaginative insight into a radiant personality who lived in a seminal period of American culture, it has seemed to Dartmouth College and the Duke University Press that its publication was a duty at once obvious and compelling.

Contents

Introduction

Richard Hovey's gravestone bears only his name and the dates 1864-1900, epitaph enough for an American poet. To be born as the Civil War brought in the new America and to die at the turn of the century was to live thirty-five years within a culture which gave itself to material progress. Some eras are rich with an energy which creates artistic forms; others put their energy into material forms, into the shapes of invention, commerce, transportation, finance. Such was the second half of the nineteenth century. Because those few writers who came to maturity within the period have received little attention, we have not sufficiently studied the dilemma of the serious artist within that alien environment. The great figures who lived on had taken form in an earlier day. Those who were to become famous after 1912 lived in an obscurity from which they were only later to emerge. No great creative imagination shaped new symbols and images, and those young writers who are best remembered—Norris, Crane, London— adapted to prose the naturalistic vision of the time.

As a subject of inquiry Richard Hovey has the fateful advantage of being one who wanted passionately to be a writer and an American in the great tradition and whose life was entirely bounded by the years between the Civil War and the new century. He rejected the one viable attitude of his period as below the level proper to art. As an undergraduate of twenty he declared that the poet is "the anointed priest of God," and he never changed that Whitmanesque faith. He was a high-minded and intensely dedicated man who explored and judged the art and life of his time and sought to preserve the vital virtues of the past by a radical attack on the present. As such he gives an understanding of the young artist in America broader than others afford, for he met life and art on a wide front and sought what he thought highest.

If this study seems too concerned with Hovey's intent and not sufficiently detailed in analysis of particular works, it is because the mind of its subject saw more perceptively than it could create artistically. This is, of course, a common fault, but few men brought to that particular time the high endowment, the versatility, and the earnest purpose of Hovey. Because we know the American poetry of the "twilight interval," as Stedman called it, only in anthologies, such a statement will seem indefensible. Even where Hovey is most remembered, at Dartmouth College or in literary histories, the impression of him is almost totally incorrect. The constantly emphasized good-fellowship was real but concentrated in time and limited in company; and the virility and intensified Americanism which are patronizingly smiled at were needed by a nerveless and derivative poetry.

Because the *Songs from Vagabondia* volumes and the college songs have been his most widely popular work, his function as an intermediary between Europe and America has been forgotten, although his own time was well aware of it. He knew many of the leading writers of Europe and as translater of Maeterlinck and publicist for the Symbolists he was one of the important few who made our literature aware of subtler desires and devices. This attention to a highly developed art sought balance with his inheritance of the strenuous social and ethical genius of this country. It was his purpose, therefore, to combine a healthy, social American poetry with a skilled, self-conscious art. He tried to follow beauty without denying reality and to hold life to ethical account without dealing in the ugly and inhuman, and so create a harmony between beauty and truth, the opposing forces in the literature of the time. It was his faith that man might attain a synthesis which would accept the facts and ideas of the modern world and yet see them transformed by art into beauty and joy As an artist he failed that ambitious intent. He tried too hard to carry into the future the full tradition of the past and to make the poet lawgiver, priest, and seer. It was too ultimate a task for the poet, or for any modern man. Such an overextension of the Romantic definition of the poet led him too frequently into abstraction and vague idealization instead of into poetic vision. At the same time that insistent definition of the poet's function led a courageous and gifted man to an intense activity which measures his time in many ways.

Hovey's early death startled men into recognition of his work and personality. Notices appeared in a hundred papers from San Francisco to Portland, and the large papers in New York, Boston, and Chicago gave two or three columns to his work. Soon tributes and estimates by Roberts, Page, Carman and others appeared in the literary journals, and his poems were printed at a remuneration he never received in his lifetime. The praise was high, even to declaration that he was "the greatest poetic consciousness that this country has produced," or Maeterlinck's statement that he was one of the two or three great poets of his day.

Literary judgments change with time, and the rise of a new and vivid poetry about 1912 blurred the memory of all poets of preceding decades. Man's judgment of his fellows, however, is less the servant of time, and the sincerity of the affection and the respect for the man stand unchallenged. However high the estimate of the poet's achievement within his brief life, the faith in his human greatness was still higher.

My thanks are due to Miss Mildred Saunders, Miss Hazel Joslyn, Mr. George Liscomb, Mr. Kenneth M. Kingsbury, men of the class of 1885 at Dartmouth, and others. I wish particularly to thank Hovey's cousin, Mrs. Agnes Cook Gale, for her constant interest and generosity, and Mr. Harold G. Rugg, without whose constant and painstaking efforts to collect Hovey material for the Library of Dartmouth College no study would have been possible.   A. H. M.

Abbreviations used herein: *DAM—Dartmouth Alumni Monthly;* DCA—Archives, in the possession of Baker Library, Dartmouth College.

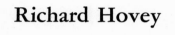

Richard Hovey

CHAPTER I

A Son of New England

> They have the still North in their souls,
> The hill-winds in their breath;
> And the granite of New Hampshire
> Is made part of them till death.
> HOVEY, "Men of Dartmouth," 1894.

In the fall of 1881 Richard Hovey rode up the steep raw-banked hill from the station and entered the class and the college he would always love. The coach reached the "gilded corner" of the common, where town and college merged, and he could look around on his new home. On the short southern side of the rectangle were the hotel and the gymnasium; then, stretching north, the simple white buildings of the old college, Reed, Thornton, Dartmouth, and Wentworth, already too precious with sentiment to be ripped down and replaced with ugly stylish buildings, as the rest of those squaring the green would be. Then, returning chastely toward him, came the pleasant row of homes broken only by the simple dignity of the church raised in 1795. Here was New England, a classic clarity of line domesticated in a northern land and softened by the villagers' love of wine-glass elms.

This was an unhappy time in Dartmouth history. Plot and counterplot, suspicion and resentment poisoned the college. President Bartlett presided over a general faculty of thirty-one, which included the faculties of the allied schools of Engineering, Medicine, and Agriculture, and men smarted under his sharp tongue and arrogant manner. Half of these men and forty-four of the sixty-one members of the class of 1881 had asked that the president be removed. All the previous spring and on into the summer investigations and trials had been in session. Though the squabble was declared closed, the bitter distrust still fermented. The college was not growing. Far off in the hills it could not compete unless, as a contributor to *The Dartmouth* said, "it can offer inducements other than the dry bones of a somewhat superannuated reputation." It was not enough to have produced Webster and Choate, nor to call "the bitter hostility to progress" conservatism.

Hovey was one of the youngest of the forty-eight boys of his class, three years younger than the average. The smallness of the class and their common cause against the sophomores quickly united them. As always those who most lacked protective coloring felt the heaviest hazing hand, and Hovey quickly aroused notice. He wrote a poem, or poems, against the sophomores which classmates had printed secretly and, after stealing into the chapel during the night, slipped into the hymnbooks of the sophomores. So when he was initiated into Kappa Sigma Epsilon, one of the two freshman literary societies of which he was later to be secretary, editor, and president, Hovey and his classmate Bryant were scapegoats for the rest of the eighteen. For a quarter of an hour he was walked blindfolded in "Bedbug Alley," the upper corridor of Dartmouth Hall, before he was presented to the sophomores and announced as "Hovey! Hovey the Poet!" The hazers hooted and yelled, tossed him in a blanket, set him upon a cake of ice, branded him with nitrate of silver, poured water down his pants, made him recite an extemporary poem, and chose him to reply to the "welcome" of the retiring sophomore president. Hovey enjoyed it, he told his mother, and surely it was sweet to hear even taunting voices calling "Hovey! Hovey the Poet!"

In this same month of October he was pledged to Psi Upsilon fraternity, into which he was initiated in the spring. The accident that Patterson happened to know Hovey was fortunate, not only for the local Zeta chapter, but also for the national organization. Hovey had more than an undergraduate loyalty. He held masculine friendship in an Elizabethan esteem. For him the fraternity, like class and college, was a symbol of love of comrades. That word "comrades" comes into his work again and again. No one but Whitman has ever used the word so often, and not even he experienced the

actuality as Hovey did. In his mind the idea reached back
to the Renaissance and forward into the new democracy Whitman hoped for, but Hovey exulted chiefly in the fact of comradeship in the vivid present.

In the room on Faculty Row which everyone admired and
which had everything civilization offered from heliotypes to
feather duster, but into which it was hard to steal without wak-
ing Professor Hazen's midnight sleep, Hovey wrestled with
the algebra which gave him colic whenever he looked at it.
He wrote to his mother that "Quinby's Algebra is the most
concentrated essence of pure, concatenated, complex, double-
back action patent oath-compelling cussedness I ever struck."[1]
The history and Greek and Latin were better, though at the
close of the first term Johnny Lord gave the boys so long an
examination in Latin that they serenaded him with horns.
Imperturbable, he came out onto the porch and made a speech
and gave them taffy, until they sang "Bye, Baby-bye O!" to
express their gratification. It was a rehearsal of a more serious
horning.

Gradually the winter cold crept in. After the rich coloring
of October came the clean intellectual austerity of November.
It was the first time Hovey had known the northern winter
with its shrewd cold, the blue shadows in the softly folded
fields, and Orion stepping into the heavens from the shoulder
of Velvet Rocks. Living in the way they did, Dartmouth men
dreaded the winter, and he was himself slow to catch the
symbolism of the emerging Dartmouth which he was first to
fashion. When "the great, great white cold" stalked down
from the hills and breath was a white plume and the dry snow
squeaked beneath cowhide boots, he shivered and was glad to
spend an extended vacation in Washington. The cold belonged
with the granite and the pines and hemlocks. It belonged to
Dartmouth, but no one had yet netted it in words, and he had to
be away from New Hampshire before he could make it serve
the uses of imagination.[2]

[1] Hovey, Oct. 9, 1881.
[2] Cf. this letter to his mother (Nov. 19, 1884): "Snow is on the ground
now; no fields and hills and brooks to stray and rest and gladden in,—in such
a situation, you see there is no relief."

When the winter was at its height, the class left for the traditional freshman supper. The sophomores kidnapped Arthur Lucas, one of the '85 men, locked him in a White River Junction hotel room, and sent his trousers to the tailor's, but the others boarded their special car for Montreal when the midnight air was already thick and hushed with the snow which piled up a foot by the next day. The unheated train burrowed its slow way, but station waits were so long the boys invaded dances and sampled the local inns' prescription against cold. After twelve hours without food and nineteen hours after leaving, they reached Montreal, stuffed themselves with food and wine, and lustily sang Hovey's class song to the tune of "It Was My Last Cigar." Next day the curious visited Notre Dame or less holy places and by evening were back in the car singing and cheering and making forays against the surrounding country in that mania for souvenir-collecting which has always marked conquerors and college students.

At home on that Sunday the Washington *Post* had insulted a Wilde it had not seen or heard by printing his face beneath that of a "*Wild* Man of Borneo" to whom, it asserted, he was undoubtedly akin. The next night a bored and polite audience gave him as dull a reception as he would receive as he toured the country. But his short-time disciple was frolicking with a hearty vulgarity which would have brought a condescending smile to Wilde's heavy face.

Whether or not it is true that Hovey had disturbed the morning sleep of the Professor of Theoretical and Applied Mechanics by his late homecomings, in the second term he moved into a more congenial fellowship of wit and intellect. To balance the popular name of their district, "Rum Hollow," his group hung a sign above the door which proclaimed the house "Saints' Rest." He wrote home that "the fellows about me are bright literary men of the class and when we are together it is truly a feast of—well, not exactly wisdom, but say, *culture,* and a flow of the soul."[3]

Hovey was always writing. Words and verses bubbled

[3] Hovey, April 23, 1882.

from him in a stream, good and bad, serious and gay. First official notice came from *The Dartmouth,* to which his class had already elected him in the minor capacity of reporter. The board had declared its intention of enlarging itself by the addition of contributing members of the lower classes. From editorial comment one judges that Hovey alone of his class turned in material. His first signed poem was "The Class of '85."[4] This is not a work of art, obviously, but its subject has kept it alive while better verses have died. In the issue of February 3, 1882, his position as associate editor was announced, and henceforth his name was carried on the masthead. One supposes that he contributed frequently, but no contributions were signed by him during this year, and the style of the verse is so orthodox to a college publication that one dares not guess at authorship.

After vacation the boys returned to the sucking mud and the boom of ice breaking in the river. Spring came as unbelievably as it always does in Hanover. Without warning maples were red with buds and the stark elms suddenly soft with young leaves. Hovey liked his work better, finding Horace beautiful, Plato's *Symposium* charming, and surveying at least interesting. But under the laziness of spring the college made its annual attack on the marking system. The editors of *The Dartmouth* made their perennial suggestion that "all the benefits of college life do not come from a study of textbooks," and noticed that "the senior class was cutting recitations recklessly." So the days of freshman year passed and with summer the boys went home with what Hovey called in his sophomore class history "serene and unconscious self conceit," since they were men now, no longer pea-green freshmen.

"Home" for Hovey, that summer of 1882, was Nantucket, the island of his mother's birth. "Very little," he said, "happened that was worth recording," but as he wandered the barren moors and acquired a summer tan along the margins of the sea, he had ample leisure to reflect upon his forebears, both in Old and New England. His blood was in fact pure Yankee,

---

[4] *The Dartmouth,* Dec. 9, 1881.

going back in every branch to the early settlers of the seventeenth century. Among them could be mentioned John Coggeshall, first Governor of Providence Plantation; Peter Folger of Nantucket, Franklin's grandfather; Isaac Allerton, *Mayflower* passenger and first Lieutenant Governor of Plymouth Colony; and Robert Cushman, his son-in-law, whose father hired the *Mayflower* for her trip. Including John Howland on his mother's side, five of his ancestors had been passengers on the *Mayflower*. Behind these were shadowy figures, Welsh kings and Saxon knights such as Gamelbar de Spofford, whom Bliss Carman celebrated in "The War-Song of Gamelbar."

He was of the eighth generation of the Hovey family to be born in America.[5] Daniel Hovey, whose Dutch forebears had migrated to England in the sixteenth century, came to Ipswich in 1635. His father, Richard, was a prosperous glover in Waltham Abbey, Essex County, but the seventeen-year-old boy adventured to the new world and married Abigail Andrews, daughter of the master and owner of the famous *Angel Gabriel*, built for Raleigh, which was wrecked at Pemaquid on her passage over. With Abigail he founded a large and vigorous line.

His son James, one of the first settlers of Brookfield, Massachusetts, was killed by the Indians in his twenty-fifth year, before he had acquired either goods or children in large quantity. Richard Hovey spoke of the descendants of James as the vagabond branch of the family: "eight generations of pioneers, each one settling in a new country." That restlessness drove them from Brookfield to Mansfield, Connecticut; and from there as early settlers to the newly granted township of Norwich, Vermont; and then, again as early settlers, a few miles north to the township of Thetford. There in 1827, in a large unpainted house still standing, was born the poet's father, Charles Edward Hovey, one of a family of eleven children.

[5] Daniel Hovey Association, *The Hovey Book, Describing the English Ancestry and American Descendants of Daniel Hovey of Ipswich, Massachusetts* ... (Haverhill, Mass.: L. R. Hovey, 1913).

The family was typical of Vermont. With high purpose but little money the sons worked their way to college. As a boy of fifteen Charles Edward taught school in a little hill community where many of his pupils were older than he. Later he cut logs, teamed, built barns, and was a blacksmith before he entered Dartmouth as an experienced man of twenty-one, to be graduated in 1852.

To one who had known him in his younger days in Vermont and New Hampshire, this same Charles Hovey would have been nearly unrecognizable when he came back from the war to his adopted town of Normal, Illinois, in the spring of 1863. He had been shot through both his arms, had lost considerable weight, and was shivering from a fever contracted in the swampy morass of Chickasaw Bayou, north of Vicksburg. He had enlisted as a private and was now Major-General-by Brevet for "gallant and meritorious conduct in battle." But he was too ill to rejoin the brigade he had commanded under Sherman, part of that famous "Brain Regiment" recruited from his students and teachers and other intellectuals who joined them. He had to decide whether to go on with the career which had carried him in a half dozen years from Dartmouth student to President of the State Normal University of Illinois or to pursue the study of law. All through the years of his Vermont boyhood he had hoped to be a lawyer, but though he had taught school throughout his college career, the payments had no more than covered his meager needs and left no surplus for further study. Now he took the chance and went to Washington to establish himself in that confused, war-swollen city.[6]

His wife stayed on in their high-studded, stylish house in Normal. It had been built when at last his unrelenting struggle to furnish a better education for children had resulted in the Normal University.[7] She had at first followed him to

[6] For further information, see Allan Macdonald, "Charles Edward Hovey," *Dartmouth Alumni Magazine* (hereinafter referred to as *DAM*), XXXIX (April, 1947), 21.

[7] This house is now numbered 202 West Mulberry Avenue. In front of it is a monument to the memory of Richard Hovey erected in 1931 by the Alumni Association of Psi Upsilon Fraternity.

camp in soldier's cap and cloak until ordered home by the authorities. Back in Normal, she had waved from the window to troops going South on the Illinois Central Railway, had cared for the sick and for escaped slaves. Her extraordinary energy took her into all sorts of activity. She nursed a fleeing colored woman through smallpox, but with equal energy she danced with Lincoln's young secretary John Hay when "Dixie" was first played in Normal. Her first child had died, but Alfred was now four and she was heavy with another child.

Richard Hovey was born on the morning of May 4, 1864, in the sunny southwest bedroom. Unlike Alfred, who ceased to look like an angel only to look like a Greek divinity, Richard was dark and olive-skinned, with rich warm eyes. It was ironic that he who was to be so colorful and legendary a figure should be born in a town called Normal. But in the baby's first summer, they left Illinois for good, and Mrs. Hovey went to North Andover, Massachusetts, to live with her parents until a home was ready in the capital. Though she had been born in Nantucket, where her father was teaching in the South School, the Spoffords had always lived in Essex County, and her grandfather's house was a second home.[8] There she remained with the children for two and a half years, until her husband's law practice was sufficient to support them.

The war boom had pushed Washington into fast growth. It was no longer quite as the French minister, de Bacourt, had described it: "neither a city, nor a village, nor the country; it is a building-yard placed in a desolate spot, wherein living is unbearable." Still, the civilized looked upon it with suspicion. It was for Henry Adams "the dullest place in Christian lands."

Such a thin veil of varnish over so very rough a material one can see nowhere else. From my room I can as I sit see for miles down the Potomac, and I know of no other capital in the world which stands on so wide and splendid a river. But the people and the mode of life

[8] Jeremiah Spofford, *Spofford, Spafford—A Genealogical Record* (Boston: A. Mudge and Son, 1888).

are enough to take your hair off . . . . Alas! I fear I shall never eat another good dinner.[9]

Yet Adams admitted that it was an easy society and that no one seemed to miss the usual comforts of civilization. When the public works program under Boss Shepherd began to tear up the city in 1867, the year the Hoveys established residence there, many must have wished the casual ways back. Graft, jobbery, and waste were everywhere. The recklessness with public funds was only an image of the national spree under Grant. The city became the hunting ground of the new businessmen who were prepared to dominate the ethical collapse of the war. The Gilded Age was on, but by that recklessness in public expenditure on streets, parks, trees, and public works a modern city began to appear. In his annual message to Congress in 1873 Grant could say: "Washington is rapidly assuming the appearance of a capital of which the Nation may be proud."[10]

All this, though it was shaping his environment, the oval-faced boy with dark eyes and well-defined lips could not as yet understand. Life came filtered through his family and through books. His health was precarious, so that for a time his eager mind outran his physical development. Even before he could fashion words into phrases, he could spell. Soon he was reading beyond the usual level of his years. He read so eagerly that he was impatient with the slowness of study. One of his later friends remembered that he first heard of him when General Hovey, a member of the school board, seized upon a book he was surreptitiously reading in class and reproved him by saying: "You remind me of my younger son Richard, who is always reading a storybook when he should be studying."[11] Nevertheless, his parents considered him better off at home than at school, and his mother remained his sole

[9] W. C. Ford, ed., *The Letters of Henry Adams* (Boston and New York: Houghton Mifflin, 1930).

[10] W. B. Bryan, *A History of the National Capital* (2 vols.; New York: Macmillan, 1916), II, 621.

[11] Walter B. Patterson, "Reminiscences of Richard Hovey," *Dartmouth Magazine*, XXIV (May, 1910), 223.

teacher. Indeed, he had no formal schooling, except in the two years before college. His father was too busy to give him attention during the daylight hours, and used to say to his wife: "If the boys ever amount to anything, you should have all the credit, for your consecration to them has been complete." "Consecration" was not too strong a word, for Mrs. Hovey, so far as one can discern, never counted cost to herself through the years of her son's life. From beginning to end she was the quiet heroine of his story, but with wisdom and with faith in individual freedom she avoided all that might have been maudlin and repressive. From her he unconsciously learned his high regard for woman, but he learned also an honesty and maturity which did not hesitate to hurt her if the cause was good.

In summer the mother and children visited her parents. The North Parish of Andover is rich in history. Here Anne Bradstreet, America's first poet, had lived, witchcraft had flourished, and famous fighters had gone forth to every war. About a mile and a quarter from the wide and unspoiled common by way of the Great Pond Road one came to the Spofford place, a handsome house set in tall locusts.[12] Around it were pastures, brushy woods, and old roads. The pasture before it dropped toward the clear pond where fishing and swimming were good. Hovey's grandfather had always been concerned with the young in Nantucket and in the local Franklin Academy, the first incorporated academy in the state to which girls were admitted. His grandmother had grown up in the great day of Nantucket whaling and knew stirring stories. The Quaker neighbors of her girlhood had objected that "she showed the whites of her eyes too much," but that spunkiness gave her character. A boy could not have asked for better hosts than this large devoted family living on its rolling acres.

Like most precocious boys, Hovey stammered in numbers long before he had anything to say. The result was a great

---

[12] The Spofford home burned about 1870. Part of the pasture is now incorporated in the North Andover Country Club and Mr. Russell Tyson of Chicago has transformed the wild land near the pond into a handsomely planted estate. A remodeled house stands on the site of the old home.

production of nonsense verse. Perhaps unfortunately his invocation was answered.

> Oh Heavenly Muse! Thy aid unto me bring
> Bestride thy Pegasus, and with velocity
> Fly to assist me in heroic verbosity!

On the flyleaf of an intended travesty of *The Swiss Family
Robinson* he listed such works as: "Othello, the Negro of
Washington," "William Tell, a Burlesque," "Hamlet or the
Dane from Dublin a fragment of a Burlesque," etc., etc. Such
unattractive sport with matters beyond his ken shows only
a flair for words and styles and a boy's discomfort before
greatness he cannot wholly grasp and so must belittle. Other
verses of a more serious sort began to take his time, but they
were either destroyed or later rewritten.

When he was about fifteen years old he turned eagerly
to natural science. By his frequent visits to the Smithsonian
Institution to look at the birds and insects and minerals exhibited on the ground floor he got to know many of the
scientists. Professor Henry and Dr. Coues took particular
interest in him, and fostered his decision to become a naturalist.
He made his collections and read elementary texts, but he also
read the nineteenth-century scientists and essayists. Though
he remained fascinated by the scientific exploration of the world,
he began at that early age the insistence that life is more than
scientific determinism can explain. A boy of fifteen is, of
course, no judge of such matters, but the indication of temperamental dissatisfaction was the childish sign of what became the man's conviction. Out of the double disillusion of
Byron's *Don Juan* and Tyndall's materialism he wrote such a
youthful protest as his "Address to an Atom by an uncom-
fortable conscious Automaton."

> If conscience be but chemic combination,
> And Love a mere molecular affinity,
> What boots all Life's superfluous botheration
> Of mad and painful dreams, that limn Divinity
> On fool-projected limbos? Life's a swindle
> If taken à la Tyndall.[13]

[13] MS, Archives, in the possession of Baker Library, Dartmouth College
(hereinafter referred to as DCA).

Though he refused such a swindle, his reading deepened his perception. He was trying to get his mind around the beauty of life. As he told his friend Loring Chase in a long piece of doggerel verse, he loved the hawk that swooped and the dove that received the blow, both the panther and the stricken deer. He was realizing that nature is a tomb and that he himself must sometime die to make room for another.[14] There is nothing extraordinary in this except that a boy of sixteen should be consciously striving to meet the problems of the age and that he should think of himself as "philosopher poet." However playfully he might speak, his ego saw him as naturalist, philosopher, and poet, one who must consider life in its broadest implications. It was at least a good start for an education.

Though his mother had begun his studies in all subjects, he now went to Dr. Hunt's School for more advanced instruction in Greek, Latin, and Mathematics. His father was worried at the undisciplined enthusiasms of his son, and told Dr. Hunt that he never stuck to anything. "Just as if I didn't always give up everything and go back to Natural History," Richard wrote to his brother.[15] Since he attended classes for only an hour or two a day and liked everything but mathematics, the schooling did not interfere with his reading and verse-making.

He had by now developed a violent hay fever which demanded that he go to the mountains in August and September. In the country around Bethlehem, New Hampshire, he found all the nature he needed as laboratory. From the top of Mount Washington he brought back a piece of rock which served his interests by doubling as a mineral specimen and as a subject of verse—"an impecunious poet's paper-weight." Such cold stone, however, hardly satisfied a young versifier

[14] MS copy of a letter to Loring A. Chase, March 7, 1880. DCA.

[15] Alfred, more extroverted and physically adventurous than Richard, moved out to Idaho Territory. Richard envied him the chance for scientific investigation in so uncivilized a place, and his brave display of Latin names shows that he had been reading up on the flora and fauna of the West. He was proud that his brother should drive a stage coach and fulfil the pioneering tradition of the family.

who had been reading Byron, and he found also a human subject for his curiosity. This lady, "quite a woman," as his
mother called her, was a rather sophisticated companion for a
sixteen-year-old boy. Indeed she led a college professor into
indiscretions which gave the rocking-chair observers excitement second only to Garfield's assassination. His mother
wisely kept quiet, and though the two were in correspondence
for some years nothing serious came from the summer flirtation.

He had intended to enter Dartmouth in the class of 1884,
but his weakness in mathematics suggested that another year of
study and maturity would be good. The great excitement of
that year was the publication of his first book. Richard brought
together seventeen of his poems and he and his friend N. B.
Smith printed them on a press in the law office of Smith's
father. Smith, some five years older than Hovey, must have
had experience in printing, for the booklet has no sign of the
amateur. The whole task of setting type, reading proof,
cutting and binding was done by the boys with complete secrecy.
Probably one hundred copies were printed. Only when the
book was copyrighted did he present his surprise to his family.
The celebration was somewhat damped by his father's cautious
warning that some day he might regret this permanent relic of
poetic apprenticeship. He was too young to see the point and
gave copies to his classmates at college. Later, as an established
writer, he could smile at the volume. As he wrote in a copy
which General Hovey had given to Laurens Maynard, his
publisher: "Who can be ashamed of having been a boy?"[16]

The poems show considerable skill in versifying for a lad
of from fourteen to sixteen, but they are otherwise without
character. The quality of the author is lost in the family
resemblance to all such young versifiers. Though Milton,
Byron, Shelley, and Poe are the most obvious models in his
mind, the verses are full of the poetic diction of the eighteenth
century. Occasionally, however, tricks of Romantic phrasing
seem well learned. The wind speaks of the lake thus:

[16] Quoted by Ernest Marchand, "Hovey's First Flight," *DAM*, XXXI (June,
1939), 15. Maynard's letter is owned by the Stanford University Library.

And when the night has fallen,
I sleep upon her breast,
For I weary of my burden
Of odors and must rest—
For with surfeit of sweet odors
My spirit is oppressed.

Explicit praise is given to Shelley, "a spirit beautiful and free," to whom the serious part of Hovey seems for some time closer than to any other poet. Shelley appealed to him both as lyricist and as seeker after visionary truth.

There is, in addition, a section of verses avowedly humorous. These come closer to actual happenings in the boy's life, but the humor is coy and polysyllabic.

Whatever his father's opinion of the little volume, it did the author no harm. The books were never put on sale, and the gift of one by the parents finally became a sign of admission to the number of those who gave faith and loyalty to him. In the ironic way of book-collecting, these are now many times more valuable than any of his other volumes.

After returning from Bethlehem late in the summer, he set out for Hanover with his friend Patterson. There had apparently been no discussion of a college other than Dartmouth. There remained the choice of fraternity, and Patterson sang the praise of Psi Upsilon. Even though his uncle, a trustee of the college with whom they stayed in Manchester, suggested the virtues of Alpha Delta Phi, Walter Patterson won Hovey's agreement to join his fraternity.[17] It was the luckiest stroke of chance Psi Upsilon ever enjoyed, for though members die, songs and poems live.

[17] Walter B. Patterson, "Reminiscences of Richard Hovey," *loc. cit.*

CHAPTER II

Pass the Pipes, Pass the Bowl

Here by the fire we defy the frost and storm,
Ha, ha! we are warm, and we have our
hearts' desire.
HOVEY, "Hanover Winter Song," 1898.

In his sophomore year Hovey became a legend. The scholar and poet had not yet grown dominant in him, and his energy flared in gay and reckless living. He was only eighteen, and he was already having his fling against the stolid aspects of middle-class culture. In the little country town of Hanover, he set out to shock the bourgeoisie with all the verve of a very youthful Gautier. In a day of manly hairiness, his hair was longer than that of others, and his carefully nurtured mustache more studiedly romantic. The boy went out of his way to cultivate the poetic, the reckless, the carelessly dandified, and the witty, according to his sense of European standards.

Richard Hovey's grand manner, his indifference to social conventions in dress and success, his sometimes amusing affectation of such cavalier prerogatives as the wearing of a sword obscured his New England origins to those who knew only the middle-class Northerner. His pride in these origins, however, may somewhat explain his social democracy, his ethical earnestness, and his vigorous Americanism. He was never content to define the purposes of American life in the terms of that economic materialism which in his time had begun to overlay some of the governing principles and ideologies of the Revolution and the earlier national period. If he fought the Puritan misunderstanding of life it was only to reassert the meaning of the coat of arms of the English Hoveys, which shows a hand and pen above the words *"Hinc Orior."* Writing was his effort to make environment satisfy ethical principle. Whatever his ancestors had transmitted to the body of the young Hovey, his knowledge and memory of them was always to be a spur to social and individual action.

The men of his acquaintance began now to use Hovey as they would have used a figure of drama—to act as a substitute symbol for their own unrealized daydreams of brilliant egoism. They took vicarious delight in Hovey's stand, whether real or factitious, for he served to assault conventions they did not dare to attack in their own names. Then, by a subtle shift of ground, many joined the mass and pointed the finger of respectability at the rebel from custom. Such an ambivalent attitude was not sinister in its intention, but it helps to explain the building-up of the legendary image which shadows the real Hovey, sometimes obscuring him and sometimes giving him more solid outline.

So, in his sophomore year Hovey emerged as a figure. He lived now in the J. G. Currier house at the top of Nigger Hill. His landlord, who farmed and carried on a stage and livery business, raised the compact little Morgan horses which were the real aristocrats in the country north of Boston. The farm was on the edge of town, where the land dipped southward to Mink Brook and rose again far down the valley to the blue balance of Mount Ascutney. There was no better place round the area for one who loved this country, for he was close to the sharp pitch down to the Connecticut River, was within sight of a superbly modeled mountain, and close to the gullied fields which cup the winter shadows.

Hovey roomed with the group which he had joined the year before. As he boasted in his class history, none of this group belonged to such turbulent associations as the Y.M.C.A., nor had radical ideas about the prohibition of liquor, nor had been affected by recent faculty rulings on unexcused absences from class attendance. As his fellow-roomer and friend Hudson recorded in the "Class Chronicles," Hovey "returned with his mother and a bad attack of hay fever." His mother was unrecognized, and his friends called out, "Hullo, Old Man! Did you bring back any of the 'Old Stuff' with you?" (A receipted bill for $1.80 from C. B. Barrett and Co., Importers, suggests that he did.) Such references to drinking turn up frequently—as they are likely to do in college chronicles. One should not make much of them except to note that Hovey is the drinker most often celebrated. If a supposed quartet is singing its favorite selection "Drink Rum, Drink Rum with Me," Hovey is his class representative. He is referred to as "that constitutionally thirsty mortal." It is Hovey on whom the tag is pasted: "Great Bacchus is my deity." Yet as one picks up such bits, he detects less the smell of rum than that of youthful rebellion and warm-hearted companionship, and, most of all, the capacity to dramatize the moment.

Hovey took the role of gentleman too seriously ever to have been an ugly or an excessive drinker. Though no snob, he had the aristocrat's fastidious scorn for any vulgarity of action. In these early years among the Yankees he carried a Southern and cavalier manner as if his family had never tilled the stony slopes of Thetford, and high-spirited drinking was a part of that attitude. Unfortunately the undergraduate joking of his friends followed him with evil persistence.

One of the most famous Hovey stories, picked up by the newspapers and perpetuated at the time of his wedding, shows his capacity to enter into a fantastic situation with evident earnestness. Sam Hudson, his warm friend then and always, had criticized a character in one of his poems and Richard flared into defense. Through O'Brien he challenged Hudson to a duel to be fought at sunrise in the Norwich hills. According to the story Hudson and O'Brien planned to load the pistols with blanks. At the sound of Hovey's shot Hudson would fall, the attendant would make a swift examination, diagnose probable fatality, and before Hovey could gather his wits, they would rush him into a sleigh and hurry him onto the train for Canada.

The story's projected ending is rather better than the actuality. Hudson, making the whole matter absurd, declared that as challenged party he would exercise his right to choice of weapons. He named cannon. Hovey, however, would use only the cavalier rapier. So they went on. Hovey, seemingly determined to charge the cannon with his gallant weapon, made his farewells. Only Hudson's refusal to go on with the game called halt to the vivid fancy of the gentleman from Washington.[1]

Hovey's qualities appear in all sobriety in the most famous episode of that year and decade—the horning and class suspension which are written up in *Hanover by Gaslight, or Ways That Are Dark*, his history of sophomore year. Professor "Johnny" Lord had given a make-up examination to a conscientious student who had necessarily missed classes for some time. To cap the length and stiffness of the exam, Lord had called the student an ignoramus. So the class got together to horn this classical tyrant.

> But hark, far off the blast of a horn
> And the far faint sound of hurrying feet
> Seems slowly moving toward College Street.[2]

Through the snow that lay glazed by the February moon the sophomores came disguised and raising hideous clamor on conch shells, tin pans, and tin horns.

> Even Prexie heard the din afar
> And thought the Alumni'd opened war.

The horns blared, snowballs beat against the house, the door was pounded, the fence broken, and finally Professor Lord gave chase, only to fall in a snowbank and lose his shoe.

This excitement Hovey missed, perhaps because he was in his room at the other end of town, but President Bartlett singled him out as the first to face faculty inquisition. Questions failed as one classmate after another stood by the agree-

[1] It is characteristic of the growth of the Hovey legends that by 1898 the Boston *Evening Record* (Sept. 1) should write: "His friends will tell you of the gray morning that he looked at an opponent over the barrel of a duelling pistol and of the six or seven other mornings that he acted as second in other men's affairs."

[2] Hovey, *Hanover by Gaslight, or Ways That Are Dark* (Hanover, N. H., imprinted for the Class of 1885 [1883?]).

ment to give no clue. The president called upon the godly and worked on their religious scruples by "appeals to reason, manhood, and piety," but his luck was so poor he announced that there was not a Christian in the class. "He actually wept," said Hovey, "but whether with rage or hypocrisy I do not know." The suggestion of family espionage failed miserably with the General, who stood by his son's manly decision. Finally, in baffled rage, the president suspended the whole class indefinitely, and wrote to the parents that he did so "for the present and future order of the college, for the peace and safety of the village, for the good of society, and even the welfare and destiny of the young men themselves."

The less determined began to falter, and there was factional conflict within the class. Fiery speeches were made in a class meeting at which it was voted no minutes be kept, but finally the majority decided to give in, though twenty stalwarts voted to leave college rather than submit. A petition for forgiveness was handed to the faculty by "the frightened wretches" and for most of them the contest was over. But Hovey couldn't forgive "the great squeal" or the college administration. He wrote an explanation to the Washington alumni and wanted "to leave town forever." His upper-class friends argued with him. Patterson wrote to his mother that "we Psi U's cannot afford to lose him." Only his father's financial difficulties kept him from immediate withdrawal, but he wrote to his father, "I will not complete my course here under any circumstances. I would rather be a clerk in the headquarters of Mephistopheles."[3] Though he hoped for transfer to Johns Hopkins, he preferred to give up college altogether than stay on. He asked for an honorable dismissal, but "the sly old fox" would not grant one until three months from the date of suspension, too late for entrance elsewhere. Hovey was stumped. Yet he felt that he had acted rightly, as he insisted to his mother.

I can have no respect longer for the faculty, and least of all for a man who is a liar and a scoundrel and who nevertheless pretends to say what the duty of a Christian is. If this is Christianity to be a liar

[3] Hovey, Feb. 27, 1883.

and a traitor to your friends, I will never be converted from my in-fidelity.[4]

These are harsh words, and perhaps unjust, but they are char-acteristic of youth's first tilt against an entrenched authority which does not know its own cynicism and stubborn righteous-ness. The fierce pack loyalty and honor of youth are seldom met with understanding.

After a while even those who had agreed to leave began to feel the pull of acquiescence, and, even more, of the college itself. One went to Harvard to arrange entrance and rooms, but in ten days he was back, a true Dartmouth man, crying, "I squeal! Rah for Dartmouth! Old Dartmouth is good enough for me!" Only a few adamants still gathered round Hovey, and the kindest of the faculty felt a natural admiration for such high-souled intransigence. They began to give invitations to call and to flatter him. "They have soft-soaped me until I can hardly recognize myself." They tell him "they want to graduate a poet; and all that kind of twaddle. In fact I am beginning to feel a slight symptom of nausea in the abdominal region."[5] Too many circumstances conspired against his leav-ing, as he would still have done had he been financially inde-pendent. He stayed on, though the affair nearly broke his love for the college and left him tired, nervous, and unhappy.

For most of the college the great fire on Lebanon Street changed the topic of conversation. For all "The Hanover Squirt Gun Department" could do, the flames ate up building after building. The students were everywhere, Hovey pump-ing for two hours and senselessly rescuing the legs from the piano and billiard table in the Psi Upsilon hall, then in the "Tontine." An undergraduate named Hatch, seated on the ridge pole of a threatened house, called out to the President: "Hello, Prex.,— —— — — ———, why don't you come up here and squirt?" Somehow rum began to flow and the scene gave a certain authenticity to the fellow who sat on a fence playing a rescued banjo and insisting he was Nero.

[4] Hovey, Feb. 22, 1883.
[5] Hovey, March 25, 1883.

Instead of doing the routine jobs of *The Dartmouth*, Hovey simply handed in poems, stories, and essays which, being better than the editors otherwise received, were published. The poems must have been particularly welcome, for Hovey's only real rival was John Ordronaux, M.D., L.L.D., Professor of Medical Jurisprudence, who rendered Latin poems into English, or with equal facility, rendered English poems into Latin under such titles as "Translation of Nearer My God to Thee into Isometrical Latin Rhymes." While an issue of the paper might start with "Shadows of the Tempter" ("Some shadow crosses every day/The sunpath of our Christian way"), it went on to Hovey's celebration of "sorrow's nectarean wine," "College Days," an inscription for an autograph album, an article on aestheticism, and a sonnet on Rossetti. This is only a sample number. But it indicates the fact, which was that Hovey sometimes wrote almost all the "literary" content of an issue.

There is nothing unusual in his verse at this time—unless it is the very excess of the usual. With the rapturous excitement of the young, Hovey quotes, addresses, imitates the whole family of singers from Homer to Baudelaire. All his verse is literary, fertilized by literature, with little of his own heart's blood. If he writes a love poem he borrows the lilies and languors of Swinburne, or else sweetly imitates young Keats imitating Leigh Hunt. Always he is divorced from his physical experience, weaving on from image to image and metaphor to metaphor, never cutting straight to a tight economic statement. He is playing those graceful piano tunes which serve as finger exercises preparatory to art. Yet one detects already the skill in metrical experiment that sets him off from other college writers. He is trying out the elements of his craft, perfecting the use of alliteration, internal rhyme, and scansion, but is still too enamoured of the realized grace of others to dare a new organization. The singing poets, Catullus, Shelley, Swinburne, Poe, elicit his most enthusiastic admiration, and though good masters of craft they are not encouragers of new poetic statement. He could catch the trick of "the red rose withers and the lily pales," but he couldn't put much of the experience of an eighteen-year-old boy living in a country village into such terms. He was too conscious of poetry as something apart, existing by itself, yet his passionate desire to enter into the fellowship of poets drove him forward.

In the spring of this year 1883 he wrote "On the Mountain," his longest and most ambitious poem up to this time. In it he sees the shapes of the great poets rise about him. He alone is without a crown until the Muses weave him a wreath of woodland sorrel and the desolation leaves him.

> And, however lowly be my station,
> I am conscious I am one of them.

A poet's business is with both words and experience. If he has a quick ear and a facility with words, the experience lags behind. As it is his own, whether of thought or sense, it finds its form and expression slowly. So Hovey's intense love of the north country and his college were developing in slow gestation while he threw off poem after poem in borrowed dress. Since he never again lived in Hanover the material of his later poems must have been harvested and laid away then. He loved with inarticulate love the dark hills shaggy with growth, the granite outcroppings, and the upland pastures. Too close yet to the aching cold to let it freeze into form, he held for later singing "the fierce white cold" and "the wolf wind wailing" outside the door of fellowship in pipe and bowl. He felt fully enough the comradeship of these days, but his practice exercises in art were not in the key to celebrate it. His masters elevated the lonely and melancholy man. It was his own distinction finally to find the key of lusty brotherhood.

The strongest and finest force in Hovey's life always was the search for beauty, and the freedom to follow beauty. Naturally enough in that day he placed himself in the aesthetic tradition. He could not then see the anemia which attacks too narrow a search for loveliness. He could not know that he came at the end of that school and that its great contribution was already made. The spent cult which boomeranged back to the country of Poe from Paris and London was no longer like

Poe except in its worship of beauty and its tradition of drinking and misunderstood genius. Gautier, Baudelaire, d'Aurevilly, and Wilde had fashioned the wit and dandy who talked and lived against the stodginess and utilitarianism of the middle class. The associated diabolism, with its reversal of Christian teaching and ritual, was never successful apart from Catholic-bred writers. Wilde's "purple" sins are sophomoric boasting thrown against Baudelaire's tragic sense of evil. So Satanism made no appeal to young Hovey, but he came naturally to *épater le bourgeois* by dress, wit, and dandyism, and to think of himself as an aesthete. Even in the December of his freshman year he had written to his mother:

Have you seen *Patience* yet?   I want to very much as I am informed by Miss Sprague that Bunthorne is a capital burlesque of (to quote her words) "Swinburne, Rossetti, Wilde, Hovey & Co." I want to see this satire on myself and feel quite complimented at being classed with the much despised aesthetic school.[6]

Hovey's local fame as an undergraduate came largely from the aesthete's desire to shock the staid by following his own definition of beauty. He might pretend to be deep in sleep during class, but when called and punched by his neighbors, he would rise and turn the text into a skilfully designed verse translation polished the night before. Yet another time "the supreme cheek of Richard Hovey" delighted his classmates when he calmly told Professor Richardson that he couldn't translate the Greek because he had only the text with him. In his senior year he and some friends brought hashish to his room and recited Swinburne hoping to evoke the warm, flesh-colored visions they expected of that weed, but after eight hours of determined smoking and after two of the men had fallen asleep in exhaustion, Hovey and the remaining explorer of narcotic imagery had to give it up. Even in clothing Hovey could put on the romantic pose like a young Gautier. If the others wore odd clothes for economy, he wore them with an air.

Wilder Quint, momentarily thrown out of a freshman-

[6] Hovey, Dec. 4, 1881.

sophomore football rush, heard a rich voice say, "Up, boy, and at them."

Such a command, a sort of cross between the genial request of old Horace for more Falernian and the order of a French marshal to his troops was interesting. The man who made it was more so. To my young fancy he seemed Alcibiades turned cowboy. He wore a dark-blue flannel shirt, fastened at the neck with a great, black bow, and his remarkably handsome head and face were set off by a gray felt hat with a flaring, bandit-like brim. Tweed trousers were tucked into long riding boots, immaculately polished.[7]

This distinctly, even if theatrically, American costume did not startle Hanover as much as the aesthetic costume Hovey later affected. When he appeared, as his friends remember, wearing knickerbockers and black silk stockings, and sometimes graced with a monocle or sunflower, the town gasped with amused derision. To the lazy, the proper, the unimaginative, these little jests seemed clever and breathtakingly daring. This was something different from the usual undergraduate deviltry. Though famous for this flaunting of custom, Hovey never joined the college brawls and mass pranks after his freshman year. He invented his own jests and for the rest held himself rather aloof, refusing even to use slang or take part in the rather cruel joking which has always amused Americans.

Beneath the posturings and pranks there was the same earnestness his predecessors in the art-for-art's-sake school had originally felt. Aestheticism was a high cause, a revolt against the moralizing of recognized literature and the narrowness of a period which worshiped monetary success and ugly comfort and forgot the Muses. In an article published during his sophomore year Hovey traced the aesthetic school to the praise of beauty in Shelley and Keats and defended it from the sarcasm of "impudent penny-a-liners and hireling caricaturists." He declared that even its most bitter revilers must base their tastes upon the school, and hoped that the day would come when the critics would cease their hostility and all would unite

[7] Wilder Quint, "Richard Hovey in College," *Dartmouth Magazine*, XIX (May 1905), 294.

with "the immortal Keats, the first of the Esthetes, in declaring that 'Beauty is truth.' "

By his junior year he could deny God Himself in defense of Keats.

> If through the whole allotted period
> Of thy brief life thou wert allowed to dwell
> In endless bitter ignorance of thy fame,
> Then must we yield it that there is no God
> Or else that he is crueller than hell.[8]

The mature realist may smile at such pious sacrilege, but the young poet was very much in earnest.

Hovey returned from the long summer holiday after sophomore year, a holiday lengthened as usual by the weeks in the mountains, in time to hear Matthew Arnold, critical leader of the great Victorians. Arnold was just beginning his lecture tour of 1883. Like all Englishmen since the Puritans he followed the British tradition of coming to America to better his financial condition. Like all cultural ambassadors he brought his own superiority and he was met with a humble anxiety to explain our cultural deficiencies. Though disappointed at seeing no Indians in New York harbor, he spoke in New York and Boston, and then came on to Dartmouth. The boys bought their tickets and flocked into the College Church to hear the distinguished essayist, "this out and out Englishman" with his mutton chops, monocle, and spats. His subject, "Literature and Science," should have interested them, for the pressing problems of a modernized curriculum and the relationship between the college proper and the scientific schools of medicine, agriculture, and engineering were still tender. But, despite the eager quiet of the audience, few could hear Arnold's Oxford singsong as he dove into his manuscript and then lifted his head to swallow a phrase "for all the world like a chicken taking a drink," as one of the boys said. No doubt they were curious, but one hundred and fifty dollars seemed a lot to pay for the privilege of watching a lecturer

---

[8] Hovey, *The Dartmouth*, V (April 18, 1884), 294.

stumble through an essay they might have read in comfort in the library any time in the past year. Hovey's friend, the writer Kate Sanborn, was hotly indignant at the cool and cheeky presumption, and a professor boldly declared that he could remake the speaker in five lessons.

At a reception at the home of Professor Parker, who was later to conduct Hovey's marriage service, Arnold was eager to meet a representative of the Indians he had missed on the Hudson. Young Charles Eastman, a full-blooded Sioux who later became famous as writer and lecturer, walked into the room with a native dignity which transformed his borrowed dress suit. The apostle of culture was as obviously embarrassed before the gracious Indian as the fops of eighteenth-century drama were before the noble savage. "He coloured up like a boy, held out his hand, and stammered out—his British egotism coming up unawares, 'Ah, eh! ah! You were there— you were there. How did you like it?' "[9]

Arnold wrote to his sister that he enjoyed his visit to Hanover more than anything he had yet experienced in America. Just as he was to be amazed at the absence of "workers" when Whittier showed him the Essex County countryside where all were workers, so he was struck by the decent living of those "in a small way of life"—notably the professors! Even the cold, dreary rain did not trouble him. Indeed, it seemed homelike. "I like the climate of Hanover," he said; "it is so much like dear England." This choice remark was cherished by the undergraduates, and whenever they shivered through the autumn rains they comforted themselves with the happy thought that the weather was like that of dear England.

Arnold's belief that literature was profoundly ethical and his interest in statement rather than form were shared by Hovey's new friend and teacher, Charles Francis Richardson, called "Clothespin." Richardson even resembled Arnold, and he came into a mustached and bearded faculty clean-faced except for his tidy sideburns. Tall, erect, with high forehead,

---

[9] J. D. McCallum, "The Apostle of Culture Meets America," *New England Quarterly*, II (July, 1929), 351-381.

he looked of the very school of Matthew. He was a man of large and gentle heart. Since he was the English department in his single self, the college was fortunate in his presence. A Dartmouth man, like Hovey a member of Psi Upsilon, for eleven years he had held editorial posts on the New York *Independent*. Already he had published his *Primer of American Literature, The Cross,* a volume of religious and devotional verse, and his often reprinted volume of essays, *The Choice of Books*. Despite limitations of literary sympathy, then, he was a rare teacher, for he combined practical editorial experience with creation and scholarship, and was to touch generations of boys with his enthusiasm and friendship.

One day in an autumn drizzle, "Clothespin" offered part of his umbrella to an unprotected fellow crossing the Common. Somehow they got to talking about *Atalanta in Calydon*. The teacher was surprised to discover a student who had read it. So they introduced themselves and were soon friends. The only teacher of English and American literature in the college found more delight in the talk of this clever undergraduate than he could in that of his colleagues. Richardson later wrote: "Altogether I would call him, as student, reader, writer, and speaker, the most generally conspicuous undergraduate of his time." So Hovey found a home to go to and someone to talk to and against. He always remembered Richardson's comments on his Swinburne poems in *The Dartmouth* as his first praise from a critic. Of course, he welcomed the chance to take advanced courses in literature and took all that his friend offered. The blunders of taste and judgment in his teacher could not have been so obvious as they are now. The older writers were safe, naturally, but Richardson liked to poke fun at Wilde and "the gently-distilling inanities" of Walter Pater. In the American field, his specialty, his judgment betrayed him most palpably. By that year his *Primer of American Literature* had sold a respectable 39,000 copies, yet all he found to praise in Herman Melville was the fact that he had "written lively sea tales." To Whitman's poems the writer grudgingly allowed some strong and fine lines, but he went on to say that "many of the poems in *Leaves of Grass* are grossly indecent, and the 'upward look' is conspicuously absent from Whitman's verse. The world's great poets have been morally in advance of their times; Whitman lags behind the average sentiment of his day and country." Such a view as this was probably natural to one who believed poetry "man's call of kinship with the eternal," an eternal already defined. Still, for all his conventional blindness, Richardson was a pioneer in the encouragement and study of American literature, and his very prejudices were the product of an earnest consideration.

Tasks such as the editorship of Dartmouth's yearbook, the *Aegis,* and the class history of sophomore year cut down to very few the number of poems Hovey published in *The Dartmouth.* Those few, however, are of interest as his first serious attempts in a vein he was to work most successfully. "Bohemia" is a first draft for the opening poem of *Songs from Vagabondia* and in some respects a better poem. It is less conscious of society and the lifted eyebrow. There are no Myrtles and Wandas, no kisses, and less self-conscious devil's advocacy. The poem is one gay celebration of the joy of free living, a surprising *tour de force* for a boy of nineteen. The last stanza was so good in its kind that when he and Carman were putting the *Vagabondia* poems together a decade later, he let it stand word for word.

> I tell you that we,
> While you are smirking
> And lying and shirking
> Life's duty of duties,
> Honest sincerity,
> We are in verity
> Free————
> Free to rejoice
> In blisses and beauties,
> Free as the voice
> Of the wind as it passes
> Free as the bird
> In the weft of the grasses,
> Free as the word of the sun, the sea
> Free![10]

[10] *The Dartmouth,* V (March 14, 1884), 248.

In the same issue of *The Dartmouth* appeared "A Song without a Theme," a poem Hovey had read in February before the Alumni Association of Washington. This is admittedly an occasional poem which rambles on in search of a theme and eventually discovers the only method of bringing poetry and an alumni banquet together—a celebration of the college. The poem makes no pretense of being more than a compromise, but here, for the first time, Hovey practices his laureateship to "Old Dartmouth, of all colleges the manliest and best."

Many of his college mates have commented on the beauty of his voice and laughter, a rare comment on a student. He loved the quality and flavor of words and spoke them with respect. The pages of poetry he memorized he would roll off, almost entranced by his own voice. He would drop into Quint's room in the Rood house and lying on the floor before the flaming fireplace would talk and recite for hours in his rich baritone. Poet and actor and ritualist, he found his fullest expression in poetry recited. He was appointed one of three to represent his class in the forensic contest of commencement week, 1884. This was no great surprise to the boys, for they had hidden two of their number in the organ to overhear faculty discussion at the preliminary hearing. Hovey later won the "dramatic prize" for his recitation of *The Bells*, which, however meretricious as a poem, is an obliging vehicle for the wide-ranged voice. *The Bells* had impressed him as a boy and his freshman grind had been a parody of it. Hovey performed again at the Fraternity Prize Speaking, this time using Twain's "Jim Wolf and the Cats." During senior year he again won the prize for dramatic speaking, but at no time did he win a prize for writing.

The memory which helped his recitation was a product of constant reading—too much bookishness. The man who was to praise the strenuous life was, like his predecessor Whitman, no great lover of the strenuous. Indeed he stayed so much in his room that his friends worried about him. Once they decided they would no longer bring him his meals, for he had cut classes for a week and lost himself in books and ventured out only at night. O'Brien and Allen set out to cure him by bringing him only the kinds of food he never ate. At noontime dinner they brought over a plate of corned beef and cabbage, which he thought supremely vulgar. When they returned for the dishes before supper they found the food untouched. "Why, Dick," said O'Brien in simulated surprise, "You didn't eat much of what we brought you. I don't see that you—What did you eat?" "Crockery, by God!" answered Hovey. That night he joined them at supper. It was the only time Allen remembered Hovey's using an oath.[11]

In senior year Hovey moved into his room in Reed Hall with Tom Leigh.[12] He was close to the heart of the campus, as he had been in Wentworth the year before. His windows looked out on the old buildings of Dartmouth Row and across the dusty road toward the fields and Velvet Rocks. It was his favorite room, though the country quiet was broken by the building of Rollins Chapel across from Reed and of Wilson Hall just behind it. The college was being invaded by progress with its insistence on taste and elegance divorced from native simplicity. Fine old buildings were going down before the newcomers, which would be out-of-date before they had felt a score of seasons. Reed stood above the ground with all the uncompromising character of the Yankee at his best, but the chapel slipped into the earth as if it had already sunk a story. Latter-day Ruskinians were to call it the "Seven Lumps of Architecture."

During the autumn Hovey went through the conventional family squabble over politics. He had been offered the presidency of the college "Cleveland and Hendricks Club," but the office work and his own legal minority decided him against accepting. Nevertheless, the very thought that her son—"the scamp"—would vote, if he could, for a Democrat, called out a strong protest from his mother. Hovey was adamant. The Republican party, he wrote, might have produced great men,

---

[11] Dr. Edwin H. Allen, letter to the author, Oct. 9, 1942.
[12] E. O. Grover, ed., *Dartmouth Lyrics* (Boston: Small, Maynard & Co., 1924); this contains a short biographical sketch.

but that did not prove that Blaine was of the same sort. Cleveland, by contrast, was fanatic on the subject of honesty in government. The platforms were the same; one had to vote foɪ
the men, and, said Richard, he stood where his father had
stood twelve years ago—an independent.

> The young men of the country will not be thoroughly identified
> with either party until they enunciate some principles on which men may
> rationally disagree.[13]

It was the perennial cry of the idealistic young, forever misunderstood by the defeated realism of the old.

As he looked out to politics for honesty, he looked more and
more to religion for some crystallization of beauty and faith.
There was nothing of the Calvinist in him. Except the demand
for freedom, he found nothing good in the old Puritans who
"thought no place so fitting for divine worship as a bare rec-
tangular meetinghouse, in one end of which the black-gowned
minister stood out in bold relief against the white-washed
wall."[14] Righteousness of the middle-class sort was a dull
enemy to be made sport of. College chapel, with its restless
compromise between spiritual education and compulsory attendance, meant little to him.

As an aesthete he turned naturally toward the Episcopal
Church. The light in the new Saint Thomas's Church was to
him both dimmer and more religious than that in the clean
bareness of the Congregational meetinghouse. He talked often
to the rector, the Reverend Robert Berkeley, and with his
undergraduate friends Ed Allen and John Lawrence. He and
Allen were both admirers of Edwin Arnold's immensely popular *Light of Asia.* Hovey particularly delighted in the last line
—"The dewdrop slips into the shining sea"—as a summary
of earthly life. He did not at first want to accept the doctrine
of Jesus Christ's divinity. He told Allen that he would have
been more impressed with Jesus Christ if he had been more
human and if physical love had entered his life. Gradually he
gave over this romatic leveling and took a stricter discipline,

[13] Hovey, Oct. 21, 1884.
[14] Hovey, "Eleutheria," *Dartmouth Magazine,* XX (Jan. 1906), 120.

but here he had stated much of his final disagreement with the Church and hinted at the place which earthly "profane" love was to occupy in his final regard. He was not ready for that insistence as yet, and so he studied Church history and Christian doctrine under the tuition of the rector. Finally he decided to become a communicant.

He wrote to his mother, an hereditary Congregationalist, an explanatory letter which combined boyish egotism with close reasoning.

Ever since I entered college—indeed, long before—theological ideas played a conspicuous part in my thinking. I have read and studied the philosophies of all ages and of all climes. I have speculated much for myself. I have toiled and moiled over musty volumes of ecclesiastical history. I have passed through agnosticism, pantheism, deism in sequence.[15]

This exhausted medieval scholastic who had most certainly been reading Poe as well as theology had now reached certain conclusions. They reduced themselves to the triune nature of God, the divinity of Jesus, and the apostolic succession of the Anglican Church. He had decided to be baptized, with Professor and Mrs. Richardson and his friend Lawrence's mother as sponsors.

Few of his friends knew anything about his long period of indecision and internal debate, and so his confirmation set the college by the ears. The "Class Chronicle," read at the Class Day exercises at the end of the year, records the effect of this nine days' wonder and suggests the chaffing which, Hovey admits, was not easy to endure.

On Friday, December 5th, 1885 [an obvious mistake for 1884], Richard Hovey walked up the main aisle of St. Thomas's Church, decorated with one eye-glass and just the cutest little knee breeches imaginable, and denounced the Devil and all his works, though he still continued to room with Tom Leigh. Of course Dick's "change in life," as Critchell would say, was not instantaneous and it will not be scoffing to tell one little anecdote. Dick had been going round with that literary expression of his all Holy Week and on Good Friday he

[15] Hovey, Dec. 3, 1884.

was especially broken up.   A friend dropped into his room before dinner that day and asked Dick to walk down to the club with him but Dick shook his head with a martyr-like air and said, "I am fasting to-day."   "Why," said the friend with credulous surprise, "haven't you eaten a damned thing today?"

"No," replied Dick with unconscious earnestness, "not a *damned* thing today."

There is no truth however in the report that Dick was intoxicated on Easter, and it all arose from his remark that "there was nothing in the Episcopalian creed that forbade a good quiet drunk on any Sunday during Lent."[16]

If the confirmation as here recorded stood alone one might take it as only a momentary impulse, the sowing of another Wilde oat.   The dandy and the ritualist were often one in the aesthetic tradition.   Yet even if religiosity in knee breeches and monocle was not quite original, surely no one else in America, least of all in a New England village, would have dared this balance of pose and sincerity—or even been accused of it. Whether or not he wore this costume, it would still be truth to say that Hovey's God did not ask a contrite and a humble heart so much as a bold declaration of the divinity of beauty. He was suffering from the same unfashioned desires which had troubled the young fellows at Oxford a generation before when their immense longing to live fully stumbled about between Reform, Church, and Art, before it finally found itself in Art. The artist was looking for a form upon which to hang the garments of holiness, but he was still an artist delighting in an ordered form and rhetoric, just as a young lover may speak his shapeless love through the ornamental words of Romeo. Beneath the surface he was altogether sincere, but he was not so single as the usual convert.   He still believed with Keats that "beauty is truth," and he demanded that even religion accept his understanding of beauty and truth.   He was not different from many modern men in his desire to bring beauty, truth, and goodness together in harmony.   He was different, however, in the dramatic quality of his imagination and the intensity with which he projected himself into situations.

[16] *Chronicles* from the "Exercises of Class-Day of the Senior Class of Dartmouth College—Tuesday, June 23, 1885," pp. 52-53, DCA.

The "nine day wonder" and Christmas holiday over, Hovey settled again to the work and friendship which alone sustained the students through the winter. There were occasional entertainments at the "Op'ry House" on College Street, where the entrepreneur doubled in the role of town bootlegger. There were oyster stew and ice cream at Lib Carter's in the Tontine. There was Freshman Beer when the freshmen set up kegs at both ends of Bedbug Alley and invited their betters to a night of rioting. As the hilarious boys looked out on the hill behind Dartmouth Hall, Hovey appeared with a coffin he had purloined from the Medical College. Unsmilingly he slid down hill on this improvised toboggan, and then solemnly trudged up the hill again.

The biggest piece of work he had yet attempted he called *Eleutheria, An Essay on the Growth of Democratic Ideas in English Poetry.* This is an astonishingly good essay for a college boy of twenty-one. It covers the whole field of English literature from *Beowulf* to Burns and shows an intimate knowledge of all the prominent writers and the moods of their times. He announces in the first line: "The poet is an anointed priest of God," and in the poets he finds the leaders and pioneers of that democracy he believes inherent in the Anglo-Saxon tradition. He immediately rejects the dictum of Oscar Wilde that the single end of art is beauty. "The error is the more widely spread that it contains a great deal of truth. It is a fact that the poet is, perhaps, above all things God's prophet of the Beautiful!—Let no man overlook it!—but it is also a fact that he is God's prophet of the True and the Good. Nor is this all. He is not only the seer, revealing the Divine to man; he is also the priest offering the prayers and aspirations of man to God."[17]

This exaggerated understanding of the poet's holy task, which spoiled the quality of so much nineteenth-century poetry, was always a danger to Hovey's critical judgment and to his writing. It led him towards that vague and tenuous kind of poetry of statement into which American poets were politely

[17] Hovey, "Eleutheria," *Dartmouth Magazine*, XX (Jan. 1906), 96.

sinking. But at the same time it encouraged his serious dedication and led him out of an art too narrowly aesthetic. As the senior said, "The battle for the rights of man is not ended." He felt himself preparing to enter the great tradition. The essay was written "because its author believes with all his soul in democracy, in poetry and in the Anglo-Saxon race,—because he believes that the principles of liberty, equality, and fraternity are truths of the highest order,—because he believes that poetry is the expression of man's loftiest genius."[18]

It was easier to declare this intoxicating faith than to fulfil it in verse. Writing became harder as he reached for his own expression and felt the pain of life more personally. He was growing up, and the process is seldom happy. He had to become a man, even though the change hurt those he loved. His mother naturally did not want to lose her boy and she felt that he was neglecting her as well as a certain Emma, of whom we know no more than the name. He replied to her with that Byronic pose natural to his age:

There is a devil of pride in my heart. It has bruised me often and seriously. Take heed lest it bruise ye also. If you meant by your remark in your last letter, that there was danger of my losing Emma,—I speak plainly but it is to you only, Mother, and in confidence,—I reply that I *demand* trust and confidence of her, and, if she fails to show them, though she were as dear as my own soul, I would bury my love in my heart. If she deserts me, it will be harder for her to bear than for me, for I have a nature strong as iron cables, and, though I can be loving as Leander, I can also be as inflexible as rock.[19]

The letter ends with the redundant postscript: "Are you aware that tomorrow I am twenty-one years old?"

He was happier when spring came and the mud grew firm beneath his boots. By his window the elms began to swell their buds and on Velvet Rocks to the eastward the birches and poplars were emerald patches. In the Vale of Tempe north of the campus arbutus broke its buds, and hepatica and bloodroot blossomed in the College Park. Though he disliked

[18] *Ibid.*, pp. 138-139.
[19] Hovey, May 3, 1885.

exercise for its own sake, and had been dosing himself with quinine to break headaches brought on by his sedentary life of constant reading, spring took him out-of-doors. His quick response to wind and hill never lost its edge, partly because all his life he was to make swift and complete changes from city and study to holidays in the presence of nature.

Now Commencement week arrived. The seniors planted the class tree and walked back to the campus for a yell. Then came Baccalaureate Sunday, prize-speaking on Monday and an uncontested prize for Hovey in dramatic speaking; then Class Day with the *Chronicle* calling Hovey a wild young blade, and the Prophecy forecasting an aesthetic career in the theater.

That year they laid the corner of the tower which would annually mount upward, substituting a column of stone for the ancient and dying pinetree around which they smoked their last pipe together,[20] listened to an ode Hovey hadn't written, and went away. The Chapel was dedicated, and Wilson Hall was opened. On Commencement Day, 1885, Hovey received honorable mention in history and English. Alone in his class, he was graduated *cum laude*. His dissertation on Victor Hugo drew praise from the distinguished who had come to accept honorary degrees. Hovey's diploma was put into his hand. There was a reception and ball at the Dartmouth Hotel Parlors. Then it was over and he was out of college.

He left behind him a legend and took with him a vast amount of reading for a man of his age, as well as some loyal

[20] Hovey's sonnet of 1895 is worth printing here:

The Old Pine

It stood upon the hill like some old chief,
And held communion with the cryptic wind,
Keeping like some dim unforgotten grief
The memory of the tribesmen autumn-skinned,
Silent and slow as clouds, whose footing passed
Down the remote trails of oblivion
Long since into the caverns of the past.
Alone, aloof, strong fellow of the sun,
We chose it for our standard in its prime,
Nor—though no longer grimly from its hill
It fronts the world, like Webster—wind nor time
Has felled its austere ghost, we see it still,
In alien lands, resurgent and undying
Flag of our hearts, from sudden ramparts flying.

friends for life. He had never been truly popular, for he was too strikingly different from most of the New England boys who made up the undergraduate body. He had sobered in the last two years and his undisputed ability had won him admiration if not wide friendship. Those who knew him well gave him respect as well as love. One of them later wrote: "I always felt in his presence warmed and cheered and delighted in every way. One endowed with a strong artistic temperament might have a little of that feeling in the presence of a consummate work of art. His nobility of manhood, his kindness and gentleness to his friends and those he loved, were beyond description, although he was one of the 'mettled breed' whenever the proper occasion arose."[21] For mere acquaintance he never cared, and he stayed too much apart to be the typical student. His aristocratic manner and reserve impressed some as snobbish in that very democratic institution. No man, however, left Dartmouth that year with greater possibility of future fame.

[21] Arthur Livermore, letter, June 2, 1912. DCA.

CHAPTER III

A Crown of Laurel

> I take the lyre with steady hand
> But reverent, knowing well how long
> And bitter are the ways of song,
> How few that reach its promised land.
> HOVEY, *The Laurel*.

Hovey had set his heart on being a literary man, but like others with the same desire, he had to hold in reserve the possibility of teaching. His professors gave him letters of high recommendation as a potential teacher of Greek or English, and friends like Harriet Prescott Spofford and General Eaton gave him letters of introduction to editors. No offer came from the colleges and only rejection slips from the editors. One decision seemed final, however; he would not be a journalist as his mother's friends suggested. "Don't they know that I would not be a journalist on any terms?" he wrote. "Have they the insane idea that journalism is literature or literature journalism?"[1]

He stayed on in Hanover ready to act upon any letters and filling his time with a local production of *Patience* in which, of course, he played the part of Bunthorne. Nothing of this production has come down to us except the program, but it is easy to believe that Hovey threw himself with vivid delight into that most skilful caricature of the aesthete. For the audience there was the double pleasure of seeing the "ultra-poetical, super-aesthetical, out-of-the-way young man" caricature his own pose.

In middle August he went to Bethlehem. Howells was spending the summer there. Hovey introduced himself and found Howells a very genial fellow. He went over often to talk about literature, although Howells's definition of roman-

[1] Hovey, July, no date, 1885.

ticism as "a stuffed dummy" nearly provoked a clash. Howells advised going to New York and plunging into the profession of writing.

When Hovey left the mountains after a month, he probably fulfilled his intention of stopping off to interview the editors of *Harper's* and the *Century*, as Richardson had urged and Howells advised. They had nothing for him, however, and in the fall of 1885, he went on to Washington, a young man without a vocation. Although he had once talked about taking a government job, and although the family was not very prosperous, he kept to the arts and enrolled in the Art Students' League. He enjoyed the painting and drawing from models, and though he never spent the time to develop skill, he sometimes later turned out drawings of people and places. He was always interested in the work of others and his quick faculty of understanding the problems of the painter made him an acceptable friend, as his striking head made him a popular model.

He did little writing during this year, for he was ill a large part of the winter and gave the big share of his time to dramatics. In the spring his amateur group presented Robertson's *Caste* at the Hovey home with Richard in the leading role, later giving a performance for the benefit of St. Mark's Church. Since the testimonial of gratitude was addressed to Hovey, one supposes he must have been the leader of the group.

While he studied the stage, a deeper drama was enacting itself within him. He had not found a place in the literary world, nor any discipline for his expansive faculties. His mind turned again to the church, the only channel of ordered beauty in that day. An Anglo-Catholic aestheticism had been growing in America. Its tangible symbol one might see in Phillips Brooks's Trinity Church, built by Richardson in 1877 in the very Boston founded by those who had fled popish ritual. Through rich windows designed by Burne-Jones and William Morris the sharp New England light fell warmly on the divine service. The fierce Old Puritan ethics and faith were being

softened and sweetened.   Form, ritual, and vague religiosity
were drawing men, and particularly women, from the bare intellectual creed that had fought to free men from these but had descended to a mere preaching of orthodox morality and a proper
humanitarianism.   Religion had been taken out of energetic
daily living and had become an oasis of emotional response to
order, dignity, and beauty in a society which had little of these.

By June of 1886, a year after graduation, Hovey had submitted himself as a candidate for priest's orders.   Bishop Paret
approved his purpose of going to the General Theological
Seminary and promised to nominate him for a vacant scholarship.   To prepare himself for his work he spent part of the
summer studying Hebrew at Newton Center, Massachusetts,
in the seminary of which his uncle, Alvah Hovey, was president.   He worked hard, for he found Professor Harper, later
to be president of Chicago University, an inspiring teacher.

In September he was enrolled in the General Theological
Seminary of the Protestant Episcopal Church at Chelsea Square,
New York City.   Because of his excellence in Hebrew and
Greek he was excused from those studies and faced an un-
relieved program of Exegesis, Ecclesiastical History, Pastoral
Theology, and Systematic Divinity.

His classmates noted his quiet reserve and rather fright-
ening dignity.   For a time good fellowship was out of it; to
one of Hovey's sort, "religious" good fellowship was incongruous.   He had no use for that bastard offspring of middle-
class Protestantism which was beginning to bolster a weakening
church.   If he was to be a man of God he would be so completely, even in outward sign.   He saw himself set apart from
worldliness and devoted to God and His worship through the
church. Attracted by the grace of ecclesiastical speech and motion and the tangible signs of devotion, he moved quickly
toward an advanced Anglo-Catholic position.   Probably at his
instigation, some of those who shared his tastes began to wear
the cassock and cord under their academic gowns.   Whenever
possible Hovey added the flat ecclesiastical hat.   The somber
clothing set off his liquid eyes and handsome head, so that he

resembled the holy young priest of tradition. Some whispered that beneath the cassock he wore a chain to mortify the flesh. He himself later said that he "meditated becoming a monk and spent some time in a monastery," though that was certainly a dramatic exaggeration. With his friends he revived the old offices of tierce, sext, and nones, and the service before sleep, compline. In his room was an altar set with crucifix and candles and here the group would gather to read the offices. At other times he took part in services at the ritualistic Church of Saint Mary the Virgin, assisting Father Brown, and sometimes sang matins himself.

That Christmas he gladly gave up the celebration at home to assist in church services which seemed elaborate superstitions to his family. Letters went back and forth and his father visited him, though without dissuading him. In March, 1887, he wrote:

I was very glad to have father come around when he was here, of course. As for our arguments, you know I do not expect any of you to look at things in a Catholic way at once. Protestants have been trained from their very youth with such strange and erroneous ideas as to what Catholicity is, that they spend a great deal of their time fighting monsters of their own creation.[2]

Hovey could not accept the conventional middle ground. Whatever he did must move toward completeness and bear the outward sign of an inward grace. He could not respond to the great Separatist and American discovery that the simple hard-working Christian was a better man than the medieval monk. A Christian should look like a Christian, as a poet should look like a poet. There was no emotional advantage in becoming a clergyman if one simply dropped onto the cold floor by the bedside and prayed each night as his ancestors had been doing since 1635. Prayers like Uncle Alvah's bored him, but compline was a miniature drama within which the acting soul achieved beauty.

If Hovey had been most of all an imitative actor he might have stayed in the church, but the need of self-creation and

[2] Hovey, March 2, 1887.

direction toward the future began to trouble him. This res-
tiveness is apparent in one of the notebooks in which he set down
outlines of sermons required in one of his courses. These
sermons were, naturally enough, orthodox expositions of Christianity, though with a stronger Catholic bias and closer reasoning than most sermons. With the actual job of composing
a set piece he found it easy to fulfil his duty, but at the same
time there was growing an inescapable awareness of what he
was neglecting in this process of narrow application. So he
began to lay out chapter headings, pages, and paragraphs for a
study of Christianity that might use more of him. Immediately
he stepped into a freer world, although his effort to think
logically and precisely is apparent in the frequent deletion and
rewriting. At the same time a brightness emerges from the
theological gloom and the quotations set at the head of proposed chapters are from Shakespeare, Dryden, and Robert
Ingersoll, rather than from Holy Writ.

The mark of the rebel appears in this comment on Genesis:

[Adam and Eve] were punished for scientific research. Eve was the
first schoolmistress in the world and was cursed for it. For my part
I feel indebted to the serpent. If it had not been for him, we should
all have been orthodox savages today. And for this great benefit to
humanity he was cursed by his creator.

Hovey finally decided that he could not accept the Christian doctrines of natural depravity, Hell, the Atonement, and
Creation. He scrawled on a slip of paper that the mind of
man had long enough been clothed in the garments of Christianity, which were becoming tattered. "The eye can easily
see through their flimsy texture. Our reason has outgrown
them and we want a new suit. We need new garments woven
on the loom of genius by the weaver reason."

These were private intellectual doubts bred by an "in-
compatibility of temper." They had to meet his realization
that in leaving religion man was resigning effective checks on
behavior and an awareness of high destiny which nothing else
so far provided. His mind forced him from the old position
but he could not take that shifting stand of enlightened self-

interest and legal honesty which was the poor substitute of his time. He never made a clean and final decision to quit the Church, but when hay fever held him in the mountains long after the new term had begun, he let allergy excuse him. In the first week of November, 1887, he wrote to Bishop Paret making his health the prime cause of his dropping out of the school. He wasn't yet ready to declare himself. Although he was no longer an enrolled seminarian he intended to continue his studies privately under the Bishop's direction, but he had other needs and, as he said, "I gradually drifted out of the intention of becoming a priest without exactly knowing how or when I did."[3]

On some day about this time he wrote in his notebook:

My Will
I, Richard Hovey, by the grace of God Poet—
I have believed much and much disbelieved.
I have been atheist, pantheist, Catholic,
Broad Churchman, New Theology, what not,
Even a worshiper of forgotten gods,
Whose names were potent once in Askalon,
Delphos, Dodona or by the centuried Nile,
And now I believe today—no matter what,
For I shall change my mind before tonight.

He had started the summer of 1887 in good faith by going to Newton to study, but new friends turned him again to poetry. In Cambridge he met Thomas Buford Meteyard, a young artist, and Bliss Carman, then a student at the Graduate School. Carman, three years older than Hovey, was as blond and tall as Hovey was dark and solid. Born on the middle day of April, he described himself as a cross between an April Fool and a Maypole. He felt immediately the strong quality of Hovey's personality, but was embarrassed by his "Indian silence." After some one-sided small talk Carman decided to hold his tongue also. Hovey saw the process with amusement and accepted him into a friendship that was the richest and closest of his life.

With Meteyard he cemented friendship by taking a walk-

[3] E. O. Grover, *op. cit.*

ing trip to Newburyport and along the coast, later visiting the family summer home at Scituate. There he met Thomas William Parsons, who must have seemed a figure out of another age, for he had been born in the year 1819 with Melville, Whitman, and Lowell, had stood model for "the poet" in Longfellow's *Tales of a Wayside Inn,* and had been publishing his translations of Dante since 1843. It had been unfortunate for his fame that he had released the *Inferno* in 1867, the very year of Charles Eliot Norton's translation of the *Vita Nuova* and of Longfellow's translation of the entire *Divine Comedy,* but he cared nothing for fame. This shy, gentle man, never at home in modern America, had put forth verse which Longfellow described as "tender, musical, and terse." He was a perfectionist, without mesage or social content, trying to record his meaning in what Hovey later called his "precise and unsuperfluous line."

It was a happy meeting for Hovey, who responded immediately to the scholar-poet with his deep religious feeling and his devotion to Dante. Here was one who might take Richardson's place as teacher and friend, and whose interests were even closer to his own at this moment.

> Art's knight of courtesy, well pleased to commend,
> Who to my youth accorded the dear name
> Of poet, and the dearer name of friend.
>
> *Seaward*

With the hay-fever season he went to the mountains. Since *Harper's* had recently turned down three of his poems, he turned "lecturer" to provide bread for himself. He went the rounds of the hotels, reciting pieces or reading from his own work. One of his Dartmouth friends remembered his costume:

His stage, or better platform "get-up," consisted of a black or brown velveteen coat with trousers of knickerbocker style, a broad flowing tie à la Elbert Hubbard, either red or black, with sash to match. A soft black hat completed the ensemble.[4]

[4] F. P. Cleaves, "Richard Hovey,—Barnstormer!" *DAM*, XXI (March, 1929), 295.

The lecturing gave him money (he wrote that he was "flush"), and his poetic rig drew the eyes of the girls. But aside from all this was the joy of the mountains and of the long tramps from place to place. It was to him the modern equivalent of the life of troubador or itinerant ballad singer. A day's tramp along the mountain roads, then the hotel, dinner, and the excitement of being the center of attention, and in the morning the romantic scholar-gypsy again took to the road.

When he returned to Boston in October, 1887, after deciding not to register in the Seminary, he had to find some employment. As he said, he had no respect for journalism, but necessity drove him to work for the Boston *Advertiser*. He worked at space rates and so hoped to have independence. When the work ate into the time he wanted for writing, he gave it up.

If there was money in his pockets he feasted with his friends and went to the theater. When there was no money he fasted and looked for a job as supernumerary. Added to the fifty-cent payment was the intoxication of the theater. He made the traditional entry onto the professional stage as a spear carrier and later was one of the mob in Booth and Barrett's performance of *Julius Caesar*. The mob was well trained, and the critic of the *Transcript* found the handling of the supernumeraries the only part of the performance to which he could give high praise. "Very rarely," he wrote, "have masses been drilled to such good artistic performance." Unfortunately this orderly movement did not last. The job of "super" appealed to stage-struck boys, of which Harvard had its share. With a little liquor in them they added collegiate deviltry to the usual fickleness of "the stinking mob." Box-office sales were boomed by those who enjoyed this comic relief from the noble periods of Booth and Barrett. The boys repaid them and by the last night of the run Caesar's Rome resembled Harvard Square during an undergraduate riot, and Antony had to quit his violently shaking rostrum before he should lie beside Caesar at its base. Hovey always referred to his experience very solemnly as his first appearance on the stage, and outside

Boston this association with Booth and Barrett was impressive enough.[5]

Obviously he could not earn his support at this rate, and so he left Boston for home, almost penniless but not at all sorry for the months which had given him "some excellent friends and a good deal of knowledge of men and life." He had an idea of working in the Smithsonian Institution or in some one of the Washington bookstores. There was a flurry of excitement about the headmastership of the preparatory department of Kenyon College to which Richardson had recommended him. Nothing came of these schemes.

Meanwhile he tried his hand at stories, sketched the plots of plays, laid out a program of essays, and tried to round out a volume of poems tentatively called "Songs and Monologues," which he hoped to publish. He wanted to dedicate the volume to Professor Richardson, but felt that he was going beyond the pretty limits of conventional verse.

I have not hesitated to treat every subject in life—the evil as the good, by no means omitting such themes as are nowadays particularly associated with Swinburne and Baudelaire. . . . This I am sure of, that while it is natural for me to seek a heart of good in things evil, my book, as a whole, fairly read and understood, teaches but one solution to life's riddle—obedience to God and to all God's laws, physical and spiritual.[6]

Understandably enough he did not want to trap Richardson into being a sponsor for a book that might be distasteful to him, but surely he was oversensitive about the projected contents. One cannot tell what he intended finally, but lists in his notebooks of the poems to be included and the poems already published in the *Darmouth Literary Monthly* give an indication. Only the most timid modesty could have forced a blush at such verses.

Many of the poems of the year 1887/1888 were prompted by "Miriam," of whom one can now find little more tangible than this fictitious name. It is only through hints and oblique

[5] *Ibid.*
[6] Hovey to Prof. C. F. Richardson, Feb. 8, 1888.

lights that one can detect even a shadowy woman. His wife later said vaguely in a note to the dedication of *Launcelot and Guenevere* that "she was a beautiful personality of his acquaintance." The half-completed poems in his notebooks suggest that Hovey met a woman, seemingly older than he, for whom he had a reverent love. For her he sketched a group of conventional and chivalric sestines which were to be presented as from the poet Delecour to the Lady Louise. Other more direct verses tell of a summer idyll by the sand pines and the sea. In these he has won her only to lose her. There is at first no more than a kiss of the hand as recognition of their love. The affair reaches its high moment of declared love on their last day. The woman is "won to be lost," lost by his own high-minded renunciation.

Behind the vague fictions there was a more intense story of love, perhaps for a woman already married. Meteyard's letters from France express a deep concern at Hovey's entanglement in an involved affair which would necessitate subterfuge and might not be happily simplified for some years. Whatever its nature, the romance may be left unriddled.[7] The actual person was important only as she meant something to Hovey as man and artist. As he wrote four years later:

Whether or not Miriam be a portrait is nobody's business; for all artistic purposes she is a type, and therefore a creation. If she had no generalized significance she would not be a proper subject for art.[8]

More important than the person was the effect of love on him. The experience went deep and he was most unhappy. One night during the spring of 1888, he read to a friend his story "Tomson," which had the same plot as the poems. A thundershower kept him, and in the need for release he told

[7] The material on this time is scant and one suspects that much of it has been destroyed. Hovey wrote for the third report of his class (writing in July, 1891): "I cannot write a long letter, though what I have done and experienced in the last three years would make volumes. These things I leave to my biographers." Biographers are altogether willing but the materials on which they might work have been lost.

[8] Hovey, no date [1892].

her that only a hatred of cowardice and a desire to use his God-given gift kept him from suicide. There was nothing else in life worth living for. Discount this as the histrionics of a romantic youth and one must still believe that Hovey suffered and that he sought in expression a way out of that suffering.

One day that spring as Hovey left a lecture on Sappho at the Columbian University, he heard someone calling "Hi! Halloa, there!" He turned to see with amazement that a dignified gentleman was chasing him and making frantic signs that he should stop. The panting pursuer was the Honorable Horatio King, who had been Postmaster General under Buchanan. Hovey's likeness to Giotto's portrait of Dante had so struck a friend that he had sent King to capture him. The friend was Thomas Davidson, one of the greatest men Hovey was to meet. Now forty-eight, he had worked himself up from an obscure Scottish farm boy to a man of encyclopedic knowledge and great linguistic skill. He had come to this country in 1867 and assumed the position of a medieval teacher with no fixed position. For six years since that time he had lived in Italy, almost as a religious hermit, while he studied the work of Rosmini. His hatred of dogma kept him from conversion and he remained "a knight errant of the intellectual life," as William James called him. In London he had founded the Fellowship of the Good Life, later metamorphosed into the Fabian Society, and had gone his way, earning only enough to live comfortably while retaining "intense individualism." Energy, laughter, spontaneous friendliness, and a delight in the out-of-doors kept him a fresh and vivid man. He had great faith in youth and genius. He believed in Hovey at first sight and on the spot engaged him to lecture in June at the Summer School of Philosophy he had instituted in Farmington, Connecticut, to carry on the spirit of the School of Philosophy Bronson Alcott had founded at Concord in 1879. He had been on the program of the first lecture series of the Concord school, and he, with Harris, had planned the last series. This was his second independent school, and he carried along not only the tradition but many of the men: Frank Sanborn, W. T. Harris, Percival Chub, and others. Hovey was invited to step into the company, though he was a man of only twenty-four. In the preceding summer his friend Frank Kavanagh had taken him to Concord to look reverently upon the school where Davidson and Harris were lecturing. Now he would share a program with them.

Hovey set to work on his lecture, "The Spirit of Revolt against Scholasticism as Shown in the Mephistopheles of Marlowe and the Mephistopheles of Goethe," or, as he familiarly called it, "The Devil." The topic was probably his, for he had always taken a deep interest in the problem of evil and in the conflict between authority and freedom. In his undergraduate essay on the growth of democratic ideas he had defended Marlowe as "no vulgar atheist" but the first free thinker and a man who dared to look into Hell in independence of thought. He also sympathized with Milton's magnification of the Evil One by his intense sympathy for freedom of will and judgment. Later, on one of his trips through the mountains, he had lectured on "Mephistopheles and Other Kinds of Devils." So the subject was not new to his mind.

On a June day in 1888 he told his audience that the devil of the sixteenth century as seen in Marlowe's Mephistopheles was the spirit of revolt against truth, whether true or not, and that of the eighteenth, in Goethe's Mephistopheles, a denial that truth could be known. Marlowe's Faustus was damned by religious revolt; Goethe's by very skepticism of the existence of truth, the final negative product of the Renaissance. Contemporary man's temptation, he added, is philistinism, mere respectability which does not revolt but conform, not deny but pretend to believe.[9] As he stopped, the audience applauded roundly. The generous Davidson, in the discussion which followed, said that the lecture was the best thing that had even been written on the subject and one of the best essays ever written about Goethe. Farmington was full of interesting

[9] MS fragments in Hovey's notebooks.

people and endless discussion. There was enough holiday spirit to draw the wealthy and refined, so that Hovey met not only impecunious scholars but the members of "the swell crowd." He was young enough to be flattered by their praise of his readings from Dante, Goethe, and Tennyson.

The climax of his success came after a reading of his own poems when Mrs. Sidney Lanier placed upon his head a wreath of laurel which had been sent from the South. Crowned with the sacred leaves by the beloved of America's most lyric singer, Hovey was ecstatically happy. It was almost "a laying on of hands."[10]

Mrs. William B. Keene was also impressed by the young scholar-poet and invited him to the School of Philosophy and Literature which she and Father Denton J. Snyder had founded in Chicago. Hovey was delighted with the opportunity and at Christmas he was in Chicago. Mrs. Keene was the first woman he had known who, like him, expressed her sense of beauty in daring dress. They were a striking pair as they stepped onto the streets, he in his velvet jacket, silk shirt, knee breeches and flowing tie, and she in a white Empire gown and Robespierre coat. One evening as they walked their aesthetic way a drunken Negress, outraged by such impropriety, followed them along the street denouncing them with loud cries of "Dress reform! Dress reform!"

His discussions on Dante successfully finished, Hovey went on to his birthplace and the relatives who still lived there. The normal child returned, a most out-of-the-normal man. His cousin, Agnes Cook, was breathless over his apparition, though in a more flattering way than her mother.[11] Richard gave the family and neighbors informal lectures in spirit not

[10] There were many interesting parallels between Lanier and Hovey. They were students and translators interested in other literatures; they believed that mastery of form was necessary to art and devoted themselves to the close study of verse forms and techniques; they shared a high ideal of the artist and sought a harmony of religion and art; their early deaths limited their opportunity to reach that ideal.

[11] All who have ever been interested in Hovey are grateful to Mrs. Agnes Cook Gale for her infinite patience in answering all queries about her cousin. More than any other she has acted as a focus for the continuing interest in Hovey and has been his most faithful admirer.

unlike those Wilde had delivered seven years before. If anyone criticized the aesthetic way of life he was ready to defend it, but within himself he had outgrown it, even if he had not yet shed its outer trappings.

America lagged behind Europe in discussion of the dominant artistic problem of the time, the relation of art to truth and to society; but before the nineties opened Hovey had worked out the first statement of that balance of forces in which he would always believe. His fully developed understanding of the artist's function attempted social advance without resigning the high position of art. He tried resolutely to maintain the spiritual hegemony of the poet both against those who withdrew art from social utility and against those who reduced it to social subservience. He carried on the faith of Shelley and Whitman in the "legislative" and even divine mission of the poet, although there is no indication of conscious discipleship.

Perhaps because he was a young American, and so further than the English or French from narrow adherence to either the party of art or the party of society, he could make a large and satisfying synthesis which, while in a sense more traditional and conservative than theirs, was broader and less of its immediate time. He was not trying to settle an argument with others so much as with himself and the pressure of debate did not distort his conclusions. The victory of one or another coterie or school was unimportant to him. He sought objectively a philosophic basis for making realism and idealism one in the service of life. This, he felt, was the distinguishing mark of great literature, whether one examined the Greeks, Dante, or Shakespeare. Like Tolstoy, he believed in "art for life's sake," as he said, but behind that simple statement was massed a solidly reasoned and progressively achieved body of thought. One remembers no other American who made so thorough, articulated, and conclusive a study as Hovey carried out in the series of articles he wrote for the *Independent*. Those were still some years ahead, but the early essays and lectures are more meaningful if one realizes that they are not discrete *obiter dicta* but the developing thought of one moving from aestheticism to a broadly explored and highly organized philosophy of art.

His first approach was a frontal attack on the time. In an essay called "The Dying Century," partially printed in the *Dartmouth Literary Magazine* (February, 1888), he evaluated his day of pragmatic acquiescence in the single worship of material multiplication and economic success. He found the stress on mere existence everywhere in business, society, science, and art. He regretted this turn from a deeper perception, but the cure was not by a more limited adherence to beauty.

Whenever the artist withdraws from the religion, hopes and aspirations of his fellows and from their actual sufferings and wrongs, he becomes a mere dilettante. He turns his high calling into a foppery. The people ask for bread and he gives them bonbons![12]

He blamed avoidance of the coarse tough stuff of the day for the preoccupation with external form. Only as art comes down from its aesthetic pedestal and finds meaning for men in the circumstances of their day will the people cherish art. It is not, of course, art in itself which is important, but art as that which finds meaning in existence.

That men lose faith in goodness, and beauty, and truth, in some great final purpose in things which shall make all the struggle and anguish of life rational . . . is a calamity so great that all others are little in comparison. Something of this sort is at the bottom of Philistinism.

There is no art without artist, and America's rejection of the artist and man of creative culture seemed to him a costly stupidity.

We are a great country. We touch two oceans, and count our population by the millions. We have railroads and telephones and cotton gins. We have daily newspapers and public schools and printing presses. We have a protective tariff—God make us properly grateful—and a surplus. But we are not so civilized a nation as the Greeks were two thousand years ago, and there are more slaves in New York City to-

[12] *Dartmouth Literary Monthly*, II (Feb., 1888), 208-211.

day than in all Europe in the middle ages. Our society is based on money-getting, not upon the eternal Harmonies. Men who waste time in the elevation of their souls are left behind in the great grab-bag struggle. As a result, we have the discouragement of culture, the survival of the nincompoop.

Such an uncompromising understanding of the general degradation of the spirit makes him doubt the sufficiency of a purely aesthetic position. Some, like Wilde, could denounce the whole utilitarian attitude and turn toward the contemplation of beauty undefiled. Hovey was too strenuous for that, and too moral. Behind him were the men who settled the new world, laid out frontier towns, and farmed upland fields. Nothing could satisfy him but an active social purpose made vivid by art. So he turned impatiently to the new century, in which social and individual life might be no longer barren and unprofitable. "Let us be men of the Twentieth Century."

The essay was directed at the public. Only a more subtle investigation of the problem could satisfy his own need for understanding within the terms of art. Since Mrs. Lanier had presented him with the wreath of laurel his happiness had sobered to a questioning of his right to accept it. He asked himself how he should dare to take the laurel Lanier had worn.

> I dare not let the sacred leaves be bound
> About my brow. My song is all unready
> So soon to seek so greatly to be crowned.[13]

Yet he felt that he must take the responsibility symbolized by the gift.

While he wrote *The Laurel* his mind brooded on Davidson's words to him. Davidson had faith in him but demanded a militantly idealistic devotion to purpose. He had the right to make such a demand for he had always made it of himself. Years later Hovey told a reporter for the Boston *Sunday Herald*: "Once I wanted merely to write good poetry; later after something had been said to me one day which altered my whole life, I wanted to do as great work as had ever been

---

[13] Richard Hovey, *The Laurel, An Ode* (Washington, D. C.: Published by the Author, 1889), p. 2.

done."[14]   Surely he was thinking of Davidson, to whom he wrote in 1892: "If I have any ability in accomplishing anything, it was in great part brought to a point by a certain confidence in myself which you did much to suggest the first summer I was in Farmington."[15]   Davidson believed in active work in the world.   Beauty was not enough.   One had to throw oneself into the effort to reconstruct society so that man's divine potentialities might be fulfilled.   In this great effort art should be a purposeful, if imaginative, solution of man's problem.

Hovey's decision to be all that he meant by poet came out of many conflicts, but it struck with dramatic suddenness and was an act of full acceptance, something on the order of an epiphany, coming, of all places, aboard a train.

On Jan. 1st. 1889, only passenger in a parlor car on train from Chicago to Bloomington, Ill., watching eclipse of the sun from car windows, what had been forming in my mind for many years took shape.   The love of writing and the love of acting, both almost passions with me even from ante-collegiate days, spurred up by many talks with Davidson in which he attacked me for too much humility and self-mistrust, and more or less dared me to try the highest, and focused by other private matters which I cannot write about—all came to a head on that long lonely railroad ride.   And I then and there decided to be a poet and playwright, and to attack the biggest problems I could find to undertake, and to begin with a series of six plays and three masques on the story of Launcelot and Guenevere.   Within a month from that time I had the whole scheme of the Launcelot series laid out, a scheme that I have in no material way altered since, and am not likely to.[16]

Hovey's feeling about his decision is clear in the dedication which he wrote to stand at the head of his Arthurian series.   Indeed that act of dedication was so important to him that he lost his sense of proportion and opened himself to the obvious gibes of the reviewers.   The dedication begins by making a double invocation to God and Apollo, not troubling to

[14] "A Typical Modern Poet," Boston *Sunday Herald*, Oct. 30, 1898.
[15] Letter of Aug. 2, 1892, Davidson Collection, Yale University Library.
[16] Hovey, autobiographical letter to Walter Rice, Feb. 4, 1899. DCA.

resolve this dual allegiance, and moves into an allegory in which Shakespeare, in the company of Dante, Aeschylus, Homer, David, and Goethe, asks him to set free the poetic drama. Again, as in *The Laurel,* he would evade his responsibility by humility, but finally declares, "I will sing."

This dedication is the expression of a young man overcome by the wonder of his own high purpose. He undertook the great task of a lifetime humbly, but in his very sincerity left himself ridiculous. He, the untried, among the greatest, with Shakespeare and Goethe alone of the moderns! This was offering vulnerability to the critics and they struck when the *Launcelot and Guenevere* volume appeared in 1891. It did seem, as the *Athenaeum* said, that Hovey was not aware that anybody in the world but him was writing verse. With biting mockery the *Literary World* made laughable the whole dedication and the writer's seeming vanity. Yet it is the fault of those who take themselves seriously to feel that a great cause depends upon their single effort. It is a fault that may be an inspiration. Meeting rebuff and indifference and poverty Hovey had to feel the very Red Cross Knight of Art to keep his spirit bold.

Through the spring of 1889 he worked on his lecture for the Farmington series. He chose to advance his understanding of the problems he faced by considering the relationship of art and morality, or ethics and aesthetics, a subject he claimed to know less well than "the Devil." He began by denying literary exactness to Keats's famous line: "Beauty is truth, truth beauty." Things are not good because they are beautiful, as the aesthetes claim, with precious sentimentalism turning everything into mere prettiness. Still more dangerous and evil is the transcendental position that what is good is beautiful. Art is not the inculcation of morality but "the seeing power of intelligent Love." That love, when perfect, should incite the will to act, but art does not concern itself with that consequence. The aesthetic is devoted only to the quickening of vision. The ethical element is one of conflict; the aesthetic is one of calm.

Though art can range broadly for her material, that material must be used for an aesthetic purpose. So it is that if the artist cannot, because of limited power, solve the conflict between ethics and beauty so that the right will have an aesthetic quality itself, it is his duty to sacrifice the ethical to the aesthetic or give up the subject, for art cannot be subordinated to morality. Yet it must not be thought that there is no relationship, for the ethical enters everywhere. If art should adopt a contrary assumption—as business had fatally done—we should have "a charlatan artistry and a demoralized public." Since man is an ethical being, his ethical nature is pre-eminently the concern of art. Thus, since the world is perceived through man, ethical relations are so much a part of the subject matter of art that art cannot reject them without becoming empty.

Hovey then goes on to consider the relationship of art and ethics as it is conditioned by society. He assumes, like Ruskin, that "a great art must arise out of a great people, that no people can be great without sturdy ethical qualities, and that it is, therefore, only out of an ethical soil that great art can grow." It is a reciprocal interchange, for as the artist owes society the cultivation of his spirit, the state owes it to the artist to use his power and so save the nation from sordid commercialism and from a morose Puritanism that leaves duty a hateful necessity.

So, he concludes, art and ethics, though totally distinct, are inextricably related. Their high synthesis is in religion, and great art, like religion, reveals the unseen in the seen, the divine made flesh, a perfected incarnation. "This is the function of Art—to reveal truth in that beauty which Plato declared to be 'the splendour of truth,' as a thing incarnate, humanized, made intelligible sacramentally to the mind of man. Therefore is all art religious and all religion, though something more, artistic." If our commercialism and our absorption in the unimportant were replaced by the old religious spirit of unification in essentials and diversity in nonessentials, the spirit would again seek nourishment and expression in poetry.

The lecture is a very sound and reasoned statement. It establishes art in its central position, art accepting the flow of all life into it and returning that flux to society in an ordered and intelligible beauty. The artist takes no cloistered retreat, but becomes again the shaper of life in the humanistic tradition. Yet he does not pervert the aesthetic stasis, "the quickening of vision," to a kinetic social weapon. Art had been vacillating between two extremes, the sociological surgery of Zola ("art in sociology") and the pure aestheticism of the Poe-Baudelaire School. Hovey touches the real truth, that art is first of all art, but that since man is an ethical being the art he creates must have ethical awareness if it is to contain his whole being. He asserts again the interplay of artist and society without which no culture can be great and lacking which his own day failed.

The essay shows that he understood what he, as artist, should attempt. As usual with the poet, his mind could reach farther than his ability, but he kept working. Though discouraged about seeing himself in print except in an occasional magazine, he was more and more drawn away from the short verses such magazines would print. The large idea of the poet demanded a large scope, and the drama offered, he thought, a greater chance to achieve his end and to return man as an active agent to the foreground of art.

Though he devoted himself to his major task and during the winter and spring of 1889 began work on *The Quest of Merlin,* he knew that more than ever he needed some economic support, particularly if his "affair" with Miriam went through. Many ways were closed to him, though few realized his difficulties. He had tried the journals, teaching in the country was impossible for him during the hay-fever season, and the dust of books prohibited library work. One position seemed splendidly designed for his gifts and needs, a consular position. He thought particularly of Florence (perhaps because of comments on his "Florentine face") and also of the north coast of Africa, Tunis, Tripoli, Algiers, or Morocco. He considered himself well fitted. As he told Lindsay Swift, he was a native American, not unfamiliar with international law. He spoke French, knew a little German and Italian, and was a gentleman, "as some of our representatives are not, worse luck." That he might seem more convincingly American, he jocularly offered up "his hyacinthine locks on the altar of conventionality." And he began to pull as many highly charged wires as possible. Governor Fifer of Illinois, Professor Wright of Harvard, Senator Cullom, the Professors Richardson at Dartmouth, and several others wrote letters recommending him highly. Nothing came of Hovey's efforts. Adventure of another kind awaited him.

CHAPTER IV

Delsartism and Mrs. Russell

> As at the altar of the unknown God
> Even so we stood before the shrine of Art.
> Ignorant, we worshipped—till the hill was trod
> By the Apostle. Whom but thee, Delsarte?
>
> HOVEY, "Delsarte," 1893.

It was intoxicating to Richard Hovey in the winter of 1889-1890 to be introduced around Washington as a poet and critic. He took pride in the titles which he had not really earned. When he reported to his Dartmouth class secretary that he enjoyed the position of literary lion, he slightly exaggerated his new-found eminence. One evening he attended a social-intellectual gathering to hear his friend Harris read a paper. There Hovey had the good fortune to meet a literary lioness who had already made a considerable success by lecturing in the drawing rooms of Washington.

Her name was Mrs. Edmund Russell. She and Hovey had met casually twice before, but now she took particular notice of the handsome young lion. Later she would remember how "fine-lined" he seemed in his dress suit, and how much younger he actually was than the quality and tone of his conversation would suggest. He quoted, in conversation, some lines of verse on the Faust-Margaret relationship. "What's that from?" she asked the young man. "It's so good I ought to remember it." He laughed gaily and said, "It's from my *Launcelot and Guenevere*." Since it was natural for her to attract men to her service, she turned over in her mind how she should ask him to call and read more of the poem. It is not difficult to prompt a young poet to read, and the next day he called and read all that was written of *Launcelot and Guenevere*.

Mrs. Russell was a revelation of the physical beauty discipline could achieve. Though forty years old and solidly built for her height, she carried herself like a goddess. Her dark hair was brushed out "in Egyptian fashion" and Pre-Raphaelite bangs made her forehead low so that one was more conscious of the blue-gray eyes which looked at one steadily from beneath well-defined brows. Her nose was Grecian in its straightness, her mouth large and finely cut, and everyone noticed the poise of her head upon the full, flexible throat.

Born Henriette Knapp in Cooperstown, New York, she was now Mrs. Edmund Russell, known in England and America as leading authority on Delsartism.[1] With a shrewd courage she had made her way by conquest of self and public. The woman now described by a society reporter as "made of fire and mist, steel watch springs and harp strings, so agile, so full of nerve, and such splendid health-giving vitality" had been a sickly child. When her health broke, the doctor blamed her restrictive clothing. So she gave up tightly fitting clothes and corsets and, as a convert to physical freedom in dress, designed her own costumes. Presently, a variety of comment on her style sense urged her onto the platform as an advocate of dress reform. At one of her talks a member of the audience spoke to her about the faults in her enunciation. Unoffended, Miss Knapp went for instruction to Professor James Munroe at the Boston University School of Oratory. Munroe had been taught by Steele MacKaye, whom Delsarte had called "mon seul disciple—plus qu'un disciple; un fils d'adoption plus cher à mon coeur que mes propres enfants."[2] Delsarte, who had opened his first course in 1839, was living almost forgotten

[1] François Alexandre Nicholas Chéri Delsarte (1811-1871) was a professor of music who taught the arts of emotional expression through voice and gesture. Because he was interested in the anatomy of the larynx and in human physiology generally, his system included training in poise, breath control, and in relaxing exercises as part of the preparation for effective appearances on platform or stage. His teachings, somewhat corrupted from the master's system, had a great vogue in America in the 1890's.

[2] Percy MacKaye, *Epoch, The Life of Steele MacKaye* (2 vols.; New York: Boni and Liveright, 1927), I, 132.

when MacKaye renewed his fame, largely through the School of Expression he founded early in 1871.[3]

MacKaye was a theater man and an inventor, and the press of activities postponed his final definition of Delsartism. His associates, however, had also been spreading the method. William Rounseville Alger, who had written *Poetry of the Orient*, and had, in a sense, taken Theodore Parker's place as the most prominent Unitarian clergyman and lecturer of the country, worked with Munroe to introduce Delsarte's method in America. When Delsarte was living in exile and poverty during the Franco-Prussian war, his disciples raised two thousand francs by expositions at Tremont Temple and Steinway Hall and Alger smuggled the money by dispatch rider through the lines from Brussels to Solemes, but the old man died on July 20, 1871, before the gift reached him.

The Delsarte system had meantime entered a temporary eclipse, but Henriette Knapp was so convinced of its value that without money or friends or adequate education, she set out for Paris ready to assume discipleship. The aged Mme Delsarte was kind to her, and the master's son, Gustave, took her under his personal tuition and soon made her his assistant and interpreter to the English-speaking pupils. When he died she persevered in her studies and went on to wider investigation.

At some time, supposedly, she had married, but nowhere in the personal accumulation which was her habit is there any mention of her husband. Her child, presumably not parthenogenetic, she recorded in a genealogical table as "Harold Kenneth Krane son of Henriette Knapp Crane" [*sic*]. This son is later referred to by newspaper reporters as one of the children of Edmund Russell. Russell is also a shadowy figure, an actor who, rumor has it, split his tights playing Hamlet, and a Delsartean lecturer who specialized in interior decoration. They had struck up a business relation, given joint lectures, and then married. By him she had two children. One died in infancy in Rome; the other was named Sigurd Naourn Russell. Now

[3] *Ibid.*, II, 267. He never found a publisher for his projected nine volumes on Delsartism and expression.

the pair were living separately, although they had made no definite move toward divorce.

Mr. Russell's friends say that his wife became too much elated with her reception in London and in this country afterward to live with him as his wife, and on the other hand it is said that Mr. Russell was somewhat jealous of the attention paid to his wife, and for this reason there was constant friction between them.[4]

In London Mrs. Russell found that only four persons she met had heard of Delsarte, one of these being Oscar Wilde, a close friend of MacKaye, who had planned to produce Wilde's plays. Soon, however, she had made Delsarte a famous name among the literary and artistic. Her lectures, given in the charming studio of the painter Felix Moschelles, drew a wide group. Here came Browning, who served her her first cup of English tea, Lady Shelley, Lady Wilde and her son Oscar, Madam Blavatsky, Lord Lytton, Whistler, Henry M. Stanley, Alma Tadema, and others. Here Gladstone told her her system should be in every school in England.

In London she perfected her method of inducing patrons to invite paying guests to lectures given in their homes. This gave a social cachet and an intimacy to her performances—as well as saving public rent. So she lectured, perhaps at Mrs. Campbell Praed's, or, if lucky, had the Prince of Mantua and Montferrat preside over the meeting. At her Monday evening receptions one might meet cosmopolitan society, Indians, Orientals, a Buonaparte, an Egyptologist, painters and musicians. Some newspaper accounts asserted that one might hear as many as forty languages at one of these soirees. Others contented themselves with a modest seventeen. Through this assembly moved the complete mistress of every gesture and intonation. Later in the evening, to quote the London correspondent of the New York *Herald*, "she used to go through some of the exercises of the Delsartean code of physical culture, which showed off the lines of her limbs and figure beautifully and *en passant* revealed to many the fact that she took no pains to conceal, to wit, that she wore no corsets."

[4] Boston *Record*, Jan. 18, 1894.

Nothing brought Mrs. Russell more notoriety than the rejection of the corset, though the followers of Sylvester Graham, Mrs. Stanton, and Amelia Bloomer had published the doctrine—and widened their hips. Her sponsorship of the "short Greek girdle" which has since become universal amused and excited the public mind. Over this perilously inadequate mould she wore a plain princess slip which was the foundation of her remarkable costumes. Out of a shawl and a paper of pins, or some lengths of material bought from an upholsterer, she fashioned a costume which, she hoped, combined the simple lines of the Greek with the richness of the Persian. Such a "brain costume" she studded with brooches, coins, and ornaments in amber, coral porphyry, and jade, all in barbaric settings. These inexpensive stones, bright against metallic backgrounds, were the forerunners of the later craze for costume jewelry.

Hovey was drawn to this rebel against Victorian convention, custom, and dress who, like him, sought a fresher beauty that wedded body and spirit and made itself manifest in physical grace and expressive clothing. He found his own delight in costume, carriage, voice, and trained expression in one who was a student and teacher of such arts. Like so many creative men before and after him his spirit was aroused only by women older than himself. He had once told his cousin, "There are very few girls I have any interest in. They are like unripe fruit—no flavor." Mrs. Russell had both flavor and ripeness.

As Hovey went on with *Launcelot and Guenevere* he met two inescapable facts—that he knew little about the drama and that he needed money. Each evening after dinner he read aloud to his mother and father what he had written during the day. They would pick the work to pieces, never allowing their pride to cripple their possible aid. In the morning his parents went off to work, leaving him to the quiet of the house. Though they were as generous as ever, he realized that it was necessary for him and good for any poet to have some means of support other than the slender reed of poetry. The stage for him would be both income and schooling.

He always maintained that the great dramatists were, like Molière and Shakespeare, both actors and writers. The closet drama held no interest for him, and he saw that central problem of the drama which has remained generally unsolved. He wanted a practical but aesthetic product which would balance the literary quality which the producers disdained with the theatrical energy and skill which the literary men ignored. Poets and playwrights who were also actors were needed. "Neither a mere actor nor a mere poet will ever stand much chance of writing great plays. It was with this thought that I chose myself to go on the stage."[5]

Mary Shaw used to say that in 1890 she laughingly told her friend Hovey that she wished he were an actor. Hovey replied that he thought he could act and reported for the job. Miss Shaw was no ordinary actress. Mme Modjeska, with whom she had just been playing, spoke of her as "a studious, intellectual young woman with a great deal of talent." Ex-schoolteacher and student of Delsartean grace, she was very serious about the stage. Later she was to have great success as Mrs. Alving in *Ghosts,* carrying Ibsen to the West, which had hardly heard his name, and becoming one of Shaw's chief interpreters. This tour with *A Drop of Poison,* however, was her first starring performance, and it brought her independent fame. The play had been adapted from the German of Oscar Blumenthal by that indefatigable translator and adaptor, Augustin Daly. Hovey had the part of Fabricius, a counselor.

He met the company, liked them, and was able to write home that "everything is lovely and the goose is altitudinous." He went to rehearsal from 10 to 5:30 and found time only to call on Mrs. Russell and to see Carman and Davidson. Finally the play opened in Chicago and then toured the road for ten weeks. It was well-received as a dignified and even ennobling contribution to the drama. The critic of the Boston *Transcript* declared (May 6, 1890) that "one such play as *A Drop of*

[5] Interview in the New York *Morning Advertiser,* June 2, 1892.

Poison intelligently and sympathetically acted will do more for the elevation of the stage than volumes of diatribe and years of theorizing." Certainly the audience agreed with his praise of Miss Shaw's "Delsartean truth and facility of gesture" and "her excellent supporting company," for there were many curtain calls and Miss Shaw was burdened with flowers.

If one can accept Hovey's opinion, Miss Shaw showed the temperamental narrowness of the star and was generally rather unpleasant. When the run of *A Drop of Poison* was finished, Hovey gladly left the company. Yet, if she said unpleasant things about his ability, three years later she wrote to ask him to take an important role—that of a United States senator— in a play by Kellard in which she had the lead. By then Hovey too had cooled. Though he wanted greatly to go, he did not dare to take the time from writing to chance an un- certain play at a salary of $30 a week.

Hovey's acting pleased some, at any rate, for he carried the part of diplomat to the court of Berlin with the grace one would expect. Clement, editor of the *Transcript,* introduced him to Barrett in a note which called him "an actor of real promise." Clement said: "I had the pleasure of seeing him this winter and, though in a minor part, his poise, grace and effectiveness were remarkable, especially for one playing his first engagement."[6] He enjoyed acting and wanted to con- tinue it for a while. He tried to get a place with Effie Ellsler playing juvenile leads. He also made a hurried trip to Boston to see Lawrence Barrett. He found no opening, however, and returned to Washington to work on the plays until August sent him north to Boston and to Bethlehem, where he spent a long holiday. So he faced another season without money or position. It is very likely that it was upon his late return this year that he was seen striding along Boylston Street in an open shirt and knickerbockers during an early snowstorm. The journalists seized upon this as another colorful Hovey story, but as he said to an old classmate, "My friend, it takes time to get your clothes out of pawn."

[6] Edward H. Clement, letter, June 20, 1890. DCA.

In November, 1890, Tom Meteyard came to Washington on his way to Florida, where he was to be happy as the best of the local painters. He had already exhibited his "dazzling little experiments in the alchemy of light" in Chicago, where the *Tribune* accepted him almost as a local son by transforming his name to "Meatyard." He and Hovey hung some thirty-five of his paintings and invited guests to view them. Alone, the two talked of France, where it was possible both to live cheaply and to devote oneself entirely to work. Hovey was discouraged about getting ahead, and, like many of the other young Americans who were considering the same haven, was prompted not by scorn of American culture but by the impossibility of living decently as an artist within it. It had little place for the writer and few prizes, unless one became a merchant of shoddy verse.

Despair and loneliness were driving him dangerously close to an assumption of defeated greatness. He had faith in himself, and, he said, was free of mean ambition, but he wanted success. The very frustration of his desires made the great work he felt ready for seem easier to achieve than it was. Though he tried the magazines, the work to which he had put his mind was not magazine verse dictated in style by Gilder and Aldrich. Carman was now on the *Independent* and received some poems with enthusiasm; but there was little payment to maintain Hovey while he gave his major effort to drama. He was working on *Columbus*, had written part of a comedy called "Bohemia," and had *Launcelot and Guenevere* ready for printing. But where were public and publishers?

Mrs. Russell put her faith in converting the upper classes from whom culture would filter down to those lower on the social ladder, but Hovey, too penniless to get to New York to see the theatrical people who might help him or, indeed, even to buy horsecar tickets to get around his own city, would have nothing of this theory. He wrote in February, 1891:

I am thoroughly disgusted, for more reasons than one, with your philanthropical elevation-of-art people. They sympathize wonderfully, but if you ask how much they sympathize that is another story, as Kipling says. They use Art for their own glorification, are enthusiastic for it in meetings and discussions that give them social and newspaper prominence, and are ever willing to have their names in print as Lady Patronesses, God save the mark! But when you say "What will *you* do for Art?" . . . And yet with this material we must work, as you know as well as I. Of one thing I am convinced,—if the American drama is created, I must do it almost if not quite alone.[7]

Mrs. Russell had returned from London in the autumn of 1890. Reading *The Laurel* over and over had brought Hovey near to her and she wondered if something "is in Fate." Still the queen, she commanded a court performance. "I am come to my homeland and no poet is near to bring me any song." Cryptically she concluded her letter: "As I am yours, so am I yours."[8] Hovey sent her the manuscript of *Launcelot and Guenevere* and they began a kind of spiritual and literary flirtation, that heady excitement to the young and unpublished. She wrote to him at the end of the year:

The recent past put women in two classes, those who loved and those who knew. . . . Your women love instinctively, intuitively, holily, with the worship of their bodies and their souls; and they know it and know it is the highest living and know why.

The woman whose passion fires her intelligence; whose heart guides both, has at last found her poet. In the name of the best I know of my sex I send you recognition, greeting, gratitude. Poet heart and artist brain, you may claim as your own all the Miriam, the Adela, the Guinevere of womanhood. To it you have spoken. It will always hear you.[9]

It was an invitation—let him speak! And let him speak to her, the very type of modern Guenevere.

Somehow he got the fare to New York in February. He had a satisfactory interview with Gilder, got Daly to read his play, and saw publishers. Mrs. Russell asked his editorial assistance on the book she was writing, a book which, with splendid disregard of the opening it offered the critics, she had en-

[7] Hovey, Feb. 5, 1891.
[8] Mrs. Russell, Oct. 19, 1890.
[9] Typescript copy initialed by Mrs. Russell ("H. H."), no date, DCA.

titled *Yawning*. This was the first volume in a projected series dealing with Delsartean principles, which Mrs. Russell believed to be "rooted in the essential nature of things," and so discovered rather than made by man. In it she used the yawn as an example of the instinctive sanity of the body, which manages the gymnastics of the yawn with admirable economy, producing the greatest motion with the least motive, and so leaving the higher centers at rest. Like a wave it passes over the whole body from outstretched legs to lifted arms, yet leaves the mind unused and the body strengthened and refreshed. In this motiveless motion, called "gymnastic," she found a salvation for a civilization which has released a large class from physical work, but left it weary in brain and emotion. The muscles need building, but not in the wasteful way of athletics, which create only bulk. Rather man must discover through the laws of the body the laws of the mind, discover that life is an art if the dormant and unawakened impulses are released into harmonious action and if grace frees the imprisoned spirit.

The manuscript of the book was typical of its author, a muddled confusion which preached a disciplined control. Like so many books put out by the physical culturists since that day, it was timid with the physical and pompously clumsy with the cultural. It was full of the phrases and clichés of professional body-trainers. Yet behind its weaknesses it stood for healthy harmony against the evil dichotomy of body and mind which had so long crippled America. It understood that the best education is that which develops all of man and that mere knowledge is no proper end. It called for a return to that wholeness the Greek made his ideal, but perhaps it is to its credit that it began not with a learned classical theft, but with a yawn. Unfortunately it ended in the same way.

It is, of course, impossible to know how much order Hovey brought to the manuscript as they worked through the spring evenings at Mrs. Russell's 12th Street apartment. One who knows anything of her lack of system, her reliance upon Sibyl-like utterances, suspects that Hovey introduced a good deal of clarification. Whether or not it was his original idea, he added quotations from the poets to precede chapters. Even in that brief quotation from Hovey's own work which heads the chapter on grace:

> O sweet as only vigour can be sweet
> O strong as only loveliness is strong

one sees something of the similarity in desire which drew these two together.

Finally they became lovers. It was no seduction. Hovey's nature simply focused on the one woman who became Love. Her poise and experience carried him safely over the unhappy blundering of young lovers and yet left him ecstatic. The painful tangle of relationships never touched his wonder at what had come to him. To Lindsay Swift he wrote:

Am I not an unlucky dog? As I have been lying here thinking of my unfortunate liaison, my asthma, and my debts, I have said: Verily am I not afflicted in mind, body, and estate? I retract the adjective unfortunate, hastily used above, though. I will tell you more of that affair sometime, having told you, by that little piece of indirection in the library, so much already. But although it has been anything but unmixed joy and promises a very red-hot Purgatory indeed before it reaches Paradiso, yet "unfortunate" it never was nor will be. It is the one thing in my life that has made it worth living. For talk of art as we will (and I did faithfully walk by that light alone for tedious years, trusting) yet it is a hard thing to devote our lives to an abstraction. If it is to be Art, we must make Art a living God, an Apollo in whose tangible reality we believe. We must have a religion, in other words, about which our works (of art or otherwise) may cling. Well, I have found my religion.[10]

Later, after the summer, he wrote again:

As for me, although I suffer more pains and perplexities than ever before in my life, I really have no feeling of sorrow—only a mad kind of joy—Carlyle's "inarticulate shriek of the human soul." I am, in a manner, drunk and want to throw my arms about everybody and tell them all about it.[11]

[10] Hovey, no date, probably July, 1891.
[11] Hovey, no date, probably Sept., 1891.

When Mrs. Russell went on to Newport, she summoned him there by telegram. He hated Newport, "the stupidest place I was ever in. All fuss and feathers and stately emptiness." The old town was "a repetition of Nantucket. Same architecture, same people, same occupations, same general look of things," but *fashionable* Newport had changed from a quiet and exclusive resort into an extravagant and widely advertised showplace of plutocratic display.[12] As one writer said: "At no time since Cleopatra carried off Anthony for a 'season' in Asia Minor has so much money been spent that a group of people might take sea baths."

On Ocean Drive or Bellevue Avenue one might see Mrs. Astor, Mrs. Kernochan, Mrs. Stuyvesant Fish, Mrs. Frederick Vanderbilt, or Mrs. W. C. Whitney. It was a perfect hunting ground for Mrs. Russell, who organized a class at the home of Mrs. Whitney in the famous Travers villa. The circular ballroom was redecorated and a platform was covered with oriental rugs to set off Mrs. Russell's yellow and silver gown as she stood under a palm tree. Every day the room was newly decorated with some particular flower. The reporters noted that Mrs. Whitney had paid "a crisp new $100 bill" to "the lithe-limbed priestess of Delsarte." "Henrietta's hour has come." It had indeed.[13]

Seventy-five or a hundred of the wealthiest and most stylish women of America used to attend these morning classes at Mrs. Whitney's or Mrs. Chief Justice Gray's where, as large headlines proclaimed, Mrs. Russell "taught Mrs. Astor to faint and Mrs. Vanderbilt to cry." When Mrs. Astor said to Mrs. Russell, "You have opened a new world to me," the latter filed the remark in her mind for future and frequent use in a world too easily impressed by names. Everyone was enthusiastic except Mr. Ward McAllister, the moral snob, who was slightly put out by having another steal the show and who, it was said, did not like to have women taught the most

[12] Hovey, July 21, 1891.
[13] Unspecified newspaper and magazine quotations are taken from a scrapbook kept by Mrs. Russell, DCA.

graceful way of laying a head on a masculine shoulder, for knowledge encouraged experiment.

Mrs. Russell's rooms on Kay Street, decorated in taste illustrative of her theories, were popular at tea time. Yet she never ruled her tongue diplomatically, and criticized her fashionable guests with unblunted honesty. To be set straight by her was a fad.

Of course, those newspapers which were not subservient to wealth rightly suspected Newport of following something new for the sake of the novelty only, even of losing republican simplicity. One writer, who signed himself "Cynic," wrote a pair of quatrains called "The Newport Fad."

> At Newport now Delsarte is on,
> The Ladies' minds grow plastic,
> While those whose youth is not quite gone
> Are getting forms elastic.
>
> And what's it all for anyhow?
> Why show this craze such loyalty?
> Perhaps it's just to learn to bow
> More deeply still to royalty.

Undoubtedly Mrs. Russell's easy introduction of noble and famous names did a good deal to attract the Newport ladies, and, of course, her costumes drew every eye. Out-of-doors she wore little Florentine caps made of gold, copper, or silver passementerie and carried a yellow and red parasol. Her gowns, as almost every one of innumerable newspaper and magazine articles noted, were without seams. Above the slip each piece of richly colored material was held in place only by brooches and decorative pins. This warm and striking effect was set off more vividly when her husband, "the white-robed Edmund," arrived in August.

> The high priest of Delsarte is he,
> A type of wan flaccidity,
> Our dear devitalizer.

While Mrs. Russell was the rage of Newport and the fad of the journalists everywhere in the East, Hovey was reading proof on *Launcelot and Guenevere*. Lovell had accepted the drama which had been promoted by some of Hovey's friends, notably by E. C. Stedman, who was always a generous helper and believer in him. He had given Hovey a note to Lovell that suggested he strain a point and print the drama.

He has a head on his shoulders, and will be likely ere long to make his mark. He will make a hit with something ere long, you may be sure.

Lovell strained the point and agreed to put out *Launcelot and Guenevere* if the writer put up $360 of the $560. This was the accepted contract. Hovey signed and returned it with the note:

> Here's Cakes and Ale for us,
> Prosit and Hail for us,
> And a great sale to us.

Meanwhile Hovey was getting his affairs in shape to leave for Europe. He expected to live abroad for less than it cost in America and tried to get newspaper work which, with the possible help from his father, would support him in the meager way to which he was now accustomed. He was also writing articles on poetics and language for the *Independent*. By the end of July he was in a confused bustle, sending for trunks, making arrangements with Lovell, and writing hurried notes of leavetaking.

He went up to Boston, where his friends feted him and praised his play. Newspapers notices were now appearing so frequently that he engaged a clipping bureau to collect them. His friends, Sam Hudson, Lindsay Swift, Wilder Quint and the others, kept swarming in to see him at the Parker House and to wish him *bon voyage*. Finally, on August 8, 1891, the Cunard liner *Catalonia* nosed out of the harbor and set her course for Liverpool. Hovey was intoxicated with the excitement of friendship and praise. The last days had only increased his certainty that, as he wrote his mother, " I am evidently on the eve of success."

More than any other American of his time Hovey strove to analyze the craft and technique of poetry, so entering the tradition of the poet-aestheticians Emerson, Poe, Whitman, and Lanier. Indeed, he is no more remarkable in his exaggerated sense of dedication than in his scientific curiosity about the mediums of expression. For the last decade of his life he was a constant investigator, believing that art is something artfully made and therefore demands study.

All good art is a growth as much as all Nature is, and every poet writes by a method that is the result of his own personal development. The natural method is his own method. But in order to use this natural method, it is necessary to have a great deal of instinctive and acquired knowledge. "A good poet," says Ben Jonson, "is made as well as born."

A poet must have something to say, and he must know how to say it. What he has to say depends on how great a man he is, and how wide and deep is his experience of life. How he says it depends on his knowledge of the laws and the possibilities of expression in the language he uses. It is true that his knowledge of these laws and his command of these possibilities must have become instinctive and unconscious before what he writes can be called poetry. But instincts are only knowledge become automatic. All that man does unconsciously he had first to do consciously. What we possess we must first conquer. There was a time when Shakespeare could not say *ba-ba*, not to speak of saying "Hamlet."

The development of a babbling baby into that crown and summit of human genius, a poet, is, in the strictest sense of the word, a matter of education. The greater part of the education of poets (and, indeed of everybody) has been left for the most part to chance and blind experiment. But if it could be shown that all Art rests upon necessary principles of expression, and that many of these principles are known, it would be clear that the scientific study of such principles would, to put it at its mildest, save the artist in words, as well as all other artists, from much waste of time and unnecessary groping.[14]

Despite the absurdities of the Delsarte cults, Hovey took from the primary tenets of the French teacher a direction and a

[14] Hovey, "Delsarte and Poetry," *Independent*, XLIII (Aug. 27, 1891), 1267.

vocabulary, though not a system, for that did not exist for poetry. Delsarte, a teacher of singing and acting, had concerned himself most with dramatic expression, but a method sound for one art should be sound for all. Though there was little in Delsarte's literary remains or in the complicated definitions of his disciples to clarify poetry itself, there was the provocative idea that within all art is a discoverable science of expression based on laws which can be uncovered through scientific analysis.

The other most fruitful suggestion from Delsarte was the triune nature of all life. This, of course, was not new to so religious a man as Hovey but pushing the logic of trinitarianism to its furthest limit made the principle useful in the smallest matters. One might be divided into three and the three again subdivided into nine, and so on. The Launcelot and Guenevere series, for example, was finally based upon this scheme, the whole divided into three parts and each part divided into three works of different but complementary method and meaning. This could become a *reductio ad absurdum,* but it gave a disciplinary method and emphasized the interplay of the physical, ideational, and spiritual, so enforcing the deduction that each should include or lead to the other two, even in a phrase of poetry.

Delsartism had degenerated into innumerable "gymnastics," and Hovey wanted to affirm a metaphysical basis for its particular techniques. Taking the trinity—opposition, parallelism, and succession—he held that opposition is physical, affirming the particular, parallelism is intellectual, affirming the universal, and that succession reconciles the two into a spiritual synthesis. This metaphysical significance he insisted upon, since it related his theories to those of the Hegelians and cut him off from the faddists. When he sent his essay "Delsarte and Poetry" to the *Independent,* he wrote to Carman:

If you use it, you may edit any of it except the metaphysical paragraph to which I attach great importance. It separates me from the "Delsarteans" with whom I do not wish to be confused, since they teach many things which I regard as superficial and chimerical. I want them and Delsarte especially to have all just credit for suggesting the line of investigation, which is yet all my own, beyond the initiatory suggestion, but I want to be sharply discriminated from them.

I hope Steele MacKaye won't, for the thousandth time, justify his baptismal name by stealing all my work and saying he taught it to me—for *no Delsartean* has ever done this work or thought of it.[15]

The general scheme of Delsarte's thinking was useful, then, because it gave a terminology and diagrammatic laboratory method for experiment, and because it gave a new approach to the synthesis which was Hovey's life search.   He was no partisan disciple to exclude other help or to limit himself to agreement.   He took what advantage he could from others, particularly from Sylvester's *The Laws of Verse* and Lanier's *Science of English Verse*, which he believed "the first and only substantial contribution to a study of poetry that has yet been written,"[16] but he wanted to go beyond mere forms to the relationship between verse forms and their metaphysical expression, as he does in the essays on the technique of poetry.[17] He thus intended an exploration of poetry which would discover the means by which tones, rhythms, and meters make their effects and also the means by which the spiritual content and the larger forms make theirs.   He wished to study scientifically and to understand philosophically.   This is indicated by contrasting the title of Lanier's book, which undertook a careful study of verse forms, with that of his projected book— "The Science of Poetry."

Hovey filled page after page of his notebooks with experimental analyses.   Much of this work was in phonetics, concerned with the precise sound of vowels, diphthongs, and consonants.   Some of it was a minute breakdown of the great lines of English poetry and a study of the effect of rhythms. He held that verse is a sequence of speech tones in conformity with law and hence can be profitably studied in this way.   He

[15] Hovey, Jan. 10, 1892.
[16] Hovey, "Delsarte and Poetry," *loc. cit.*
[17] The essays published in the *Independent* are: "The Technique of Poetry" I and II, XLIV (April 7 and 21, 1892), 473, 544; "The Technique of Rhyme," XLV (Oct. 19, 1893), 1399; "The Elements of Poetic Technique," I and II, XLVI (Sept. 27 and Oct. 4, 1894), 1241, 1275.

was, of course, always careful to distinguish between poetry and versification, the latter of which is physical and so examinable. Like music, verse is an art of time and uses the meanings of sound as music does, whereas poetry also uses the meanings of words. The two are indissoluble in that fusion of symbolic and physical which is true poetry, but they may be separated for the purpose of study without killing the life of the whole.

The Delsartean emphasis on opposition, parallelism, and succession suggested a dialectical approach to a harmony enriched by resolved dissonance. To put it another way, the physical force of opposition and the intellectual calm of parallelism in thought or sound might merge in the equilibrium of succession in which variety exists within unity. Although he was concerned, like Lanier, with turning prosody from a rhythm too narrowly based on accent, he did not exaggerate the precedence of music over thought, as did Poe and Lanier. The flow of melody was not the aim, but a symphonic totality. He defended assonance when it was misunderstood in even such great poets as Emerson and Dickinson, so accustomed was the ear to simple melody and exact rhyme. Protesting Howells's objection to an impure rhyme in an otherwise gracious review of James Whitcomb Riley, he wrote:

To my ear *months* and *once* . . . gives more pleasure than any exact rhyme could possibly give. "There is no exquisite beauty without some strangeness in the proportions." The perfect agreement of the tonic tri-chord is a harmony, it is true, but a harmony too simple to cause delight. The intervals must be augmented or diminished, an element of dissonance must mingle with the element of concord, before there can be real music.[18]

This understanding of the texture of verse coupled with his preference for the interplay of physical, mental, and spiritual brought Hovey to a preference for that rich and complex poetry which the century had steadily rejected in its love of the exclusive single-minded lyric mood. In theory, at least, it placed him with the moderns.

[18] Hovey, *Daily Tatler*, Nov. 9, 1896.

Hovey always intended to set forth his discoveries in completed form. He never ceased his fascinated examination, and never came to the end of his learning. He lectured, criticized, and wrote long analytical letters, but the books he occasionally set down as titles in the scheme of his life's work were not to be written. This was a very real loss to art, for his scholarship, his sympathy with French experiment, his scientific approach would have made an illuminating study. Certainly it would have been far in advance of the vague and ideal books of the period. An outline of chapter contents for the book to be called "The Science of Poetry" shows a tremendous range:—comment on the students of verse from Aristotle to Alexander Graham Bell, studies of quantity in the poetry of the classical and modern languages, examinations of even such unfamiliar rhythms as the proceleusmatic and the trochaic tribrach and of meters up to the octometer and enneameter, verse form, accent, tune, tone color, all are indicated as to be present and as leading up to the study of poetics proper, that is, words as symbolic notations for ideas.

Men like Carman, themselves successful poets, believed that no one had such knowledge or such capacity to impart it. As Carman said, "Hovey's discoveries and elucidations, could they have been recorded, would have marked an epoch in poetical criticism."[19] It was not the dead knowledge of the mere student of past art, but the knowledge which desired to free spirit by greater capacity for expression. It was not the regulating dictation of the grammarian, but, as in all Hovey's effort, the knowledge of the laws which man might master in the long effort toward fulfilling his creative nature.

[19] Carman, *Criterion*, XXIII (April, 1900), 527.

CHAPTER V

Launcelot and Guenevere

> I must pity you that you are a woman, for so you miss life's greatest gift—the joy of loving one.
>
> Launcelot to Guenevere, in HOVEY, *The Marriage of Guenevere*, 1891.

It is easier to conceive a fair ideal than to give it body and make it dramatically interesting. An artist's perception of his goal is often well beyond his immediate reach, especially in the years of his youth. Though Hovey is remembered nowadays because he walked certain poetical by-paths, he never, to his own mind, deserted the main road he first set his feet upon. That odd hour aboard the speeding train, when the eclipse of the sun and the resolution to dedicate himself to serious poetry happened singularly to coincide, pointed to a destination other than geographic. He was then only twenty-four. Yet he attacked the biggest problems he could find and laid out a scheme of six plays and three masques on the story of Launcelot and Guenevere.

Only a very earnest young man would have been so rash. But it was more than rashness. It was the decision of one of the most sincere, cultivated, and promising of young Americans. Moreover, it was in itself symbolic of the general failure to find fresh native materials which might bear the weight of symbolic interpretation. The problem Hovey faced was to solve, if it could be done, certain sharp dilemmas within the *mores* of the time, yet still to place the solution at a spiritual level no lower than that of art which would really endure. To achieve this end seemed to Hovey to necessitate a familiar sustaining structure within which he might work: the same need which eventually made later writers turn to the Greek and Roman myths, or to the stories of the Old and New Testaments. Refusing, in short, the mimetic limitations of social naturalism, Hovey turned to legend.

It is instructive to remember that in our time such work as Eliot's poem *The Waste Land* around which the nimbus of the Round Table hangs like a remote halo, actually stands near the end of a long line of modern versions of Arthurian legend. In Hovey's day the Arthurian stories had been widely revived after a century of almost total neglect.

The late romantic attempt to recapture the spirit and savor of the Middle Ages had led to a popular mid-century celebration of stories based mainly on Malory's *Morte d'Arthur*. In the three years 1857-1859, for example, Algernon Charles Swinburne published *Queen Iseult*, Matthew Arnold, *Tristram and Iseult*, Tennyson, the first edition of *Idylls of the King*, while Wagner produced his ageless but typical *Tristan und Isolde*. Of course it is fair to say that these and other authors varied widely in their interests and in their use of the materials. Swinburne characteristically subdued the old story to the interweaving of lyrical digressions, William Morris to the likeness of a medieval tapestry, and Tennyson to moral judgment.[1] Unlike most readers, Hovey preferred the work of Swinburne to that of Tennyson, who made Arthur the perfect gentle knight to the loss of human sympathy and tragic nobility.[2] Certainly Tennyson too often confused Arthur with Prince Albert and after-generations damned him with the faint praise of blameless life. He found in the old mythos a counterpart to the breaking of social order he sadly witnessed in his own day. Hovey found in the same breaking a symbol of what might be if a new synthesis were to be achieved.

It is to be doubted that Hovey consciously adopted the Arthurian story simply because it was popular. The size of his original scheme and the lateness of his attempt preclude that assumption. So, even more, does the deeper level of meaning in his own life. He faced the general problem of finding a tutelary hero for man's long endurance and ultimate peace.

[1] See Margaret J. C. Reid, *The Arthurian Legend* (Edinburgh: Oliver and Boyd, 1938).

[2] MS notes for a later lecture at Barnard College, DCA.

He faced also the particular problem of finding a pattern of illicit love within which his own position might be imaginatively projected. In our time heroes and myths are not made. The secular and middle-class modern world thinks in more closely conditioned terms. Yet to the artist myths furnish familiar figures and situations through which he may work in terms larger than life. The aristocratic and ancient personae of mythology and legend allow the artist in whatever medium to be free of the petty slavery to time, place, and economics which has dominated our social literature. They can act singly, as ethical beings, in the unreal purity by which literature simplifies existence. So it was natural, almost inevitable, that Hovey should reach back to so celebrated an example of his individual problem.

One cannot positively say that at the beginning of the work he filled a position parallel to that of a chivalric knight in love with one who was married. He had not met Mrs. Russell at this time, and such a typical situation can be supplied only by the assumption that "Miriam," to whom the first volume of the series is dedicated, was married. This is an assumption easy to make in the light of his suffering, his evident devotion, and the secrecy with which the affair was handled, but it must stand at present unproved. Nevertheless, he had not finished the first play of the series before he was most certainly in Launcelot's position.

From the very beginning he conceived the Launcelot story as one of spiritual growth. At the inception of his resolution to write the long series of pieces, he set down a draft of that speech which, although written first, was intended to stand at the very end of the work.

> It doth not now repent me of my sins;
> They oft were my salvation. But for them
> I might have lain forever in my dream
> In the child-hearted valleys. They, like wolves,
> Roused me from my as yet unearned repose
> And drove me toiling up this arduous hill
> Where from the summit now mine eyes look out
> At peace upon a peaceful universe.

Nay, sweet, our sins are but God's thunderclouds,
That hide the glorious sun a little while;
And afterwards the fields bring forth their fruit.[3]

That ultimate peace demanded that the love triangle be capable of some more positive solution than Tennyson's immurement of Guinevere within the convent of Almesbury while Arthur "admonishes her like a curate," as Meredith said. The ethical and social problems drew him, rather than the picturesque possibilities which delighted Morris, Swinburne, and the Pre-Raphaelites. He hoped to free himself from the temporal limitations of both historical romance and modern realism. The legend furnished him "a modern instance stripped of modern dress," as Carman noted.[4] It gave possibility for freer imagination in opposition of old and new, individual and social, and for a resolution unconditioned by the legal possibilities of the contemporary. It gave the image of a known society with definite relationships, loyalties, and duties, but an image that was pliant to manipulation by the writer.

The major problem to Hovey was that of woman in her legal and love relationships. He saw Guenevere as he saw Mrs. Russell, "a new woman" too far developed for the limitations of an old and formalized society. Either the woman and her lover had to be sacrificed to the society, or the society had to change to admit a new definition of human rights and needs. All these possibilities he intended to work out dramatically in separate plays and groups. The Arthur-Guenevere-Launcelot relationships gave him a rich field to cultivate because the legal and social conventions of husband and wife, king and knight, lover and mistress were strictly defined in the Middle Ages, and so granted a system rigid enough for social evaluation

[3] Compare the note left for "Astolat." "Central idea—the necessity for experience in order to come to one's self" (*Holy Graal*, p. 69). It is interesting that Hovey should have written this ending first, as Tennyson had first written the concluding "Morte D'Arthur" (later enlarged as "The Passing of Arthur") a half century before the poems of the *Idylls* were concluded.

[4] Carman may have had some punning intent. Howells's *A Modern Instance* (1881) was the most successful of those novels which attempted the question of divorce. As a novel, that is to say an action severely limited by time and scene, and as a study of divorce, a current subject of discussion, its approach and spirit were instructively different from Hovey's project.

and criticism. The denial of those relationships demanded a more integrated solution than mere process of law or individual withdrawal from society. As Mrs. Hovey said after his death:

The "Poem in Dramas" was undertaken less to excuse Lancelot's act or Guinevere's, or to show Arthur's very natural psychic blindness, the blindness of a good and trusting nature, than to impeach the social system that had not yet—and has not yet—gone far enough in evolution to become a medium in which all lives can move at all times and in all respects in freedom.[5]

He was, then, attempting the problem of the sensitive and moral modern man and woman caught within an intolerable social situation, but using the archetypal figures of legend which transcend the accidents and tangential remedies of the modern example. He was concerned with examining and enlarging that great central ground where individual freedom forever struggles against social restraint to win recognition for man's increasing consciousness. As he saw the story it was not, as for Tennyson,

> this old imperfect tale,
> New-old, and shadowing sense at war with soul,

but a story of sense and soul allied against rigid social usage. Therefore the lovers are no longer romantic adulterers, but the agents of man's advance, and their unhappy dilemma is the proving ground of the future. Though most of the writers of the century were sympathetic to the illicit love and sought to excuse it, as even Tennyson did, none of the others thought of that love as a breach in the wall of custom and law through which man might advance. To Tennyson the lovers offended against the marriage law; to Hovey that law offended against them.

Obviously so large a program as Hovey conceived called for more than one play and demanded methods which could not be limited to conventional drama. Hence Hovey, at the very beginning, plotted an ambitious program of preludes, plays, and interludes. His plan continued to develop symmetrically

[5] Typescript copy initialed by Mrs. Russell ("H. H."), no date, DCA.

until by the end of his life he conceived it as including three subdivided parts. Each part would include a long introductory masque, which would serve as prelude and suggest the symbolic and ethical overtones of the parts. In each division a tragedy would follow and this would be followed in turn by a "drama" which, in the first two groups, would effect a partial solution, and in the final group achieve a synthesis and reconciliation of those inadequate solutions. Thus, the individual parts, though they might be played alone, were to be members of an organic whole, culminating in a final "harmonody." Of this nine-fold whole only two masques and two dramas were written.

Part One is introduced by *The Quest of Merlin*, a masque, or more exactly a libretto, for Hovey intended the masques for music and hoped always that someone would undertake their musical scoring. Often, as in the work of the admired Lanier, the thought gets strangled by the intricately woven strands of song. Image, metaphor, and musical phrase break, shift, and re-form until the pattern of thought is lost. The libretto concept has led him into confusion, though often the individual songs and themes have a charm of their own, particularly where Hovey's ability to handle the short line is most evident.

The poem concerns the quest of Merlin for foreknowledge of the outcome of Arthur's projected marriage to Guenevere, as Hovey spelled the name. First he arrives magically among the Norns beneath Mount Hecla and hears their boast of the final weaving of the fate and their riddling runes of woe for the fated three of Camelot. Then with a fade-out and fade-in he is transported to the world of Greek myth, of fauns, satyrs, naiads, maenads, Titania, Ariel, and Aphrodite. With Aphrodite appear the Valkyrs, so that the sterner strength and will of the North can be added to the passionate heart of the South. Then to Merlin speaks the Lady of the Lake in Avalon, who, like the Norns, prophesies pain and sorrow, but finds in that unhappy fate the divine dissatisfaction that drives man on to larger spirit. Finally the angels speak the ultimate truth, the third truth beyond that of the dwellers in Avalon who originate action and that of the Norns who conclude it. Though both have seen grief and sorrow, the transcendent angels descry the ultimate victory of spirit.[6] Launcelot and Guenevere will win through to calm and fulness of soul and by the nobility of their endurance will open a greater realm to love.

The first play, *The Marriage of Guenevere*, begins by setting the conventional chivalric problem, the choice of love or friendship. Arthur is about to wed Guenevere, a strange, self-willed, and wayward girl. Few of the critics would accept Hovey's heroine, whom he tried to make a modern, direct, humorous girl capable of independence, frankness, and sincerity, that is, a type of modern woman as he conceived her. She runs the hills, a rebel against woman's subservient place, and is quite unawakened to love. She has simply given in to her father's promptings—"as well Arthur as another." Launcelot, absent on a knightly errand during the wedding, returns to find that Guenevere is that very Lady of the Hills with whom he has been in love since he once saw her. Though he has not known her name, in that name he has done valiant deeds. To him Guenevere gives her heart at first meeting. There is little attempt to make the love convincing. The sketchy story is accepted as time-saving motivation so that the action can get on to the immediate consummation of their desire, the plot against them, the public accusation before Arthur, now returned from the war, and Arthur's kingly refusal to hear aught against the guilty lovers who cannot bear to repay his love with confession. So the play ends with foreign war declared against Rome, and Launcelot at civil war within his soul. Guenevere, who has come virgin to Launcelot's love, suffers no real conviction of sin, since she has never sinned against love.

Hovey afterwards wrote a series of sequels to the volume of 1891. *The Birth of Galahad* (1898) moves from the secret event which gives it title to the capture of Rome and the Pope's blessing on Arthur as Emperor of Rome. Between these events come domestic scenes, clashes of armies, an interlude, the tak-

---

[6] As Peacock said of the spirits in Byron's *Manfred:* "It is difficult to conceive where this heterogeneous company could have originally met, except at the *table d'hôte,* like the six kings in *Candide.*"

ing of Rome, and all the mechanism of involved plot and intrigue. The love of Launcelot and Guenevere is a pawn in
the international struggle and finds only one rapturous scene
for itself. Any advance in its larger meaning is lost in the
crowding of martial action and the play ends with no external change in the positions of the central three. Launcelot
is still torn by his divided loyalty; Guenevere is still no more
than Arthur's legal spouse, with all her love and imagination
given to Launcelot; Arthur is still the trusting friend and un-
perceptive king.

Hovey's introduction of new meaning into the old story
brought certain changes. Launcelot suffers least metamor-
phosis, for his position between love and friendship is the stock
heroic dilemma. He does, however, lose his characteristics as
a typical lover within that tradition of courtly love which was
set up to sweeten and make romantic a feudal rigidity no courtly
lover wanted seriously to destroy. In Hovey's reading of the
triangle, Launcelot is the true husband, and he and Guenevere
and their bastard son make up the true family, that is the
family held by love rather than by legal bond and social
acceptance. Launcelot alone feels the full force of broken
allegiance, since he only is aware of it. Yet, though he suffers from deceit toward his friend and king, his love is before
that of the king's in time so that he feels:

> She's mine,
> And by a higher title than the King's.

Thus, though he believes himself justified by the high power
of love, loyalty to Guenevere forces him into daily deceit and
self-torture which deny his fealty and force him toward the
decision of the uncompleted plays in which he would, for
a time, renounce love to follow religion.

Guenevere suffers from her clandestine love for Launcelot, but not from guilt, since she has never sinned against love.
As far as the plays carry us she has known no man but Launcelot, for since the marriage night when Arthur honored her
shrinking, he has been busy at war or content to leave her her
own mistress. She is really the true wife in all but name, and

Hovey, alone of all the tellers of this old tale, has made her the mother of Galahad. In his story Ylen (Elaine), the legendary mother by Launcelot, becomes the pretended mother to conceal the secret of her dear friend.

The birth is illicit and hidden, and a haze of sacramental mystery is thrown over it. Hovey intended that sexual love at its highest, as here, should exist in its own right, and that the product of that love should borrow something of the quality of immaculate conception, since all conception in exalted love is holy. To carry such a symbolic burden Guenevere, the type of advanced spiritual woman, is placed in a situation where she must break the existing law of family and society to fulfil her function as individual. The unsuccessful attempt later to put the legal family above this true family and to bring Arthur and Guenevere into closer union in a husband and wife relation is not written. We have only a scene in which Guenevere fiercely rejects Arthur's hope for a royal heir.

The king is most changed by Hovey, for he falls from the Tennysonian position of "ideal manhood closed in real man" to a kind of spiritually ungrown boy who refuses to entertain the suspicions which others try to force on him and who cares less for his queen than for his empire. He is a man of state; more a king than a man. Therefore Launcelot can assuage his conscience for taking the queen by fighting magnificently to win for his king his greater desire for world power. Arthur's hold on the reader's sympathy had to be limited so that he might not intrude too sharply into sympathy for Launcelot, but it is evident that his limitations are intended to typify a stage of human development lower than that the wife and lover have reached. Arthur is in some sort the embodiment of a static society unaware that man's growth demands new values.

The trouble with this rewriting is not that it denies the traditional relationships of the three, but that in granting the supremacy of love Hovey implied rather than elaborated the psychic motivation. Realizing within himself how true to love was his own affair, he turned too far from the problem of individual character toward a social reorganization that would allow the expression of that exonerated love. Thus, since the integrating "harmonody" is not written, one misses the final ethical and social solution as well as the strict examination of motivation which might have saved the individual plays. The investigation of problems of character is less than in Arnold or in Tennyson, or than in E. A. Robinson at a later date. The very freedom from sin, except in Launcelot's friendship for Arthur, lessens the poignancy of guilt and the dramatic possibilities of character. The social and philosophic problem takes precedence over the dramatic and psychological, but does not get beyond the introductory thesis that love outside the conventions of society brings unhappiness to lovers who are sensitive moral persons. Such love is tragic because it denies harmony by division within the soul and peace between society and individual.

It was fatally natural for a high-minded aspirant in drama to go back to the plays of Shakespeare for suggestion. From them Hovey took his verbal reminiscences, involved plots, his clown, his comic interludes, his broken talk, and his verse. These were only the accidents of a great art, and had now grown stale except as they could be revivified by ability, an ability no one at this time owned. However skilful at any one element, as, for example, the songs, Hovey lacked the cohesive power which could combine fragmentary excellences into a dramatic entity. He had neither maturity nor sufficient practice. Trying to bring drama out of the closet, he got it only part way to the stage.

Though the plays are replete with love, murder, lust, adultery, intrigue, and warfare, nothing seems to happen. Love on the stage must be either words or action, and since action is forbidden, words alone are left. Since the words must be beyond any verisimilitude to love's inarticulate stammering, only great poetry can make them convincing and memorable. Stage battle is a thing of excursions and alarums and reported action, and only the audible ring of steel and thud of feet upon the visible stage can endow them with life. So the published plays for all their restless action never come wholly alive,

though the second of them shows decided growth in the ability
to handle action. It has a greater swiftness of movement and
firmness of outline. The reminiscences of Shakespeare are
fewer, the speech is tighter and more masculine, the words ap-
proximate action. It might well have stood theatrical test while
taste was still in the mood for romantic drama.

One wonders if such material is fitted to a modern interpretation. Certainly to make the story "real" is to lose the charm
of the picturesque, the pathos of "old unhappy far-off things
and battles long ago." It is this light of romance which has
endeared the *Idylls of the King* and the poems of Swinburne
and Morris to generations of readers, and romance lives easiest
on the level of traditional poetry. To bring characters and
language toward the modern is to lose grace and awake the
charge of vulgarization, as Hovey did. Characters who are
endowed with a will to stand free of the medieval spell which
lies over the most successful treatments seem coarsened rather
than ennobled. Readers look to the old and romantic for a way
out of the physical realities of their own lives and are offended
by a scene which is "poetic" and yet admits the physical act.
It is somehow embarrassing.

GALAHAULT. Gramercy. Now 'tis fit you enter on Love's service.
Kiss him once before me, madam, for the beginning of true love.
GUENEVERE. Those yonder, sure, would wonder that we should
do such deeds.
GALAHAULT. No one will see (Turns away).
GUENEVERE. And if they did?—Why, Launcelot, You tremble
like a leaf. Will you not kiss me? Are you afraid? Nay, then,
I will kiss you (She takes him by the chin and kisses him).

Though it cannot deny one's critical judgment of the plays,
the fact that they are only a fragment of the large design laid
down must be remembered. The over-all pattern was inimical
to the finished effect of individual plays. They could not come
to a resolution that would satisfy the problem evoked, for they
were no more than acts within the total play. Since it was intended that the first part, which alone was completed, should
state only the thesis, its position in the dialectic of the whole

drama is left without opposition or resolution. The fragments of the other plays left at Hovey's death his wife brought together in *The Holy Graal* (1907). From these and her aureate comments we can gather something of the development contemplated. Part Two was to show the lovers renouncing physical love to seek a solution within the sanctified ways of their society, putting the world above themselves. Since denied love must find its outlet in asceticism and sublimation, this part was to find its symbol in the religious search for the Graal by Galahad, while Arthur's kingdom enjoyed twenty years of peace and greatness. But since renunciation is a denial of life, this antithesis to Part One had also to be largely tragic. Of Part Three one can say nothing except that Hovey with the greatest daring intended a synthesis and an establishment of harmony that would bring the dissonances and antagonisms and oppositions into a great tonic affirmation.

Unquestionably the finest and most enduring member of the *Poem in Dramas* is *Taliesin,* begun in 1893 but not finished until January, 1896, and not published until 1899. It is the masque intended to introduce the second section of the large work, and, in general, to give "the aesthetic drift," as Hovey said. As it opens, Taliesin and Percival, the poet and the man of knightly action, meet in the wood of Broceliande. Here voices of dream call for return to the sea of Being, where there is no strife or separateness of identity. Percival, however, is out to find an active way from the sin that besets the court of Arthur, Taliesin to make the underlife of dream itself serve the unfolding purpose of evolving man. Each is seeking the old master Merlin, who sleeps in a peace which knows no compulsion to action. Speaking in a dream he tells Taliesin that he will go on "to win from brighter powers intense wakefulness," and then glides back into the instinctive preconceptual life of dream.

The first step in this intensifying of consciousness is the disclosure of Nimue, the earth goddess, in her naked beauty. This the overmoral knight may not see, for his ascetic purity condemns such beauty, but the poet is rewarded for his long pursuit

and love, though warned that the desire for her beauty will
eat at his heart and that he must control the love of natural
beauty.

As the second movement opens, Nimue and Taliesin stand
on the slopes of Helicon. A spirit child is born of their meeting, an uncouth wild thing that speaks in grotesque jingles and
shows the irresponsible prankishness of the primitive. This,
an evident symbol of the elementary imagination, climbs
higher with Taliesin. Gay dancing damsels give the young
creature ornaments, bells, jewels, and flowers, the delight of
things without spiritual meaning. Higher they climb to the
summit of Helicon where the nine Muses move in stately
dance singing that the spirit is unrevealed unless made flesh.

> But the flesh, given spirit
> To the world, gives it as well back to itself,
> great with a world's gain.

To the beseeching Taliesin they reveal that God as a spirit dis-
closes himself in the heavens and earth and in the soul of man,
even in his body. Taliesin asks that they help him in the poet's
priestly office.

> To fashion worlds in little, making form
> As God does, one with spirit,—be the priest
> Who makes God into bread to feed the world.

The body, he is instructed, is not only a form but is fashioned for music that its loveliness may call loveliness into being and clothe the desert places and, by the magic of the word,
call from the mind new concepts and ideas. All forms and
beauties and ratiocinations, however, must ultimately express
themselves in act.

> Man, Master of an Act,
> At last and only finds whole utterance.

The Poet must sing the Hero and be he who reconciles strife
through his unfolding comprehension and capacity for unity.

Again the child, which is his poetic sense, develops, and
now, with fewer but more graceful ornaments, and with

Apollo's promise of inspiration upon him, he leaves for the city of men, that is, for the place of humanistic art and thought in which truth and beauty are one.

The final movement is in the chapel of the Graal in a white northern land some time, one guesses, about the sixth century, when Taliesin is supposed to have lived. Percival attempts the golden doors which hide the Graal, but Uriel and the Seven Angels prevent him. He is too insistently and inhumanly pure, and must learn love and forgiveness. Though Taliesin pleads for Percival, it is to him, the less pure man who yet perceives images of the unseen, that Uriel allows a glimpse of the ultimate in a crystal within which still lurks the vision of that glory too bright for his beholding. This is vouchsafed to the imperfect poet because of his greater wholeness and his office to man.

> Thou art the eye for him thou comest with, that he
> may know the joy divine;
> Thou art the eye for all thy kind, to lead them to
> the open gates of Heaven.

So he beholds the vision of joy, a reach of man's imagination beyond the limits of the old thinking and impossible to both Celt and Greek. Only the modern creative man who dares to accept evil and passion and paradox as materials of emerging good can win that final revelation.

Confusing as it may be, such a reduced outline of the machinery and "story" of *Taliesin* alone gives an idea of how Hovey's mind worked in its intensest and most characteristic expression. The masque is his truest utterance of the religious poet he wanted to be, for here are many of his beliefs about the nature of man and the universe, and here the widest range of lyric and allegoric invention. He is trying to cast into symbolic form the history of poetry as man moves from the strivings of natural instinct to intellectual comprehension and heroic song, and then to intuitive and ecstatic vision (from wood, to Helicon, to chapel). To put it another way, he suggests the movement from naturalism, to classical humanism, to spiritual insight. Such threefold developments are part of the triune nature of man and part of his development through synthesis.

Since the masque was meant to give "the aesthetic drift" of the *Poem in Dramas,* Hovey was definite in his insistence that spirit clothes itself with flesh and that the poet lives in what Wordsworth called "an ennobling interchange" with nature, receiving and giving. It is his function to make men behold the loveliness they have not seen and to be an eye to mankind. With that vision he pierces to the heart of this universe and finds that it is joy.

The work is the most variously elaborated Hovey ever undertook. It was conceived as an actual masque, the dancing an integral part of the piece, and the singing to be performed by a cast of twenty voices as well as a women's chorus, a boys' chorus, and a full choir. The ideal presentation which he and his wife projected in their most optimistic moments would have been an example of their theories of art, action, dance, and song, bringing out the union of body and spirit which the poetic theory explicitly outlines.

The songs show the range of Hovey's experiment. Verse forms range from two-stress to nine-stress lines, and rhyme schemes constantly change from song to song. Some have no rhyme, others carry the same rhyme for six consecutive lines. There is wide use of initial rhyme, assonance, and phonetic and alliterative play. A close scrutiny reveals an effective play of opposition, parallelism, and succession of sound, but so controlled by the larger pattern that they do not obtrude. Sprung rhythms and frequent use of initial trochaic feet show that Hovey thought of the lines as lines to be heard, not simply to be read. They break the metronomic music of contemporary versifying by introducing a wider range of sound and pattern than any other American was attempting.

He was aware that the Greek forms to which he went back might seem awkward because unfamiliar to ears accustomed only to the more conventional melodies. Probably they did. But his stanzaic patterns show great skill in maintaining variations from the usual in orderly recurrence. No one since

Shelley had used so wide a variety of lyric forms, and these not haphazard but based upon considered theory and a philosophy of composition.[7] Considered simply in musical terms the songs prove his skill. Beginning in rich sensuous sound that enforces the statement of poetry's beginning in dreams and nature, they move through the clearer ideational quality of the classic until they flow into a "stream of sound," as Shelley called it, which lifts into an exaltation beyond words, an incantatory utterance which stirs the imagination to reach beyond verbal meaning.

One accepts the explicit theories of *Taliesin*, which are reanimated rather than new, and one must respect the versatility of the poet. If the poem has not received its due, it is because its interest is specialized and because it attempts too much both in its masque form and in its exposition of theory. But if it attempts too much, it is partly because the means are not adequate to so sustained an exposition. Modern poets have either interjected their aesthetic theories incidentally and fragmentarily, as Browning and Whitman constantly did, or like Wordsworth, Shelley, and Poe they have worked them out in prose. Hovey had spent untold hours of hard analytical work on the anatomy of sound and verse structure, but here he overleaped all that to utter a theory which would unite body, mind, and soul, and make the poet the anointed priest of God. In that effort the language and metaphor at times fail the purpose. The words come too easily and smooth the way, where a tougher discipline of thought and a stricter vocabulary, more stringent in the use of "lover," "beauty," "soul," "God," would make the reader a participant in the problem under resolution. The beauty is too constant, the high perception too self-assured, so that the reader agrees without being won to new understanding until the final songs soar free of imagery and thought.

No other work of Hovey holds so much of him and expresses it so well. Once he had it well under way no other

[7] Curtis Hidden Page estimated that there were over thirty rhythms in the poem.

work could hold him, and when it was finished he was for days "drunk" with those final songs. The writing was the most engrossing and satisfying experience of his life as poet, because it expressed the most of his actual and ideal being. A modern might cut *Taliesin* ruthlessly, but he would be cutting things essential to the total Hovey: the high attempt, the sacramental theory of poetry, the triune structural conception, the overromantic metaphor, all those elements which the poetic revolution of our time has rejected. But there remain the extraordinary versatility and musical facility, the passages of great beauty, and a noble-minded faith in the high purpose and apocalyptic function of poetry which Hovey was perhaps the last to express.

Set within the contemporary scene the plays deserved and received higher praise than one now gives them. Of course, though they have here been conveniently considered together, only the volume bearing the dedicatory *Quest of Merlin* and *The Marriage of Guenevere* appeared in 1891. Hovey was conscious of the faults of the play but he felt that the poems would stand up to time and grow on people. Some of his friends agreed. Davidson criticized him for wasting his talents on illicit love. Though he deplored the "unpruned exuberance" and the need for severity, he still said: "He is a poet, beyond peradventure, and the only one I have met on this continent among the young men." Charles Eliot Norton, who seldom gave praise and was considered by some the most finely cultivated man in America, was likewise impressed with "the exuberance, the lack of experience, the wastefulness of youth." E. C. Stedman acknowledged "more than common talent—perhaps even genius." These comments came in reply to copies sent out by his mother; thus they had to be discounted, but there was enough praise to give him confidence. Others were more generous still, but often only irritated Hovey by "a kind of supercilious pat-on-the-head God-bless-you-Sonny air that is unworthy of serious self-respecting people." He asked for a more impersonal criticism. "I don't see what pertinence it has to remark my youth, unless it be to contrast their own unproductiveness in fifty years with my fertile twenty-five." Indeed, the only statements that irritated him were the patronizing. He was "downright angry" at "a certain pervasive Bostonian flavor of superciliousness" in many of the articles.[8] He much preferred honest dislike.

Actually the volume was a fair critical success. It had a wide press notice, partly because the family and such friends as Carman were careful to see that copies got to the right persons and places. Much of that notice was vague and irrelevant to criticism, but it brought the book to wider notice. The English reviews were the most workmanlike. William Sharp, whom Hovey knew, gave it mingled praise and censure in the *Academy*, but said "few young poets start so well as Mr. Richard Hovey. He has the freest lilt of any of the younger Americans." So too the *Literary Opinion* and the Dublin *Warder* found praise and blame, but the *Athenaeum* and the London *Times* were severe.

As many a critic began his comments, Hovey had opened himself to comparison with the great Tennyson in a daring and inescapable way. The moral comparison was particularly detrimental to Hovey but is the most interesting aspect of the book's reception since it opens a window on the time. The Boston *Transcript* found the prosaic passages as realistic as what one might hear at Franklin Park. The *Literary World* spoke of "the vulgar triangular problem He, She, and the Other Man," and declared that "Guenevere develops from a hoiden with tendencies toward the women's rights platform into an aggressive temptress of a coy knight." The *Bloomingdale Pantagraph* complained that a reader did not rise from reading "morally strengthened" as he did from the *Idylls of the King*, that the knights were "a bad lot," and Launcelot and Guenevere "not worth saving." The Brooklyn *Daily News* pointed the difference from Tennyson and declared, with lofty ignorance of sources, that "in this [that is, the intrigue] it may be realistic, but it is sadly out of touch with a story which stands

[8] Hovey to his mother, Dec. 17, 1891.

out among all myths singular in its purity." Louise Chandler Moulton found too much "atmosphere of a French novel," each character the "slave of his own desires." This and similar charges of "Zolaism" Hovey found "supremely absurd," as well he might, but they serve to point the attention of hardened moderns away from what is for them the more obvious romanticism to the realism and frank utterance of the plays. This unromantic material was on the increase in those fragments which move toward the disintegration of the Round Table and would have caused still greater indignation if they had reached publication.

Such moral indictment was an important influence on sincere young writers trying to meet man's problems with honesty. It drove the weak into a sterile but profitable acquiescence and the strong into consciousness of enmity with society. It was easy to turn into the kingdom of aesthetic dreaming away from the social responsibilities and interests of the mature artist, particularly when the paying magazines were controlled by genteel editors catering to still more genteel women readers. It was almost equally easy to turn to the bitter and angry ugliness of the naturalists. The one good of such criticism was that it posed the problem of art in unavoidable terms and this problem Hovey was attempting in those essays which he was writing at the time the reviews were coming out.

Neither praise nor blame had any perceptible effect on his great idea. Whatever else the exigencies of necessity or the moods of creation produced, Hovey always desired and intended to be a playwright. The large share of his effort went into the writing of plays, and he placed his hope for fame on the poetic drama. The combination of poetry and drama alone seemed to him to fulfil man's possibilities and bring the whole of man into artistic action, to bring thought, philosophy, religion, and beauty back to the drama, and to bring action to the beauty of poetry.

The idea of the *Poem in Dramas* was bold, but it was a mistake. Only the greatest success could lead to the reading or playing of a life-work in so many parts, yet without that con-

secutive reading the final resolution would stand without foundation, or, if accepted in itself, would throw the other parts
into the discard as unnecessary. Since the whole was not
achieved, the plays on which he staked so heavily as parts of
that major work to which all else was subservient are with the
exception of the masque *Taliesin* the least read of his writings.

CHAPTER VI

Seaward

Blow, horns of the old sea-rapture!
When your call comes from afar,
I would rise from the grave to reach you
Where the sea-dooms are!
                              HOVEY, "Short Beach."

Hovey had a happy passage to England in August, 1891. Mrs. Russell was also on board. Indeed, in that middle course between honesty and disingenuousness which he felt he must adopt toward his parents, he told them that he took this boat that he might have her companionship and the advantages of her introductions in London. He had an outside stateroom far better than he expected, and sat at the captain's table, which, he felt, was part of his faculty for lighting on the right foot. The sea was quiet and except for the fog off Newfoundland, which reminded him of Tom's watercolors, the visibility was good. Dolphins played off the bow of the ship and as they neared the coast of Ireland the sea mews cried round them.

As soon as they docked at Liverpool, Hovey went to the art gallery to see Rossetti's painting "Dante's Dream." He had not realized that the admiration of the American undergraduate who had dared to write poems to Rossetti was so little singular and was amazed at the popularity of the Pre-Raphaelites, already out-of-date in the world of painting. Even more amazing was the courtesy of everyone—customs officers, policemen, and porters. There was none of the rudeness of equalitarian America. Civilized order was part of the very countryside. Farms and forests were like gardens and parks, and, except for the manufacturing towns, the whole land at first sight seemed full of ease and comfort and civilization.

As a pious literary pilgrim, he went first to Stratford, and, wasting no time, chartered a carriage to drive with Mrs. Russell through the moonlit town and over old Clopton Bridge above the golden Avon. Next day he drove to Shottery and Anne Hathaway's cottage, where, still the sentimental traveler, he picked blossoms to send home. In London he hired for eight shillings large and well-furnished lodgings looking over Kensington Park. So strong was the impression of Dickens and Thackeray on him that he had to pinch himself to be sure he was not within the confines of a book.

Hovey was not a scholar in the earlier American tradition of Ticknor or Longfellow, nor an exile in the manner of James or Whistler. He was not part of what has been called "a great pattern of flight." He was not fleeing from anything nor looking for any particular salvation. His greatest aesthetic curiosity was about style. He knew America was less interested than Europe in the subtleties of the poet's craft, and knew that the cross-fertilization of other manners would be stimulating. Most of all, however, he kept at work as if he were at home, and whenever the chance came broadened his acquaintance in the literary world and tried to place his work.

Early in September he crossed the channel alone and went on to Giverny, the little village on the border of Normandy and the Île de France which Monet and some of his Impressionist friends were to make famous and the Germans were to destroy in World War II. Monet had come here in 1883 to find inexpensive quiet and gradually to transform his two or three acres into a kingdom. Tom Meteyard was one of the young Americans interested in *plein air* painting. Most of them had been made aware of Monet by John Singer Sargent's enthusiasm. They clustered about the master and began the American tradition in that favorite village to which few tourists came except the relatively permanent art crowd. The little Epte flowed close to the village and flooded the pool Monet was changing from a mud hole into a loosely organized composition vibrant with color. A half mile away, beyond the haystacks which changed chromatically with each hour, the Seine

ran between rows of slender poplars. The haystacks and poplars were standing as models for the famous series of paintings
Monet was executing in this and the following year.

Hovey settled into quarters in the Maison Baudy, a name
which was always good for a laugh among the English-speaking. His room high in the house had been decorated with
frescoes by the hand of some former tenant. He met the
people here and at other pensions in the village. Notable
among them were Mr. and Mrs. Thomas Sergeant Perry.
The Perrys were Boston people, as famous for their friendliness to the young and unknown as for their wide acquaintance
with the great. Mrs. Perry, born Lilla Cabot, was a painter
and poet, and her husband was a teacher, scholar, translator,
and critic. Perry had the reputation of knowing and enjoying
everything and of talking about books with wit and enthusiasm.
E. A. Robinson later called him "one of the great appre-
ciators," and Hovey always responded eagerly to such a mind.
Perry wrote to Howells, with whom he had collaborated on
A Library of Adventure, "a howling letter" in praise of Hovey
and when the latter had returned to America let him have the
freedom of his country place at Readville, just outside Boston.

The strangeness over, Hovey settled to a quiet life of hard
work. He was writing the critical articles for the *Independent*
and sketching scenarios for several plays. He felt that he ought
to get out *Gandolfo*, the play on which he was working most
enthusiastically, while the impression of *Launcelot and Guenevere* was still fresh. By the middle of December three acts
were about ready.[1] "I am not," he wrote early in 1892, "the

[1] This play, *Gandolfo*, first called *Anselmo*, is the violent story of the moral
breakdown of the once saintly Archbishop of Milan. Hovey found the subject of marital infidelity "unpleasant" and worried over the Catholic reception and his reputation as one who dealt too constantly with faithless love.
Despite a rush of events that leaves too little time for thorough and convincing
psychological motivation, the play has an energy about it which really moves
from scene to scene. Despite some Elizabethan reminiscences the passages which
suggest too retentive a memory are very few and the wit and raillery of the early
acts are entertaining and sophisticated. He has moved from the lyricism which
must be charming at any cost to a more virile blank verse and a greater use
of prose. But his development in technique is spoiled by melodramatic un-
reality. This is perhaps what Maeterlinck thought when he wrote (Nov. 3,
1896): "En résumé je trouve Gandolfo très beau, très puissant même par

comet of a day and cannot afford to rest on my laurels yet awhile."[2] He had also begun *Columbus,* of which at one time he had great hope. Perhaps it would be the first play in a New-World trilogy. If possible he wanted to get it out for October, 1892, because the anniversary interest might help to give it wide reading, and he had a slight hope of having it presented at the Chicago Fair. The research fascinated him, but he found it difficult to get material on the Indians and had not enough money to see Spain and the Gulf of Mexico as he dreamed of doing.

He pushed himself until his eyes were strained and severe headaches forced him to work less strenuously. Meanwhile he waited eagerly for criticisms of *Launcelot and Guenevere,* wondering "what dear old moral Whittier will think of it." At home his family were sending out copies for review, writing to the publishers, copying all the letters which came to them in reply to the dozens of volumes they had sent.[3] In a rather lordly way Richard expected this, and they did far more than even he could ask. They uncomplainingly answered all the business correspondence and undertook the clerical drudgery. After a day at work his father and mother would recopy most letters in entirety and paste into a scrapbook the press notices, which mounted into hundreds. In addition to a flyer made up of carefully selected statements, his father prompted a publisher's letter to all Dartmouth men after the class of 1881 which appealed to their college spirit by suggesting the virtue of support for one who was remedying Dartmouth's lack of notables in literature. Father and mother must have tired

---

moments, mais trop dans la tradition du drame passionel et pas assez *inattendu,* pas assez necessaire en quelque sorte pour le début sensationnel que vous deviez faire en France."

He put his faith in this play all his life, but it was dogged by bad luck. Though copyrighted at the end of 1892 and even printed in plates, it was never published because of the failure of the United States Book Company. Hovey read passages from it many times and tried to interest producers, actors, and publishers to no avail. Nevertheless, he felt sure that he had written a good play and one which would succeed in the theater despite possible outcry.

[2] Hovey, Jan. 16, 1892.

[3] Of the 584 copies sold the first year, his father bought 242 for free distribution.

under the dull work of transcribing, excerpting, and dispersing such praise as came in. It is rare to find parents doing all the hack work, supplying money, and conducting an advertising concern for a a fledgling author, but their faith and love were rare.

Hovey went up to Paris occasionally, still as a "conqueror," which was "very satisfying," but there was too little money for a long stay. He tried to meet the problem of living by doing odd jobs for Morton Fullerton, a Boston man now in the Paris office of the London *Times*. Carman had introduced Hovey to him by letter, but before Fullerton had received it he had read *Launcelot and Guenevere* and was enthusiastic. He and Hovey became warm friends and he found occasional assignments for the needy author. Forty or fifty francs a week saw Hovey through, and these little jobs extended the one hundred dollars his father sent.

His French was improving, but his English did not satisfy the waiters.

The French people say I get on beautifully, but when I speak English they correct my pronunciation. The last time I was in Paris I asked for a sherry cobbler, but was not understood at first. Then the waiter said that I meant a "sherrie cobblaire" and went off satisfied.[4]

At the turn of the year 1892 he was engaged in a correspondence which deserves notice only because it demonstrates a sensitive awareness of others which less intimate dealings cannot. His mother had written to him of a letter signed by "Rosa" and was troubled by its romantic suggestions. Hovey thought it to be the nom de plume of a young German poetess introduced to him by Mrs. Lanier, "nervous, exalted, sensitive, sentimental, like all Germans romantic and absolutely ignorant of real life."

Of course I don't *want* it, nor any other letters of the kind. But they come, and the responsibility of dealing with them and with their writers is one I feel unable and unwilling to shift to other shoulders. "Rosa" must not be allowed to know that her confidences have reached any other ears than those they were intended for. My experience has been

[4] Hovey, no date, probably Jan., 1892.

that this sort of thing *never* comes from bad girls or fast girls, or even questionable girls; but from girls of an innocent and romantic enthusiasm, who need to be handled very gingerly. . . . I have never yet given any one any reason to suppose me unworthy of confidence in these matters, nor did any girl ever regret making me, as so many have, her father confessor as well as ideal. I wish they wouldn't. It simply harrows up my feelings and breaks me all up.[5]

So when letters came directly from "Rosa" he answered in as kindly a way as possible and set her straight with the tact and gentleness native to him. It was easy for such girls to adore the handsome figure which fulfilled the image of poet as so few literary men do, but the man had given his heart to a woman long since beyond such adolescent tremulousness.

Always in the center of his mind was the knowledge that his child would soon be born. When the time approached, Hovey joined Mrs. Russell in Tours. They found shelter with an old couple in an ancient house. It was quiet and full of peace there. A garden walk, where Hovey paced striking out the lines of *Gandolfo*, ended in an arbor. Beyond, the path climbed to a fig tree and a little vineyard. The rose bushes and the grapes trained on the garden wall were now stark and lifeless, but they loved the place and made reckless plans of some day buying it.

Obviously the illicit relationship and the birth of the baby on February 9, 1892, could not be publicly owned without hurting his family and leaving an ineradicable stain on the woman he wanted to marry. It was, as he put it, a kind of courtesy not to throw this violation of custom in the face of society. The easiest way out was to create a marriage for himself with an anonymous woman who would conveniently die and whose loss would create a private sorrow into which no one would intrude.[6] Even Carman was told only of "the romance of the fair lady whom I first married and of her sad death at Perpignan giving birth to my little Julian." Mete-

[5] Hovey, no date, probably Jan., 1892.
[6] In his biographical letter to Rice he wrote: "I have one son, Julian, by a former marriage, the history of which is too tragic for me to wish to have much of anything said about it."

yard, however, knew more, for he had to send off under Paris postmark the letters which Hovey sent him. "A little tour through Brittany" furnished an excuse for some weeks, and Meteyard advised him, since he was so poor a liar, to return through Chartres so that his enthusiasm for the cathedral might bear the stamp of authentic enthusiasm. Mrs. Russell's retreat was explained as necessitated by a severe case of pneumonia.[7]

Prevarication and evasion because of social conventions to which they were opposed left no scars upon them. Neither lover felt guilty about the child, for they were convinced of the supremacy of love. Mrs. Russell later wrote to Mrs. Hovey (and to some future biographer!):

> History will get it straight from our correspondence. For the benefit of that historian let me say just here that I have never repented Radegund's birth. He is well born. I like to think that there is a modern form of immaculate conception. Richard is probably the purest of passionate men living. He is pure gold—no alloy even. He is an angel. And to me such love is not sensuality but the highest life of the soul. *Such* love I mean.[8]

While Hovey was less reckless with fine words, he believed in the goodness of the relationship in itself, and even saw it as a step into the future toward which his plays and his theories were urging men. To his mother he was to write in 1895:

> Don't worry about Radegund. He has nothing to be ashamed of in his birth. On the contrary, he will be very proud of it some day. And I am proud of him and have never had a thought of how he came to be that was not happy and pure and with no leaven of regret or wish that anything had been different. Of course, there are stupid and malicious people in the world, and on their account we shall have to use the wisdom of the serpent.[9]

The dark-eyed and dark-haired baby whose head was shaped like his father's they called "the Gros Pasha" because of his

[7] New York *World*, Jan. 10, 1892.
[8] Mrs. Henriette Hovey to Mrs. Charles Hovey, Sept. (no date), 1894. Compare her notes on *The Holy Graal*: "There are parents wickedly below the law of what makes a wholesome order for all. There are also those so subject to psychological law that they live above the order of the many."
[9] Hovey, Aug. 2, 1895.

dignity and stately way of sitting up. After a little his father gave him the name Radegund, anglicized and made masculine from that of Radégonde, sixth-century saint. There was a church near Giverny which carried her name. Mrs. Russell never cared for the name and they later argued the matter week after week, but Hovey returned to it always and, after their marriage, they compromised on Keith Radegund, though finally they came to the name Julian, suggested by the church of St. Julian near Tours, originally founded by Radégonde's father-in-law.

The baby's "sage femme," Mme Laborderie, was immediately fond of the little fellow, and when the Hoveys had to leave Tours it eased their distress that another loving woman, Louise Raveau, should take the baby into her home. It was the best provision they could make with the world still to conquer, but it was another break with the accepted ways of men.

In March and through April Hovey was in Paris. He was anxious to return to America, but his very debts kept him on. He was thinking of lecture and reading trips, but was irked by the casual way people expected a writer to limit his craft to spare hours saved from the really important business of earning a living. He had to accept the fact, but his purpose was strong to drop everything except writing as soon as the need for mere dollars was met. It angered him that the writer was put aside as less important than other workers and that his work brought slender returns. But he had pride and asked his mother to conceal the name of his unfashionable ship and to let it be supposed that he was coming home because of his prosperity and that engagements only hoped for were already promised.

He had not fallen in love with France. The dictatorial organization of society bothered him, as he had noted earlier.

In fact, politically France is a distorted America—with all our faults exaggerated and none of our English virtues. Altogether England is the only country in the world that is completely civilized and made thoroughly fit to live in.[10]

[10] Hovey, Dec. 17, 1891.

At the end of April he crossed to London and on May 19, 1892, he landed in New York. Because he was encouraged about getting *Gandolfo* played, he stayed on in New York after a visit of two months in Washington. Though the University Club there was enthusiastic over his reading of passages of the play, neither theatrical entrepreneur nor publisher would accept it.

Carman had suggested that he give Hovey a letter to his cousin on the Bliss side in Windsor, Nova Scotia, where he might spend the hay-fever season cheaply and quietly, and so in August he went there. Charles G. D. Roberts, later to be knighted and, in Carman's phrase, to be "the acknowledged laureate of this young nation," was four years older than Hovey, had been teacher and editor, and now held the chair of English Literature and Economics at King's College, that old Tory university founded under a royal charter by petition of the royalists who had fled the turbulent Revolution. He had already published two volumes of verse and edited an anthology. He was an enthusiastic lover of nature, though his desire to spiritualize the natural world later brought upon him Theodore Roosevelt's scorn as "nature faker." Naturalist, athlete, scholar, and poet, he made a good companion and welcomed many writers to his home.

Hovey was charmed by the lovely countryside and the college at Windsor. It was the kind of country he liked, since it offered the happy satisfaction of intimate living with nature without exacting an arduous struggle for survival. "Kingscroft," the Roberts' home, was on the edge of the college woods. The house looked out across the Avon and the Basin of Minas and was gay with the presence of the brilliant children who were to publish while they were still in their early teens. One of them later remembered their guest as "a black-browed Viking" who, "broad, black, and bearded, roared in on the gale of his own exuberance,"[11] much in contrast to the gangling and puckish Carman.

[11] E. M. Pomeroy, *Sir Charles G. D. Roberts* (Toronto: The Ryerson Press, 1943), p. 73.

Each of the young poets enjoyed experiment in form and had exercised himself in many of the more intricate measures. Hovey invented a game to use this interest. The three would agree on a form, or at times allow free choice of form and length up to one hundred lines. Then each wrote on slips three titles on which he would like to write. One title was drawn and all had to abide by it. No meretricious slapdash was allowed, yet the poem had to be submitted to criticism at a certain hour, usually two days later. Roberts has said that Hovey was best at fitting his meaning to the required form.[12]

One day Hovey was delighted to receive Dr. Parsons' last book inscribed: *Ad Ricardum Hoeium, poetam dilectissimum et amicum meum.* With it was a manuscript slip which pointed a parallel between poems by them which had pleased the scholar. With this fresh in his mind Hovey set down a little epigram which he first sent off to the *Century*, though it was the *New England Magazine* which finally printed it in November.

T. W. Parsons

The maiden knew great Hercules divine;
For while she saw him, was she not content?
So in the satisfaction of the heart
We find his praise, nor with too noisy art
Proclaim the beauty past all ornament
Of his precise and unsuperfluous line.

Four days later he heard of Parsons' death on the very day the lines were written. He had been found in a well into which he had fallen, presumably during an attack of apoplexy in his seventy-third year.

Hovey had not known him very intimately, but Parsons had been to him a revered figure. The essay he was soon to write for the *Atlantic* shows how strict he could be in his judgment on the minor quality inevitable in those who exist outside vital relationship to the contemporary world, whether that relationship is of sympathy or antagonism. Parsons had lived apart from his age, an artist marked by quality of expression rather than by imaginative insight. He was no model to be

[12] Roberts, *Dalhousie Review*, April, 1930, quoted by Pomeroy, *op. cit.*, p. 82.

followed, but a lost friend to be wept for.   Indeed, one doubts
that *Seaward* would have been written except for the fact that
Hovey was living with two poets engaged on memorial verse,
Carman writing "The White Gull" and Roberts writing "Ave,"
both for the Shelley Centenary.   Hovey had been a part of
the talk and mood of this effort, and the sudden announcement
of the death of one he warmly admired was probably the spark
that touched him to similar action.

There are few symbols for the eternal recurrence of life
and perhaps it was only by coincidence that the three poets
began their works with the tide.   Roberts never ceased to celebrate the tidal marshes of his beloved Tantramar, and for
Hovey the tide-flooded marsh was a bridge from Windsor to
Scituate, where he had first known Parsons.

> I know that there the tide is coming in,
> Secret and slow, for in my heart I feel
> The silent swelling of a stress akin;
> And in my vision, Lo! blue glimpses steal
> Across the yellow marsh-grass, where the flood,
> Filling the empty channels, lifts the keel
> Of one lone cat-boat bedded in the mud.

The best of the poem is in the early statement of the theme,
the loss caught into the daily round of life and crying through
the long accents at the beginning of the lines.

> Alas! he is not here, he will not sing;
> The air is empty of him evermore.
> Alone I watch the slow kelp-gatherers bring
> Their dories full of sea-moss to the shore.
> No gentle eyes look out to sea with mine,
> No gentle lips are uttering quaint lore,
> No hand is on my shoulder for a sign.
>
> Mourn gently, tranquil marshes, mourn with me!
> Mourn, if acceptance so serene can mourn!
> Grieve, marshes, though your noonday melody
> Of color thrill through sorrow like a horn
> Blown far in Elfland! Mourn, free-wandering dunes!
> For he has left you of his voice forlorn,
> Who sang your slopes full of an hundred Junes.

Hovey's difficulty was greater than that of his friends. Shelley's bright, wind-like spirit and the ideas and things through which it blew were far richer material than the restrained and conservative austerity of Parsons, who detested modern life and had shut himself away from even its best, as the neo-humanist sometimes does. His very death was unusable poetically and was in nice contrast to Shelley's symbolic end. Thus the subject gave little urge to the lyric impulse and the writer had only his limited personal affection and the general tradition of the form to help him. The keen and stringent criticism of the prose article shows a judgment here unused as out of place, and the field is left to be filled in by a created mourning. This sometimes goes over into an inflated but traditional extravagance of phrase, a rhetoric artfully fashioned by will where imagination finds no hold and no central cohesive mood. To give the poem reach Hovey had to invoke and invent too consciously. He calls the mourners, in the elegiac way, but the mourners, after Dante, are Holmes, Stedman, Miller, Riley, Chanler, Roberts, and Carman, poets often unrecognizable without notes and too minor and sometimes too shoddy to stand in the betraying glare of the greatness he claims for them. His hospitable judgment and intense belief in greatness in the present warp his standard of value, a generous but unfortunate fault in a writer. Whatever questionable taste Hovey anywhere shows is always the result of introducing the modern and temporal into the conventional form he has adopted. It opened him to the critics and to the stricter judgment of the time, and here, certainly, the poem could be bettered by omission of at least such poets as Amelie Rives Chanler, "Virginia's hawk of song," and Riley, "full-throated, with imagination kissed."

The poem in its movement rises above the shadowy goblins of death to the serene reach of the marshes, the gleeful shouting of the sea, and the sure voyage to Paradise, where poets welcome the newcomer to unmeasured life. But the marshes and the ships dropping down the tide of Fundy for far ports draw the poet back to an earth rich in romantic association, and he ends in a mood exalted by the sheer adventure of setting forth on far journeys.

Seaward has stretches of real beauty and flashes of fine phrasing. If it was not, as Roberts claimed, the best elegiac verse in American poetry (or as Carman later said "probably as good as anything ever said about Death"), it had few rivals, with the exception of Whitman's Lincoln poems. Characteristically Hovey tried to break the hold of the classical elegy and to be contemporary and American without resigning the values of the old form. If he had followed Whitman in working a purely native strain the result would have been a less obvious pouring of new wine into an old bottle, but of course, it would have been less true to the subject of his theme. As it was, he had created something of which he was proud and which brought him fame.

The *Independent,* which printed the entire poem on its first page, introduced it in an editorial which said:

It is certainly one of the most memorable poems which have been published for many a day, and will, we think, be remembered among the great elegies of the language.[13]

Other journals and papers which commented did so only to praise, and some of Hovey's friends made the most of the opportunity. The *Elite* of Chicago went so far as to say that the best critics were placing Hovey "in the descent from Aeschylus, Shakespere, Dante, and Goethe." If his friends didn't do that, they came dangerously close to it.

Lothrop, the publisher, evidently set out to do his best for the poem in book form. A flyer was issued announcing publication on or about March 15, 1893, at $1.50 and quoting laudatory notices. It promised a "most ornate and chaste" binding "in perfect accord with the high character of the poem." The book, when published, was very attractive, only two stanzas to each page of excellent paper and the red initial letter of the first stanza worked into some pattern of rushes, shells,

---

[13] *Independent,* XLIV (Nov. 17, 1892), 1617. Robert Frost told the author that as a freshman at Dartmouth he saw the poem displayed in the college library and for the first time fully realized that one could have poems printed. Almost exactly two years later (Nov. 7, 1894), his own first publicly printed poem appeared in the *Independent.*

waves, or birds. This the *Critic* protested against as "not a consistent feature of a memorial poem unless it be an elegy on the death of a clam digger or shell gatherer," but the publisher boosted the decorative volume as a gift book for the Easter trade.

When the book appeared its press was excellent, though by signs of an unadmitted plagiarism one doubts that many of the enthusiastic commentators had read it. The same extravagances and the same praise were repeated over and over in what were only extended book notices. The more responsible journals tempered their criticism, but on the whole were very flattering. The *Literary World,* for typical example, summed up at the end of a very fair examination by saying: "On the whole, his poem is worthy; its merits are many and decided, while its defects are those of vigorous and generous youth."[14] The publisher got together an anthology of critical excerpts from some seventy papers ranging from Dublin to San Francisco, a very satisfying record to the author.

After a happy month Hovey left Windsor for Boston, where he saw the Perrys and Charles Eliot Norton, who invited him to dinner with his old teacher "Jack" Wright to celebrate the "decline and fall of Bartlett," the president of Dartmouth College. He saw others such as W. B. Harte and Stedman, feeling an increasing respect in their attentions. The *Atlantic* had asked him to write a paper on Parsons and a poem was appearing in the *Independent,* which held him in considerable esteem for his two articles on the technique of verse which had enlarged the circulation of the magazine and brought in an ample harvest of letters. Dr. Ward, the editor, was trying to make some kind of invitation to serve as literary editor which would be acceptable to Hovey. Meanwhile they gave him sixty dollars for the right to print *Seaward,* an amount, as Hovey noted, almost equal to what Milton got for *Paradise Lost.*

Carman had given up his position on *Current Literature* to devote himself to free-lance writing, and they went on to Washington together. He was as much beloved by the Hoveys as he was devoted to them. "Bliss is my boy by adoption,"

[14] *Literary World,* XXIV (June, 1893), 187.

Mrs. Hovey said, and he gave her the title of "Mother." Other young poets took it up until she had become "Mother Hovey" to most of her son's friends. Since Carman stayed for months and was joined by Roberts for a month, one sees how deserving and how genuinely felt was the loving name. Friendship for her boy and need of her affection were all Mrs. Hovey asked. Perhaps one should say almost all, for she found it hard to capitulate to Mrs. Russell, though she was won to her more and more by her cleverness and her unhappiness. She had repeated her Newport success at Bar Harbor, Maine. Her great moment in the summer of 1892 came when she rode the streets of the wealthy resort with a Pinkerton detective beside her and escorted by the police. She was on her way to a lecture on jewels at Mrs. La Bau's home and carried thousands of dollars' worth of loaned jewelry. Though by her account she was made miserable by the staring of natives and rusticaters, this established her as an authentic success. Her lectures had taken her west to Kansas City, where the papers reported the floors "carpeted with society ladies" learning to be graceful. She was now in South Dakota to go through the process of divorce.

Unexpectedly the press and the scandalmongers kept quiet about the lovers, and the people of Washington were sympathetic. They probably prided themselves on their liberalism, but one suspects their charity might have withered if they had seen the letters which came from France with news of "Bébé" and a nice mixture of affection and demand for money. It hurt Mrs. Russell to be a begger for favor when the rest of the world recognized her as remarkable. Among other honors she was soon to be elected physical-culture director of the World's Fair and to be put on the Advisory Council of Representative Women. There she made an interesting contrast to her fellow councilor Lucy Stone, her flowing Greek drapery quite overshadowing the militant short skirt and bloomers of Miss Stone.

When Hovey began seriously to try to place his plays, he realized more keenly than ever the low condition of the American stage. The regular public was indifferent to good plays, though it would pay for a slovenly piece of farce-comedy. This confessed taste, common in all the arts, was not worth denouncing. There remained the necessity of developing a more cultivated audience and an artistic theater which would be free of the domination of buffoons and purveyors of cheap amusement so that intelligent people who now looked down on the public theater could be interested. Such an interest was lying unused, and the creative artist was ready to write for it. Doing so he could rid himself of box office concerns and stifling obedience to the demands of stock actors capable only of the most primitive effects. Hovey was not of the writers who scorn the actors' profession, "a great art." With its complexities of motion and rhythm it drew him, as Delsartism did, because it brought body and spirit together and projected emotion in movement. He was concerned that the traditional school of the theatrical gesture should go and a slower and intellectualized type of acting take its place.

The problem was to finance a theater that could promote drama of a high literary quality acted in an imaginative way. This implied "a subsidized, independent Theatre." Such a theater would free the writer from commercial influence, and because he would then become a theatrical power, he could train up actors to respond to their parts, rather than reducing the parts to the accepted stereotypes of heavy, soubrette, and juvenile.

All this was in his mind, so that when chance offered he eagerly associated himself with the Theatre of Arts and Letters recently incorporated by Henry B. McDowell, Edward Alden Petit, Eugene Wiley Presbrey, Simon F. Sullivan, and George Sheldon, and with an impressive advisory committee of seventy, including such theater men as Belasco, Booth, Daly, Fitch, and the Frohman brothers; artists such as Lafarge, MacMonnies, and Saint Gaudens; critics such as Barrett Wendell and Stedman; and a membership of a thousand important persons. He was soon engaged as secretary of the jury at a salary of fifty dollars a week and traveling expenses, was elected one of a committee of five to select plays for the repertoire. Later he became one of the trustees.

Hovey worked hard on this venture in Boston, New York, and Washington. The nervous work and the uncertainty of success wore him down. Both his personal and his professional life were confused and without reward. On one of his trips to Washington his family were shocked by his exhausted condition. Working eighteen hours out of the twenty-four and with no peace in his heart, he was "worn out and nearly sick." The venture, like others of its kind, was dying before actual birth, though McDowell sank $60,000 to keep it going. The time was not yet ready, though to young men like Percy MacKaye, Moody, Torrence, and Hovey it continued to seem on the very verge of fulfilling their hopes. Yet this examination of the professional theater and this movement toward a cultivated drama were not without effect. Many of the ideas Hovey and his friends held have not yet been realized, but the history of the modern drama has been a slow advance toward their desire.

The failure of the venture was a double disappointment, for *Gandolfo* was on the repertoire selected by the jury. Instead of being the author of an acted play, however, Hovey was an impoverished play-tinker who revised the text and wrote the songs of *A Lady of Venice* for Katherine Clemmens. Revision wasn't enough, as he knew. Though he removed what defects were obvious, the play, he said, had no idea in it to make it great. Though the revision was more than hack work, of which he was incapable, he was unsurprised when the critics roasted it as it deserved. Yet such a shabby piece could get on the boards, and his plays could not. He felt caught between the commercial theater and the hothouse gentility of the small private group. When he "invaded the strictly practical realms of Philadelphia," early in 1893, "aesthetically gowned young women with worshipful poetic fervor in their eyes, and Delsartean grace in every movement, acted as aids,"[15] according to the local paper. This was even more unreal and distant from a vigorous public art than the legitimate stage.

[15] Philadelphia *Times*, Feb. 12, 1893.

CHAPTER VII

Men of Dartmouth

> Daughter of the woods and hills, Dartmouth, my stern
> Rock-boned and wind-blown sibyl of the snows!
> First in thy praise whom we can never praise
> Enough, I lay my laurel in my turn
> Before thee in thy uplands.
>   HOVEY, "Dartmouth Ode," 1894.

The happiest hours of early spring Hovey spent working on "Comrades," the poem he had been asked to deliver at the sixtieth Psi Upsilon convention, to which all nineteen national chapters would send delegates to Hanover. Professor Richardson headed the committee and saw the chance to bring honor both to his fraternity and to his former pupil. Hovey's mind, ridden by worry and the city, projected itself into realization of what it would mean to him to be once more in the hills and walking the village streets. In mid-May, 1893, after a final shaping of the poem in Washington, he was in Hanover, seeing old friends and old places. In this limited world he was feted as a prince of poetry. On the second evening of the convention the public literary exercises were held in Bissell Hall. After prayer, piccolo solo, address, vocal selection, and oration, Hovey at last arose and spoke:

> Again among the hills!
> The shaggy hills!
> The clear arousing air comes like a call
> Of bugle notes across the pines, and thrills
> My heart as if a hero had just spoken.
> Again among the hills!
> The jubilant unbroken
> Long dreaming of the hills!
> Far off, Ascutney smiles as one at peace;
> And over all

> The golden sunlight pours and fills
> The hollow of the earth, like a God's joy.

The poem was written for vocal delivery and Hovey gave it his magnificent ability. William Jewett Tucker, who had accepted the presidency but had not yet been formally inducted, sat enthralled by the "deep jubilant tones of his voice." As he listened to those first lines he said to himself, "Here at last is a poet."[1]   As Hovey moved through his poem with its broken meters that beat into blank verse or swung into song, he carried his audience with him. It was no stodgy poem nor was it a mere piece of occasional verse. The man was in it and his praise of the love of comrades came truly and movingly.

> But more than strength and more than truth
> Oh praise the love of man and man!
> Praise it for pledge of our eternal youth!
> Praise it for pulse of that great gush that ran
> Through all the worlds, when He
> Who made them clapped his hands for glee,
> And laughed Love down the cycles of the stars.
> Praise all that plants it in the hearts of men,
> All that protects it from the hoof that mars,
> The weed that stifles; praise the rain
> That rains upon it and the sun that shines,
> Till it stretch skyward with its laden vines!

Next day the convention moved by special train to Springfield, Massachusetts, for its banquet. Those who had heard the poem wanted others to hear it and demanded that Hovey repeat the reading. Again man and poem did Hovey good. One lauded success made months of vain effort less depressing. The receptions, the hours with the Richardsons, walking the campus, and remembering invigorated him. It was pleasant, even, to walk into Deacon Downing's drug store and pay twenty-five dollars on a bill now eight years old, even if almost as much remained unpaid. Whatever other disappointments there were, this was good and a springtime renewal of an old fealty.

[1] President Tucker, letter to Willard Huntington Wright, May 21, 1912.

He returned to Washington, where Carman was in the last month of his long visit. They were delighted to be together again, planning projects, reading poems, and talking nonsense. Out of their discouragement over publication and the fun of making sport of the successful dictators of literature, they fell to making satiric verses, sometimes jointly, sometimes singly. All through the June days their minds ran off into ridicule. Woodberry, Gilder, Aldrich, Higginson, Matthews, Sherman, Underwood, Mitchell were shot at with light-barbed arrows. The verses on Thomas Bailey Aldrich, who for nine years had ruled taste from the throne of the *Atlantic* and still spoke ex cathedra, are characteristic.

> Dandy Tommy
>
> Dandy Tommy, spick and span
> Struts before the Gilder clan
>
> All the Gilder clan bow down
> To the beau of Boston town.
>
> What though like a lady's waist
> All his lines are overlaced,
>
> What though from a harmless brain
> Smooth inanities he strain,
>
> In his emptiness content
> He achieves his ten per cent,
>
> And secure in magazines
> Rules all rhymesters in their teens.

This was only the laughing face of a serious concern with a poetry which had fallen to a sentimental and gushing treatment of genteel matters. To succeed you had only to

> Turn your woes (divine or dental)
> Into anapaestic slush

and "Sharpers" (*Harper's Magazine*) would accept the pretty verses. If you rebelled, you were a barbarian. It was not the men themselves they attacked, but their oligarchic tyranny of narrow taste.

When shall the Golden Age of Song
Return to earth again?
When all the dilettante throng
Is silenced or is slain

When Tommy Aldrich is tabooed
And Woodberry's forgot;
When Gilder knows bad verse from good
And stops accepting rot.

Such verses they got together in what they called "The Book of Gibes." Several typewritten copies were made, but there is no indication that they were optimistic enough to suppose that any publisher would issue them. They were probably only for the laughter of their own group, the caustic laughter of the rebellious young excluded by their entrenched elders, though three years later many of them would appear in the *Tatler*.

Before Hovey left home he told his mother his feeling for Mrs. Russell and his desire to marry her. She was sympathetic but feared the newspapers. She had seen enough silly facetiousness about Delsarteans to dread such a chance for a reporter's holiday. He trusted her to see that such a position was cowardly and untenable. Even though she might admit that it was such in the moral realm, she had to come slowly to accept the inevitable fuss. Until she had been won over, however, Hovey said nothing to his father, who was less sympathetic to Mrs. Russell and who, he rightly suspected, would object to the disparity in their ages and to her former unions. It was an unhappy situation.

A summer outing seemed the best opportunity for the lovers to be together again, since, as Carman wrote to Mrs. Russell, he wanted no "exclusive rum and tobacco garden party" and women were to be admitted to the fellowship, even though they must have foreseen the minor scandal. So in the hot and rainy days of August they came together again in Nova Scotia, staying first at Windsor College. Carman and Roberts were late; thus the large share of work in clearing the ground and setting up the tents fell to Hovey, while the women sewed the canvas. The strips which were left he made into cots.

He rejoiced in the life, feeling "strong as an ox," and working on *The Holy Graal* in less muscular hours. By the twenty-third of the month they were in camp, and before the end of the month Roberts and Carman had joined them. The rains came again and after a sodden week under the gloomy firs they stayed much of the time in Roberts's house. This was better for literary work and Hovey did a lot of studying and reading. He could use the college library and once, as Mrs. Russell looked up from a letter to his mother, she saw him crossing with an encyclopedia "smiling and handsome as possible, with a sense of power." With this literary work they plunged into philology and undertook the study of accent, rhythm, and sound under Mrs. Russell's tuition. The stimulus of quiet and friendship drove the men to extraordinary production. While Carman filled thirty book pages, Hovey finished the *Invocation to Merlin*, which his friends thought his best work, wrote "Down the World with Marna" to Mrs. Russell, and began work on *Taliesin*.

The one unhappiness was the realization of what his mother was undergoing. A letter would come and leave him white-faced and feeling utterly helpless. Mrs. Russell was also worrying, wondering what Roberts had written to her. "I am awfully sore, sensitive, and proud about what you are all saying to each other." She never quite trusted Roberts's discretion or his judgment on fundamental values. Of Carman there was no doubt. "I rely on Carman," she said. "I think as far as he understands women at all he recognizes me. He has said some things about me, almost greater than I deserve."[2] She could not endure the slight to her nor the question of Richard, for, as she wrote too swiftly for punctuation: "He is God an angel and a man a gentleman the ideal lover and his heart is holy as heaven."

Even here in the woods of a college campus they could not escape the hard necessities of money. They were living simply,

[2] Mrs. Russell, no date [Oct., 1893].

innocently, and intensely. They were working with hands and brain as few ever work. But the man to whom they still owed money for the materials out of which they had built the tents with their own hands was demanding payment. The bill was fifteen dollars. The three intellectuals and poets, four if one counts Mrs. Russell, had not that sum among them. Manuscripts were out and going out all the time, but these honest, grown men had not fifteen dollars and Hovey had to telegraph to his father for aid. It was galling and insulting that they should be so harassed. As they talked of the hard lot of the poet in the modern world, they longed for a better life. Out of their hurt and their desire, out of their life in the woods and their free companionship, came their own world of Vagabondia, soon to be shaped and charted by their poems.

After a time Mrs. Russell moved on to Halifax to lecture. One engagement was at the Sacred Heart Convent. The dramatic contrast between her beliefs and practice and those of the audience frightened her, but standing before the nuns and the archbishop she kept calm and won them to enthusiasm. Other lectures followed and brought success. Slow as Halifax was, she "regularly took the town." She was entertained, Hovey came and was lionized, she was even the subject of a sonnet by a local Sappho. Then the maid Eliza, who had cooked for them in camp, accidentally set her clothing afire. In her desperation she wanted only to rush flaming out-of-doors. Mrs. Russell had to fight her and when it was over was bruised and burnt. Need of money was so desperate that she kept going until one day she nearly bled to death. The doctor found and removed a malignant tumor in the uterus. She lay weakly in bed for a fortnight, but then, with money all gone and none for the future, she forced herself up to address five hundred people in Halifax. With quiet courage she got on to Yarmouth, where she took a little rest between classes, but she was still unwell when she reached Boston.

Hovey, tanned and thin, had moved to Boston, where he roomed with Carman at the Thorndike. He was deeply unhappy at his father's uncompromising disapproval of the marriage. Night after night he tossed sleeplessly or walked the floor. There was no way out. If he followed his heart and his belief, he must go against all else. He wrote his father a dignified and formal letter. He said that he suffered from his father's disapprobation, but he refused all objection on the score of Mrs. Russell's age and his own exaggerated inexperience. "As yet no woman younger than myself has ever, I will not say held me by the slightest tie, but really awakened any interest in me at all other than such as I might take in a clever child that I might like to teach and train." It was necessary that his wife should be an intellectual comrade. He and Mrs. Russell were already bound in such a comradeship. "My career intellectually and practically is in any event closely bound to hers and must be. In no figurative or hyperbolic sense, she is the chief aid I have outside myself in thought and art." As for the divorce, he had long ago taken his stand as poet, and as man he had urged it. He was sure he was making no mistake; their temperamental fitness and their love were too real for mistake.[3]

No explanation could ease the difference, but his love was too deeply integrated with his whole life to be denied. As Mrs. Russell wrote to his mother in December, "Richard is not like most men. To him affairs of the heart are sacred and he would not be reasoned out of doing as his love and his intuitions prompt. It is a religion with him."[4] He was not to be put off like a schoolgirl. The life-long trust his father had given him had educated him to courage even against that father, if need be. So he kept writing, always in the most manly and mature way. He wanted to keep his family's love more than anything else except his integrity and his love for Mrs. Russell. He stood firmly on his declaration of the free right of a man and tried to keep his father from a position unworthy of him and certain to give later regret. For the family who had dreamed and worked for greatness for him, the marriage seemed a tragic fall; for the lover no other course was pos-

[3] Hovey, Nov. 16, 1893.
[4] Mrs. Russell, Dec. 14, 1893.

sible. Thus the parents had finally to make the best of it, for they would be faithful to him always.

Back Bay gossiped, Washington friends fell away, and the family were hurt by hints of evil. As Mrs. Russell later wrote to her son Kenneth, "Richard and I are too picturesque a couple not to be gossiped about. It is romantic and the world is always starving for romance."[5] Hovey hid his hurt and went ahead with plans to marry. His friend Ben Tenney, Dartmouth '83, had recently married Alice Parker, the daughter of Professor Parker, Hovey's former Latin teacher, and the Tenneys offered them their Marlboro Street house for the wedding on January 17, 1894. Professor Parker himself performed a religious marriage ceremony and A. A. Maxwell, Dartmouth '83, performed the civil service.[6] After the ceremony there was an equally impartial supper: lobster, camembert cheese, wedding cake, champagne, beer, and Maraschino. The groom had written an elaborate Latin epithalamium which he read and later, when even the bride and groom seemed more interested in talk and poetry than in leaving, recited "The Wander Lovers," written during the stay at Windsor, and soon to appear in *Songs from Vagabondia:*

> Down the world with Marna!
> That's the life for me!
> Wandering with the wandering wind,
> Vagabond and unconfined!
> Roving with the roving rain
> Its unboundaried domaine!
> Kith and kin of wander-kind,
> Children of the sea!
>
> . . . .
>
> Down the world with Marna!
> Daughter of the air!
> Marna of the subtle grace
> And the vision in her face!

[5] Mrs. Russell, no date [1895].

[6] According to the Boston *Record* the double ceremony was conducted because Professor Parker was not a resident of the state and because the bride and groom preferred "the French ceremony." Maxwell, a lawyer, was a justice of the peace.

Moving in the measures trod
By the angels before God!
With her sky-blue eyes amaze
And her sea-blue hair!

. . . .

Marna of the far quest
After the divine!
Striving ever for some goal
Past the blunder-god's control!
Dreaming of potential years
When no day shall dawn in fears!
That's the Marna of my soul,
Wander-bride of mine!

Hovey was pleased that the journals made no more foolish reports than they did, but only an exaggerated foreboding could have found them good. The Boston *Record* headed its long account: "The Delsarte Lady Married to a Poet."[7] There followed a long account of her activities, with generous borrowings from her publicity, and some paragraphs on Russell, their disagreement, and divorce. Her costumes were described but it was admitted, "she would be called handsome in any set." The paragraphs on the new husband were captioned "An Odd Genius," and "He Is Quite a Poet." They accorded him the title of "the most erratic genius and perhaps the most naturally gifted man of ten years ago" at Dartmouth.

The publicity did little harm with those who knew them. Calls and return calls were made, and the new Mrs. Hovey proudly wrote the names of her distinguished guests, Mrs. Jack Gardner, Mrs. Perry, and others. Their first "At Home" was crowded. But though she was recognized, she found few pupils. She spoke at the Boston College School of Oratory with Alger, and the Boston *Courier* recognized them as the two disciples in apostolic succession from Delsarte and Mac-Kaye. This was important to her, for while MacKaye had lived she felt she had no right to assume leadership, even though he would not. Now that he was dead she was ready to step

[7] Boston *Record*, Jan. 18, 1894.

forth as leader. As she told her audience, "I have no home. I am a pioneer. I go about spreading the doctrines of Delsarte."[8] She now listed among her endorsers such men as Mark Twain, Charles Dudley Warner, Joaquin Miller, Edward Eggleston, and as pupils John McCullough, William Gillette, Daniel Frohman, and Carman. This professional standing brought in little money, however. She had complained to Mrs. Hovey:

> I can't think of anything bad enough to say of the manners, the inhospitality, the penuriousness of Boston Women. . . . They have such great enthusiasm to get all they can in a lesson; question, tease and tire me out with their eagerness, and then wriggle in every way to put off paying good prices. You would not believe the little meannesses they stoop to.[9]

Though she found Boston "mean and stingy" and Hovey found it without manners, a course of lectures kept them on in the harsh air neither liked, though both had once looked forward to being in the town where, she said, her intellectual life had begun. Six weeks after their marriage they had moved from rooms at 15 Blagden Street, and now occupied the first floor at 601 Boylston Street, just across from Trinity Church and "under the very eaves of the Library." They kept their habit of studying together several hours a day, and Hovey was eagerly tracing his ancestry back to the Welsh kings who reigned in descent from Arthur. He was "very smiling and proud about it," but the kings had bequeathed him no inheritance. He kept on thrusting new irons into the fire as he pulled old ones out, but with little success. He had hopes that Stanley Hall might get him a place at Clark University, where they could pursue some interesting technical experiments. He even applied to President Tucker for the Professorship of Oratory at Dartmouth. Though his self-praise may sound fulsome, he had been greatly encouraged to such estimate by the words of men like Dr. W. H. Ward, editor of the *Independent*, Dr. W. T. Harris, the famous scholar, and President

[8] Boston *Traveller*, Feb. 7, 1894.
[9] Mrs. Russell, no date [1893].

Stanley Hall of Clark University. Notebook after notebook he filled with schemes and tables that attempted to put a scientific order into the art of spoken speech. So his words are not extravagant.

I have studied with the greatest teachers of expression and have everywhere met with enthusiastic receptions as a public reader. The material of speech (the physiology of the vocal organs, the analysis of articulate sound, etc.) have been a specialty of mine for many years. In the application of modern methods to poetics (and also to the technique of prose, spoken and written) I am accomplishing a work which competent judges pronounce to be an advance on what has been done heretofore.[10]

For a time, things looked promising. McDowell talked of writing music for *Merlin*. Hovey's reading of *Vagabondia* at the January Alumni Dinner in Boston "elicited a storm of applause,"[11] and the attractive circulars for *Seaward* were bringing wide notice. He made two quick runs to New York to do a "reading-acting" of a play for Lincoln. Wheatcroft wanted him to act the part of Edgar Allan Poe for him. On his return he lectured at Boston University, and his wife followed him in the evening. The Professor of English was very much impressed by his treatment of poetics as Delsartean studies had illuminated the subject and admitted that the work was "far in advance of anything yet done."[12] Still, whatever his efforts and whatever his successes, he was neither making enough money nor getting on with his desire to be a great poet.

Then came the suggestion that he write a song for Dartmouth. The Dartmouth Lunch Club of Boston had voted to "appoint a committee of three to obtain a Dartmouth song, special mention being made of Richard Hovey '85, whose marriage with Mrs. Henrietta Russell, high priestess of the temple Delsarte, has created so much interest."[13] Beyond all prize money was the chance to put his feeling for Dartmouth into

[10] Hovey, March 30, 1894.
[11] Boston *Record*, Jan. 18, 1894.
[12] Hovey, March 4, 1894.
[13] *Dartmouth Literary Monthly*, VIII (March, 1894), 293.

words. More than that, the poet's chance to lift the feeling of other men to a level of perception and expression far beyond their individual capacities. The chance might have seemed a little thing to hundreds of poets less than Hovey in ability, but to him it was as moving as any other creative experience. Dartmouth as men knew it was uncreated; he would make it. The thought took hold of him as the phrases came together. Late in March, 1894, he sat in their rooms looking out on Copley Square, thinking of the poem, "his eyes shining like two moons."[14] Then he would pace up and down the large room. "Walk walk and smoke smoke seems the necessity when he is writing." So he rolled cigarette after cigarette of Bob White tobacco and measured out the rhythm with his pacing. On Easter Sunday, two days after he began, he made his fair copy.

"Men of Dartmouth"—he threw away the outworn sentiments of the college songs that could belong to any college by mere change of name. He built his poem out of Dartmouth, but, by suggestion and symbol, he built a new student body.

> They have the still North in their hearts,
> The hill-winds in their veins,
> And the granite of New Hampshire
> In their muscles and their brains.

Out of whatever else more conventional and sentimental, these were the phrases that caught an emerging feeling for "the lone and silent North," and, by reversion of the pathetic fallacy, borrowed from nature the qualities of men. The original Dartmouth "spirit," dedicated to Christianizing the heathen Indians, had quickly died as the Indians became fewer and less important. With the growth of the country the courage of a voice crying in the wilderness of New Hampshire became incongruous. Isolation bred no virtues except narrow allegiance, and, as the student complaints of the eighties show, the college was following others of comparable size and reputation at an uninspiring distance. It needed a new idea and a new myth. Dr. Tucker gave the ethical idea; Hovey the poetic myth.

[14] Mrs. Hovey, March 23, 1894.

When the mark of poverty was muscle and rude health, the college man took no pride in them. Poe at Virginia was proud of his Byronic pallor and Longfellow at Bowdoin gave up shadow boxing with a figure sketched on the door as too strenuous. Now, however, the poorer playmates of the college man went into offices and grew flabby and pale. So the twentieth-century student was increasingly to boast his ruggedness. As the natural world retreated as an inescapable fact, its poetic possibilities emerged. When man's ecological victory was won he could glorify the old antagonist. Hovey, who had disliked the cold winter as a student, stirred now to the idea of the cold and the edged wind sweeping down from Canada. All his actual experience of cold was already achieved, and the "Winter Song" of 1898 with its wolfwind and "great white cold" were already admitted in imagination. Without the cold and the fierce wind the fellowship of pipe and bowl would be tame.

So decades before the rise of skiing, winter carnivals, Outing Club cabins, and the glorification of the North Country, Hovey's imagination leaped to set the feeling men would someday enter. It is as if he created the present Dartmouth, the Dartmouth of myth which stands any assault of reality, a pagan, Anglo-Saxon myth of primitive living and comradeship quite unlike that of Latin piety toward Alma Mater. It could not have caught and held men if it had not been in the spirit of our time. To have sensed that coming spirit was a flash of intuition.

Dartmouth was much in his mind in the spring of 1894. Just two days before his departure for Europe and too late to change his plans, he saw an announcement that he was to read a poem at the next Commencement. Even then he did not realize that the occasion was to be the formal celebration of the one hundred and twenty-fifth anniversary of the College. He remembered only vaguely that someone had spoken to him at a banquet, but, as he understood, he accepted the responsibility. When the poem was finished he forwarded it from England with a letter to Dr. Tucker.

Presuming that there will be plenty of laudation and eulogy from others, I have ventured in my verses to be a little critical; not because I lack pride in my Alma Mater; but because I want to see her, not merely abreast, but in the van of educational progress. And, however much she has accomplished, I believe there is much that *no* educational institution has yet begun to do. I should be still prouder of Dartmouth if she should be among the first to attempt the unattempted.[15]

The "Ode" begins with the voices of nature calling men from their narrow scientific studies to a more intimate knowledge. "He only that loves us and lives with us, knows what we be." It then turns to Dartmouth, "rock-boned and wind-blown sibyl of the snows," and the poet's lasting love.

> None goes
> Forth from thy granite through the summer days
> And many a land of apple and of rose,
> Keeping in his heart more faithfully than I
> The love of thy grim hills and northern sky.

But he would have the college greater. Let the boys have their games and their books, which are good, but let them waken also the "unaroused and undivined" instincts that lie asleep in them that they may respond more swiftly and more subtly to emotion and intuition. Let Dartmouth push forward through ignorance and the untried that men may know art, religion, poetry, yet never kill early man's wild intimacy with earth. Let man's love grow and keep his knowledge from sterile death.

> We . . . what have we done that the
>   heart should be taught?
> We have given men brawn—without love 't is the
>   Brute come again;
> We have given men brain—without love 't is the
>   Fiend. Is there aught
> We have given to greaten the soul, we who dare
>   to shape men?

[15] Hovey, June 10, 1894.

The "Ode" is another and quite different token of Hovey's love of his college and his devotion to what it might be. It is no occasional verse casually compounded of remembered fragments. It keeps the dignity of the form, but freshens it with new images and intellectual statement. It is less a commemoration than a philosophy of education, and sketches an ideal which the colleges forever miss. It aims at the development of all of man's possibilities acting in organic wholeness.

> Oh, train we the body for beauty, and train we
> the soul
> Not only as mind but as man, not to know but
> to be!

The concept is as old as the Greeks, but whatever lip-service it receives men sell their colleges to other ends. If one breaks through the conventional complacency that blinds us to our own indifference, one sees here in the "Ode" not a college poem, but one expression of Hovey's enduring ideal—a beautiful and interplaying harmony of man's total endowment, his godlike potentiality. This highest end of all living he asks the college to foster.[16]

The Hoveys had not found what they wanted in Boston. It was of the past, as even Barrett Wendell felt the Yankees were. The old giants had died off; even Holmes, who seemed immortally young, died in this year, and the old fighters like Mrs. Howe and Dr. Hale were only symbols. Boston was still the intellectual center of the United States. In education, in philosophy, in theology, in disciplined culture it still clung precariously to its old crown. But it turned from the new and from a serious concern with experimental art and busied itself burying the great and writing reminiscences of them. When the creative artists have left a city it cannot long keep its cul-

---

[16] Hovey wrote to Grover after the latter's review of Hovey's work: "I wish I were in a position to do more for the Lit. and for everything that concerns the cause of Art at Dartmouth. But, in every way that I can help, command me. Times are so hard that I have to practise the smallest economies. But though I cannot help now with my purse, I am ready at any time to help with my pen" (March 31, 1894).

tural dominance. At best Boston was a huge museum. Certainly it was no place for new ventures, this "old, fad-ridden, priggish, pompous, stilted, affected, ridiculous Boston,"[17] as Hovey called it. In April they had filled all the engagements they had secured. They made a visit to Washington, and then, on May 9, 1894, after a sleepy trip to Philadelphia, they boarded a small ship for England.

[17] Hovey, Dec. 20, 1894.

CHAPTER VIII

Vagabondia

I said in my heart, "I am sick of four walls and a ceiling.
I have need of the sky.
I have business with the grass.
I will up and get me away where the hawk is wheeling,
Lone and high,
And the slow clouds go by."

HOVEY, "Spring," 1896.

Although all wars are revolutionary, the Civil War was more than usually an economic and ideological revolution. Machinery, corporate finance, mass production, wealth in railroads and oil, the growth of cities and vulgarity prospered in the decades after it. Concord, Massachusetts, had lost the war as truly as Macon, Georgia. The resulting split in our culture widened most in our literature. Though, as Emerson had said, "Our people have their intellectual culture from one country and their duties from another," American writing, so far as it attained the dignity of recognition, had earlier concerned itself with the great materials and matters of Western culture. The scarlet A's, white whales, Walden cabins, and even the "trottoirs" of Manhattan were the new and recalcitrant stuffs which made more real the fundamental principles of human living. However native the idiom and homely the material, the high dignity of literature and of man remained. Indeed, the farther from political and artistic orthodoxy the writer, the more he wrote like prophet and lawgiver.

If the great writers of the earlier half of the century had kept a sane balance between native and universal, after 1865 the split which had long threatened the indivisibility of art came more and more to oppose art to reality. Men like Longfellow were too timid and cultivated for the raw impulse of either the frontier or the new industrialism and made the costly mistake of separating poetry and the day's existence. Longfellow frankly recognized "the difference between my ideal home-world of Poetry, and the outer, actual, tangible Prose world." He could not successfully merge their distinctness in a poetry which might be a new act of creative imagination.

The mistake belonged to his time, and most of England and America were with him. As the years went by, the penalty for the divorce became more obvious in the men born in the 1820's and 1830's. They were now becoming the dictators of poetry, if only because they edited the great magazines. Aldrich, Stoddard, and Taylor had lesser scope in a less "poetic" world. They watered their sentimentalism still more and defended their very right to be called derivative if that alone declared them lovers of beauty. Aldrich was finally to realize the lack of body in this material they shaped with a devotion and skill our poetry had not before been given, but he had already waged his war on realism from the editorial chair of the powerful *Atlantic Monthly*. He and his friends were gentlemen. The old Puritan and agrarian ethics had made the Yankees indifferent to being gentlemen, since to be a man was a greater act. But these, their successors, were gifted with position and income, and they were on the defensive against attack on their citadel. They were conservatives because there was no new idealism to lead them on; they were repressive authoritarians because, in all truth, there was no spiritual force worthy to dispute the supremacy of their academic and literary culture. But if one praises them as cultivated gentlemen, he damns them by the same phrase. They were inheritors, not progenitors.

Even more pure and refined were the women writers and readers who had become the great reading and writing public in a world of businessmen devoted to busyness. "The damned mob of scribbling women," of whom Hawthorne had complained earlier, had grown and produced a public. Even the fastidious Henry James bewailed the false delicacy demanded of a writer. The genteel female, except in the centers of old culture, took over the guardianship of literature, and even where "gentlemen of taste" still devoted themselves to the arts they were outnumbered and outvoted. An editor is not so powerful as his subscription list.

So this temptation to division within the educated and moral American drew him farther and farther from the earth and the people of America and found no insight into the problems presented by the social context. He became a poetaster, a dilettante, a litterateur, whatever name one gives to the class-conscious amateur of literary taste. Travel, study, antiquarianism, and polite criticism were as much his interest as verse. He fed on the Old World and its assured products. He was afraid both of the raw native power of America and of the ideological and aesthetic energy of contemporary Europe. There was no germ of new life within him.

By his middle twenties Hovey realized fully the inadequacy of this elegant art. He had himself practiced the precious forms—triolet, villanelle, rondeau—since his junior year in college and particularly in the first years after graduation. Technique interested him profoundly and was to be a constant study, so that he knew how meretricious and elementary that quality in modern verse was.

In the midst of a temporary lull in real poetic accomplishment, we have been priding ourselves on our technique. And it is undeniable that a certain facility in jingle, a certain ease in using words like the sentences of a Chinese puzzle, a certain mastery over intricate rhyme-combinations is not uncommon.[1]

Yet he found little real technical power, little "ability to use the infinite rhythmical, phonetic, and rhetorical resources of language." Indeed, he felt that the aesthetic school of the nineties was finished while it was still in fairly vigorous production. His clearest statement of rejection came in 1892, though he had made his decision earlier.

. . . the aesthetic movement which began with Keats, reached in Tennyson a state of finish which precludes further advancement on

[1] This quotation, like those immediately following, is from Hovey's essay "On the Threshold," *Independent*, XLIV (Nov. 3, 1892), 1546-1547.

the same lines. "Art for art's sake" is no longer a phrase to conjure with, and its devotees amuse themselves with poetic bric-à-brac. We are not likely to forget the lesson that a work derives its most potent beauty from its air of being a thing complete in itself; and, therefore, we will no longer put up signboards to call attention to the relations it may have with things outside of itself. At the same time, we have tired of dilletantism, and "aesthetic" has become a word of reproach. We think now more of art for life's sake, and are beginning to realize that the best art is the most human.

That side of the split, then, could not command his interest nor his faith. It denied life by an overemphasis on formal elaboration and limited selectiveness. It had already achieved freedom from utilitarian function, but it had no directing purpose to give that freedom meaning.

The other strain in our culture, the native fact, had been pushed as far from the center in the other direction. It had lost the imaginative and religious sweep of Emerson, Thoreau, and Whitman, and, unable to lift the homely commonplace to dignity by seeing through the material fact to its symbolic and artistic possibilities, it settled for the particular, the local, and the vulgar. At its best it gave the Mark Twain who in books which were flooded by the Mississippi set down a moment in our history. But the lesser Twain is almost indistinguishable from the journalistic producers of dialect verse who too often mistook illiteracy for humor and ignorance for democratic wisdom. A cynical disingenuousness grows in a Riley or a Field who can tailor his work to a familiar pattern and know that an audience will accept it as genuine. The declared homespun becomes shoddy. Even one's real affections will seem, like Field's delight in Horace, mere copy for a debasing drollery. But the public ran to this folksy, patronizing verse. Riley got out fourteen volumes of it, and the log-cabin-born farm boy, Will Carleton, had sold 600,000 copies of his books before his death. This particular vogue had no hold on the intellectual class; nor, indeed, did its material have any hold on the affections of its producers. Bret Harte's melodramatic and sentimental celebration of the West, in which the wide-open spaces are mostly of logic and honesty, was so successful that he could clear out for Europe, where he spent twenty-five years. Twain quit the West in his early thirties to live in the East and in Europe. They were symptomatic of the rejection of native culture even by those who had most profited by it.

So, in the early nineties, when the old gods (Emerson, Whittier, Melville, Holmes, Lowell, Longfellow, Whitman) died with almost conspiratorial unanimity, the young American who was serious about literature found himself without great rivals but with no energetic inheritance. Hovey was too cultivated to go directly to the crude and meaningless vulgarity of what was confused with realism and honest homespun. Even the best of Twain and the writers of local color left him cold. He was not concerned with a distinctly national literature, but with literature.

Local color threatens to become a fetish. It is the primary fundamental humanity that we want, rather than the trivial peculiarities of time and place, whose interest at best will soon become merely antiquarian. We have learned that red shirts and miners and Indians are not necessary to Americanism, but the prophets of dialect and etiquet [*sic*] are still aggressive. We shall be quite American enough if we take the world for our heritage and use it with American hearts.

As one looks back to the three decades before World War I he sees that the strongest writing in America was in the realistic novel. No poet or dramatist attained real stature. The best outlet for creative energy was the social novel which realistically attacked the problems of the time. Such realism, of course, is contrary to the very nature of poetry, and so the poet was cut off from renewal of purpose and vigor by what was almost a denial of art. Keeping his sights on the highest purposes of art, Hovey saw that the function of realism is intermediary only, that realism is not an aesthetic end but a corrective means. Unfortunately there are moments in history when the means to a new organization of insights commands the only energy capable of large social attention. So though Hovey was fundamentally right, as one now agrees, both his art form and his thinking closed to him the one literary mood which succeeded in perpetuating itself.

Hovey was not a frightened traditionalist in his estimate
of realism. He praised it for what it was. Early in his career
he called it "the most vital and most human literary movement
of recent years," and said that it had furnished "the virile element in our artistic development." When in 1895 he wrote
for the *Independent* an article entitled "The Passing of
Realism," he quite brilliantly cut through the sociological and
moral debate and declared its irrelevance. Realism he saw not
as an end, but as a phase of health. Just as when one lives too
spiritually to the utter neglect of his animal being one must
allow nature her therapeutic revenge, so overrefined art must
make its way to health by an overdose of reality.

Art having forgotten the earth too long, needed to sprawl upon it for
a while for refreshment. It is a good thing as a phase, tho in itself
something unpleasant. It is an attitude of fatigue and fatigue is
usually unbeautiful. . . .

The analytic, merely intellectual act of recognition, came to be the chief
source of esthetic pleasure, and imitation the chief artistic activity. Of
course, nothing infuriates a realist more than to tell him that imitation
is the lowest of aesthetic faculties. Nevertheless, it is true.[2]

So, because realism forgot the very nature of creative activity, it had to be rejected as an end. A compromise such as
is common in popular literature could arrive at nothing but
good form, without the merit of either realism or idealism.
There remained only the dialectic synthesis which might unite
shadow and substance, ideal and thing. This returned art to
its high function, but also set it beyond contemporary ability.

It is a very simple matter. Find the idea in the thing in Nature and
put the idea in the thing in Art, and the problem is solved. Both must
be present, the thing and the idea or we shall have a world of corpses
or of ghosts, not of men. But both must be present, not as separate
or contradictory entities, but as inextricably one. We must have the
ideal; but we must find it where it actually is, in the real, not in the

[2] Hovey, "The Passing of Realism," *Independent*, XLVII (Aug. 22, 1895),
1125.

unreal. We must have the real; but we must portray it as it actually is, as the process of the ideal, not as a meaningless and empty husk. . . .

It has sometimes occurred to the writer that, when we have learned our lesson, we shall find that Art, except when it has been twisted and deformed by the theorists, has always held the solution of this problem, that it is its very essence to incarnate ideas in forms, and that it was sacramental before the world ever heard of a sacrament.

Every artist, when he quits theorizing and is content to be simply an artist, sees things in this way. It is this which makes him an artist. He does not confuse the unseen and the seen; neither does he separate them. He delights in the world because it is alive.

Such critical estimates are worth quoting for themselves, for no other American, with the exception of Henry James in England, was writing a more perceptive and closely reasoned criticism. They have the virtue of penetration because they are so singly concerned with the ultimate problem of art. They also show how mature in reason their creator had become, how capable of an analysis free of the styles and fads of a contemporary literature in which he was greatly interested. His love of good and noble works and his metaphysical concern with the creating artist were safeguards to his judgment of ultimate ends.

This rejection of current vogues was in no way a self-glorification by depreciation of others. It was a diagnosis of illness within the body of Western art. He vigorously opposed the spiritual attitudes behind the art of the nineties, whether that art was aesthetically decadent or a realistic study of a decadent society. Either approach failed to take the step into a new and affirmative social art.

Many of us agree very heartily with Napoleon. "This old Europe bores me." Only to speak by the card, it is not the old but the new Europe that bores us, and, what is more fatal, bores the Europeans.

. . . Russia, Norway, and Sweden sit like Lapland witches about a filthy cauldron and intone the grisly literature of Despair. France, like an intellectual roué, coaxes her artistic appetite with aphrodisiacs, and ransacks the impossible for new sensations.[3]

[3] Hovey, "On the Threshold," *loc. cit.*, p. 1547.

Germany, he continued, does no more than prattle "an infantile cruelty," and England doesn't count.

He found the same pessimism, dilettantism, and decay in American literature, but here, he believed, they were importations into a naturally healthier life and thought. Here "the philosophy which conceives the universe as rational and the destiny of man as adequate" meets with acceptance and is supported on the necessary foundation of a vigorous popular life. The Americans, like the Greeks, are a democratic commercial nation with the raw material of a great literature. They were, he believed, on the threshold of a splendid period of literature, particularly in poetry. That poetry must be for life's sake, that is, it must enrich our relation to the universe and it must be written by a more stalwart and vigorous brood of men than those contemporaries who wooed the Muse with a sighing adoration which could capture none but the most refined and thin-blooded goddess.[4]

Through this thinking there is a strong reminiscence of the expectation which had run through that of the 1840's and 1850's. Although there is no indication of reading Emerson, Thoreau, and Whitman, there is the same hope for literature based upon the same faith in a sturdy democracy. Though Hovey cried against a mean-spirited money-making, as they did, he gave the same respect to the enterprise and courage of commerce. There is the same demand that the New World prove herself by a healthy, masculine, and high-minded literature, and the same call that ethics and art become one in imagination.

It is ironic that Hovey is most read as the poet of the three *Vagabondia* volumes written in collaboration with Bliss Carman. They were incidental in his writing life and tangential to his high purpose, but they reached a wide audience and, as many will admit who memorized them as undergraduates, they filled a need for poems of brave and zestful living which greater poems did not satisfy. Poems which speak to men for

[4] Laura Stedman and George M. Gould, *Life and Letters of Edmund Clarence Stedman* (2 vols.; New York: Yard and Co., 1910), II, 153.

men are worth examination if only because they show the unsatisfied desires a fully expressive culture should fulfil, and these are peculiarly diagnostic in their easy and popular celebration of virtues to which American idealism responds but which it lets go. Though they have parallels in Europe and England, they are very American poems, and though they are gay and reckless they are an expression in undress, even in motley, of attitudes Hovey took with true seriousness.

The poems are of further interest as the most memorable statement of the war against Victorian safeness and conformity which was not won in fact until the nineteen-twenties. The quality of their "bohemianism" recalls a mood of the day and distinguishes the national flavor of Hovey's feeling. There had been some vague bohemianism ever since the early seventies, but the nineties saw its fullest flourishing. Wilde's visit in 1882, James Boyle O'Reilly's often declaimed "In Bohemia" ("I'd rather live in Bohemia than in any other land"), and finally the unbelievable virulence of the Trilby craze had made hardworking and earnest Americans aware of the *vie de bohème*.[5] Bohemian magazines sprang up from Boston to San Francisco, but there was little studio or café life, and few could discover within themselves the awful vices they read about in Max Nordau's *Degeneration* or in the work of the so-called "French Decadents."

America's Bohemia was of a different sort. The groups Hovey knew best were "The Visionist" and "The Pewter Mugs," of which the former group was "the madder and more fantastic" nucleus. "The Visionist," of which Ralph Adams Cram, Bertram Goodhue, Bliss Carman, T. B. Meteyard, Herbert Small, and Herbert Copeland were members, embraced men interested in the arts and in publishing, as the names suggest. They had rooms on the top floor of an old building on Province Court. Around them were carpenter, locksmith, and engraving shops, but the hideout was the better for that. They cultivated "a certain Elizabethan tang" and "a sound taste

---

[5] *Trilby* was begun in serial publication in *Harper's Magazine* in January, 1894, and the book appeared in September, 1894. Cigars, garters, corn cures, towns were enthusiastically christened Trilby.

in malt liquors,"[6] but their kinship was less with the café dwellers of Paris than with the English aesthetes or the earlier "Oxfordians" with their union of art, religion, and economic radicalism. They were mildly socialist and high church and filled with hope to set the world right in their own decent terms. They were keen, hard-working fellows, most of whom made their mark. They were not cultists, café-sitters, nor militant enemies of bourgeois culture, but men who liked talk and fellowship when the day's work was over and who enjoyed a playful exaggeration of their limited revolt. They were cultivated and energetic men who knew the limits of their playing and knew also that it was a kind of masquerade. Most of them did not have the ready money or the taste for the epicureanism and roistering of the New York group around Huneker nor were they the mixture of theatrical and foreign-born people out of which a true Bohemia usually comes. It was their type of fellowship which Hovey enjoyed; and Carman and Meteyard, whose faces appear on the cover of the *Vagabondia* volumes with his, Copeland and Day, who published the first volume, and Small and Maynard, who published the second and third volumes, were all members of the group.

Bohemia belongs to Europe, but *Vagabondia* is Anglo-Saxon, and perhaps, as Hovey thought, peculiarly American. Even when he used the word, he returned its meaning to the original belief that Gypsies came from Bohemia. His Bohemian is the vagabond, the man untrapped by settled ways and city walls, the wanderer in lanes and fields and old roads who comes at night to the companionship of the tavern. Burroughs and Muir and the admirers of Whitman and Thoreau had opened the natural world. The mountains and the sea were coming into more than literary vogue and energy was splitting the seams of gentility's coat. The summer resort, sailing, cycling, tennis, and an active combination of body and mind were new preoccupations. As yet no one but Whitman had brought together the comradeship of the gregarious and the nature love of the lonely individualist, and his songs of

[6] Ralph Adams Cram, *My Life in Architecture* (Boston: Little, Brown and Co., 1936).

the open road became songs of himself and took the tone of his own half-feminine temperament. The success of Hovey and Carman lay in their combination of a number of attitudes and forms of expression which had hitherto stood singly: the love of nature, the joy of the open road, comradeship, physical courage, medievalism, sexual democracy, the scholar gypsy, and the vivid contrast between vital energy and mere existence.

It was General Hovey who saw that an attractive and popular volume could be made up out of disconnected verses, many of which celebrated the joys of friendship and out-of-door living. They had been written for reading to the group in Nova Scotia, where the poets first became aware of their vagabondage, or for sending to fellow vagabonds, as they called themselves. Publication let still others into the fellowship, for American men were irked by their captivity and happily took up the pleasant pretense of freedom and boisterous camaraderie. Hovey himself had little to do with the organization and publication of the books. Carman saw the first through the press in 1894 when Hovey was in Europe, and undertook the third after his death, as well as publishing another volume (*Echoes from Vagabondia*) under his own name in 1912.

The volumes leave a memory of those poems which are most in the spirit of the title, but when one analyzes the table of contents he sees how heterodox the selection was. For example, *Songs from Vagabondia*, the first volume in the series, begins with an enlargement of a poem written at Dartmouth ("Vagabondia") and ends with "Comrades," obviously conceived in terms of the project; but the other poems are simply collected from the unpublished verses which had accumulated while Hovey was engaged on particular and longer works. There are "Evening on the Potomac," the somnambulistic "Down the Songo," "The Wander Lovers" with its fantasy of worldjourneying with his beloved, the Browningesque "Contemporaries," poems from his first love for "Miriam," a song from "Venice" written for payment, and the toasts to his fellows. Obviously the relation to a central theme is most casual. Carman's contributions are much closer to singleness of mood and statement, perhaps because the idea of the volume captured

144 *Richard Hovey*

his imagination, whereas Hovey was preoccupied with his marriage and his European trip.

Songs from Vagabondia (1894) appeared in an attractive format repeated with only a change of end-papers in the volumes which followed. Tom Meteyard's cover showed the faces of Carman, Hovey, and himself, Carman's light head between two dark and bearded fellows. The design made Carman laugh, but he thought it would sell the book, and, indeed, "the quaintly covered little book," as the *Bookman* called it, still catches the eye. Inside, the drawings originally intended had shrunk to end-papers framing verses. Everything about the volume placed it as the product of the publishers concerned with book-making. It was dedicated to Mrs. Hovey in Carman's words:

> To H. R. H., for debts of love unpaid,
> Her boys inscribe this book that they have made.

There was "no one so fitting for all three of us to honour together," as her son said.

The volume was a popular commercial success. There were three impressions of 750 each in the first fifteen months, and frequent reissues thereafter even into our own day. Critically it fared less well at first because it offered so many opportunities to the prejudices and witticisms of the reviewers. It is amusing to observe the watch-dog morality of some, a vigilance which Carman feared might kill his chances of a college position.

The tone of the entire collection is vibrant with the enthusiasm of an intellectual tramp who is blessed with a steady thirst and enough small change to satisfy it.[7]

An elaborate effort to combine the love of nature with the morals of the tramp.[8]

. . . of prurient taste.[9]

Any such song as that about a soncy maid is simply indecent.[10]

Such caviling at the moral tone of gay openness was more

[7] New York *Mail and Express*, Sept. 19, 1894.
[8] Springfield *Republican*, Sept. 23, 1894.
[9] *Nation*, LIX, 468.   [10] *Atlantic*, LXXV (March, 1895), 411.

than balanced by the reviews in the New York *Times,* the *London Athenaeum, Poet-Lore,* and other publications. Francis Thompson in *Merry England* praised the verve and felicity and masculinity of the songs, but criticized their lack of finish. This is sound enough, but many balked at the far-fetched rhymes and free rhythms which are part of the very quality of the verses.

The venture called for continuation and in October, 1896, *More Songs from Vagabondia* appeared. Hovey expected the conservative journals "to jump on the book," but despite some scoffing the critics, who had had their chance at smart gibe, gave most attention to the gusto and warm cheer of the verses. Those who liked the volumes resented the imputation of moral looseness and praised the clean manliness of sentiment.

Still another volume had been suggested by the publisher, but Hovey died before the volume was put together. Carman, with Mrs. Hovey's aid, collected those poems by Hovey which might fit the general scheme, but the quality falls off and Hovey's contribution naturally has less common ground in theme. Carman was anxious not to hurt the reputation of his dead friend and so was intentionally more sober and omitted "the boisterous notes" which had given the volumes their lilt. Moreover, those poems which offered themselves were darker in mood and more tragic in implication. The game had become a mortal struggle.

It is easy to understand the popular appeal of these volumes. They fall between the carefully ordered poetry of high imagination, then at low ebb, and the vulgar versifying that in every age commands the larger audience. They have no pretentiousness and none of the assumption of moral profundity which marks the insincere homeliness of Field or Riley. They are what they are, just as Hovey and Carman themselves intended—the holiday mood of intelligent men or the brief poems of many sorts which might stand together without too great a quarrel.[11]

[11] That the poems were thought of as a kind of busman's holiday is amusingly illustrated by Mrs. Hovey's angry rejection of literal acceptance.

"I am still raging about the criticisms. To think of their taking Richard

Certain of their qualities, however, may be examined more particularly. Most striking is the out-of-doors freshness which blows through the verses. They are of the plein-air school. They have neither the acute perception nor the philosophic largeness of the great Romantic poetry, but rather the gypsy freedom of men released from city and society and more aware of what they leave than the still mystery of what they move toward. It is not nature poetry but holiday poetry, and at times too insistent on declaring its superiority to the soberly industrious, as one on holiday is apt to be. Often there are resemblances to the Georgian poetry which came later in England, but Hovey thought of this mood of field and open road as distinctly American. He shared Whitman's feeling of pride in America's emergence from four walls into the open air. He made this one of the marks which distinguish our taste from that of the English.

Then, too, we like the outdoor note in poetry. We go in for greater freedom of treatment, but more especially for freedom of atmosphere and spirit—the sort of poetry that represents free and natural and buoyant life, whether indoors or out. We don't care so much for the refinements of the scholar as for something genuine and healthy and modern and alive. . . . We prefer the sort of work that a man does who lives outdoors a great deal and has a healthy mind in a healthy body, and is free from morbidness. English poetry compares with American as the song of a caged bird with that of a free one.[12]

Hovey was more used to the out-of-doors than most writers are. Hay fever would have forced him to the mountains or seashore even if he had not enjoyed them. So two or three months of every year he was out of the centers of civilization, though not in the wild. The nature of the country road and mountain trail he knew well; so the poems are not the vicarious exercise of an armchair dreamer. It is only in the air of far

---

for a vagabond! Why, he is without exception the most aristocratic nature I ever knew or heard of! Only an aristocrat would write nonsense and play at vagabond; the real vagabond would put on kid gloves and write for the *Atlantic* and say 'it can't really matter.' Richard was really mad" (London, Feb., 1895).

[12] An interview in the Boston *Sunday Herald*, Oct. 30, 1898.

distance and high adventure that he touches the actual with considerable license. Even if not the wanderer who tomorrow must be "hull down on the trail of rapture," he was seldom in one place for more than a few months and had traveled widely in his years. Indeed, he and Carman were the least settled of men always. Neither had a home except that of Mother Hovey.

Virility is another of the obvious qualities in the poems. This again is a boisterous expression of something deeply held and truly needed then even more than now. In the seven-point program of the literary movement of young men of which Hovey later talked a good deal, virility is one of the points:

Poetry is thought to have something to say to strong men in the midst of the battle of life and not to be an elegant amusement for schoolgirls and dilettanti. More stress is laid on the masculine element in thought and life, and the effort is to be downright and masculine.[13]

This emphasis on virility is one aspect of Hovey's rejection of the aesthetic movement and of his desire to reanimate an ef-feminized poetry. He was not alone, of course, nor was he the first to make the attempt. Indeed, this sort of vigor goes back to Carlyle, perhaps, though it is most familiar in Henley, Stevenson, and Kipling. Hovey was not so desperate as Henley and Stevenson because he was more physically normal and held joy to be the very health of the soul. In some poems, particularly in the last volume ("At the Crossroads," for example), there is challenge to Fate, but most are more relaxed and make no call on will or biological survival, both because he had not lost religious centrality and because these poems were thrown off at the periphery of his mind. The reasoned and passionate utterance of philosophic statement he reserved for his greater work. There is less of the opposition of Life and Death, for the contrast is usually between life lived passionately and life lived meagerly, even if usefully. The virility is seen less in stoic endurance of circumstance, though that

[13] *Time and the Hour* (Boston, Dec. 4, 1897), p. 192.

is present, than in the fellowship of men who presuppose the heroic virtues.

It is easy for the sophisticated introvert to scoff at this playing at Robin Hood, Arthurian knight, or fellow soldier, but it is less easy to deny modern man's frustrated desire for these roles. This desire Carman and Hovey projected into lusty songs which borrowed the ideology and vocabulary of the past or into songs and toasts which gave the present the color of romance.

> Comrades, pour the wine tonight
> For the parting is with dawn!
> Oh, the clink of cups together,
> With the daylight coming on!
> Greet the morn
> With a double horn,
>
> When strong men drink together!
> Comrades, gird your swords tonight,
> For the battle is with dawn!
> Oh, the clash of shields together,
> With the triumph coming on!
> Greet the foe,
> And lay him low,
> When strong men fight together![14]

Into the namby-pamby versifying of the nineties the poems came with a gay and welcome heartiness. They are a contemporary echo of the Saxon lustiness in Carman's "War Song of Gamelbar," which celebrates Hovey's Spofford ancestors. Strength, loyalty, courage, comradeship, these virtues had been little enough proclaimed in the womanish verse of the day, or, indeed, in all formal poetry. Whitman's comradeship carried the quality of his strange nature and was always confusing itself with sexual affection. Strictly speaking, "the dear love of comrades" is not masculine in effect. It is too self-conscious and too physically demonstrative. Hovey places comradeship where men know it and accept it, as one realizes when he hears men of every social class roaring Hovey's lines:

[14] "Comrades," *Songs from Vagabondia,* p. 54.

For it's always fair weather
When good fellows get together,
With a stein on the table and a good song ringing clear.[15]

The verses are too disarmingly simple in attitude to be scoffed at as mere literary chest-pounding. They exaggerate, but any praise of masculine virtue and comradeship is an exaggeration in our unmasculine society and in a time when life and death are unheroic. That exaggeration was the secret of their success, for though in fact man is the creature of economic and social law, in imaginative escape he is the manly man. The *Vagabondia* poems combined the American longing for youth's perpetuation in a world of heroic virtue with a healthy protest against the dullness and the dishonesty of middle-class success-morality.

The outdoor mood, the masculinity, the protest against convention, the verve are, of course, only the most obvious qualities of whatever common ground the volumes have. Actually there is a tremendous range of materials and art form, especially in Hovey's work. One thinks of no other poet of the time, with the possible exception of Kipling, who covers so wide a territory, and Kipling's spread is more geographic than experimental. Many of the qualities of modern verse are there: the contemporary idiom and speech cadence, the daring in rhyme surpassed by no one but W. S. Gilbert, free verse, imagist phrase, and symbol two decades ahead of their time in America and England. To be sure, these are somewhat obscured by the dominant recklessness of tone, but they are none the less present. The facility and off-hand virtuosity refuse solemn judgment, but even the extravagant play has often a brilliant skill of its own.

The volumes are a notable experience in happy collaboration. Many who cared most for one or the other of the authors were at first critical of them for merging their talents in the first volume, in which authorship was undesignated. Almost invariably such critics spoiled their case by quoting as best some poems by the other poet. Yet now it seems relatively easy to

[15] "A Stein Song," *More Songs from Vagabondia*, p. 27.

distinguish the work of each. Carman's poems have either an almost fantastic ebullience or, if nature poems, a kind of nascent mystery which implies a religious emphasis. His have greater perception of natural loveliness and greater delicacy of grace and expression. Hovey's poems have a richer color and deeper tone. They are more masculine and earthy, Elizabethan rather than Celtic. The material ranges more widely and is more experimental in form. For all the fact that the poems are an excursion from their most earnest work, the very character of the men is written into their verses.

The usual criticism of the volumes takes them either too seriously or not seriously enough. One approach solemnly damns them for not attempting the major questions of the day; the other is content to read a few of the more "vaga-bondish" poems and put them back on the shelf of the fra-ternity library. The reading public is kinder, and the volumes are still among the most popular American poetry of their time. They need no justification. They are quite openly what they are and succeed within a limited evaluation. The very fact that poems such as "Barney McGee" and "A Stein Song" now exist unattached to any name and a part of the public do-main of familiar verse is proof enough of that. Hovey's repu-tation has been hurt not by the poems themselves, but by the careless assumption that he himself did not set the limits within which they stand successful. Indeed, their very success has re-turned like a slow boomerang to injure one whose purpose lay far beyond.

CHAPTER IX

Translator of Maeterlinck

> Not to reveal one mystery
> That lurks beneath life's garment-hem—
> Alas, I write of human hearts
> Because I cannot fathom them.
>
> HOVEY, "The Dramatist," 1898.

For days after the Hoveys took ship at Philadelphia the sea was as smooth as all their shipboard affairs. Captain Morle was very gracious and asked them to use his mahogany cabin as if it were theirs, something, they believed, he had never before done. Perhaps he was already impressed by the stylish Miss Soley, Mrs. Hovey's pupil, who was paying half price for the lessons she and her teacher hoped would make her a great actress. At any rate, before the end of July the acquaintance had become an engagement.

Hovey, just past his thirtieth birthday, "looked a picture of peace and plenty." He lay about reading novels and "soaking" the new Dartmouth poem—the "Ode." The soft languid air of May, Hovey's birth month, destroyed all energy. After a winter in Boston they wanted only to sleep and eat and loaf. They had not an idea in a week, and Hovey continued to rejoice in the sea and the release from confusion. He was "negatively content" and thought magnificently that he might rather have a yacht than a theater.[1] The weather continued fair and at length they landed at Liverpool, took a quick glance at the art gallery, caught an afternoon train to Chester, and went up to London early on a May morning of 1894.

They found quarters for a time at 160 Kensington Park Row, only a block from Sigurd, a happy and pretty little fellow much like his mother in looks. For a time the boy lived with

[1] Mrs. Hovey, May 13, 1894.

them, and the firm but gentle ways of his new stepfather made
him his worshiper. Every night there was a story from Shakespeare. But finally they had to ship the lad off to Paris, "alone
among strangers only two of whom know a word of English."
It was hard, but there was credit at the school where his half-
brother Kenneth had been a pupil, and there was no credit
elsewhere. Kenneth was now with Mrs. Hovey, Sr. The
school at which he had been a pupil had failed, and he was
without money or decent clothes, a poor tattered waif. Mrs.
Hovey's large heart took him in. His mother was troubled but
realistic:

> I never once for one minute neglected one of my boys for 'Fame,'
> but always for bread—quite a different matter. If I am less than an
> ideal mother, I am more nearly a good father than most mothers
> would or could be. . . . I have, moreover, no knack with children.[2]

The minds of the Hoveys went constantly to their own
child. They knew he now weighed thirty-two pounds and
had sixteen teeth, but what was he like? The foster mother
begged them not to take Bébé from her, but Mrs. Hovey, so
she wrote, felt as if she were holding a volcano inside her. She
wanted desperately to get to Tours, and to have the child in
America or England. The plan was gradually shaping up by
which the children would be gathered somewhere near Washington. Letter after letter was concerned with the problem of
getting "Radegond" across to England and then to America,
where Mrs Hovey, Sr., had offered to take the child. Hovey
suggested that they profit from the impression made by the
dedication to the *Launcelot and Guenevere* series that he had
been married before and that the boy was the result of the
marriage and the cause of his mother's death.

> I am not sure deceit is not justified when people pry into matters
> that do not concern them. And there is no use in defying the world
> single-handed, and so the world's false standard of reputation must be
> preserved at any cost for Radegond's mother.[3]

[2] Mrs. Hovey, no date [1894 or 1895].
[3] Hovey, Sept. 30, 1894.

As yet, however, there was no money, and when "Nounou's" doctor forbade her to bring her own child along, there was no one to accompany the boy. So the unseen heartache and confusion went on under the surface of their lives. It was a strange shadow over a first year of marriage, but it did not darken the landscape of their love.

Before they found their days crowded with society, Hovey settled to work. He had part of the "Ode" finished, but he blamed it for keeping him indoors until the buttons on his vest needed revision. Elkin Mathews had accepted Copeland's suggestion of an English version of *Songs from Vagabondia*. He was glad of this, for there were none of his books in England just when he might find sale and publication for them. He wrote for circulars of *Seaward* and for anything else which might noise his name abroad.

Soon there were many visitors. Hamilton Aïdé acted the good friend in introduction, as he had done before. This gentleman-author, son of a Greek diplomat killed in a Paris duel, was now in his middle sixties and had been publishing off and on for decades. He knew everyone and invited Watts, Leighton, Beerbohm Tree, and others to meet Hovey at lunch. He got together a crowd which included a publisher and Henry Irving's son to hear Hovey read from the Arthurian plays. Hovey always made an impression that brought him another invitation. So there were invitations to Leighton's, to Watts's studio, where he wrote a poem on an unexhibited painting, to the studio of Felix Moschelles, and to the homes of others who came to the Hoveys' "at homes" in return. Mrs. Hovey wrote. "We shall soon know enough people to fill a theater." This was no unsupported boast.

Aïdé, who had exceeded even his own reputation for kindness, asked Hovey to rework "Temptation" for him. He disliked to refuse and needed the payment of $100. Moreover, Aïdé's reputation gave some hope that Forbes-Robertson might take the play for his theater. Hovey turned the characters over and over in his mind, remodeling three of them completely, but it wasn't his own work and he was irked by it.

Aïdé's friendship and praise kept him at work, but the task dragged on for the rest of the autumn.

By this time they had moved to 508 Rossetti Mansions, a handsome studio room which looked far more prosperous than its inhabitants deserved. Hovey delighted in the place, for there was room to walk, there were water colors and fine carved furniture and books, of which he read "tons." They entertained and were entertained. Lady Brooke, the Ranee of Sarawak, became their friend and called Hovey "the Emperor of Poets." They even flirted with the scheme of going with her to Borneo.[4]

Edmund Russell came to dine, for though Mrs. Hovey hated him and saw him "building his reputation but running down rapidly in character," Hovey insisted on treating him with courtesy. It angered Mrs. Hovey that her former husband should be photographed in the costume in which he read *The Light of Asia*, plastered with jewels from chin to belt, while their child needed underflannels and overcoat. But she consented to an armed truce, partly because of the projected International Delsarte Society of which Dr. Alger was to be president, she vice-president and editor of the magazine, and Russell, whose familiar name was necessary, business manager.

Instead of working, it was necessary to meet people and make an impression so that work might be called for. It was a galling and precarious existence on the edge of society. For example, Aïdé invited Hovey to share the Royal Box with its big reception room at the Haymarket Theatre in order to impress Tree, who, they hoped, might put on *Gandolfo* in the next season. Mr. and Mrs. Tree came in after the play and were very cordial, but Hovey had ridden to the theater wrapped in a coat on top of the omnibus, and so he returned. They might walk through the rain to enter a handsome reception. Sometimes the last shilling of the moment went that he might dine with somebody who could help his work to recognition.

Though discouraged, he did not let his difficulties nor his rusty clothes spoil his happiness and his joy in meeting men.

[4] Mrs. Hovey, Oct. 1, 1894.

He met many: Beardsley, Wilfrid Blunt, Gosse, Sharpe, Meredith (with whom he stayed at Box Hill and talked of America, women, and cooking), and Oscar Wilde, who "raced after Richard all evening," according to Mrs. Hovey, who had never liked him. He had wished particularly to meet Blunt, Beardsley, and Davidson, all of whom he liked. Davidson, who had pushed the *Vagabondia* songs with Lane, the publisher, eyed him and declared heartily, "Well, you look like a man."[5] They attracted each other and continued the friendship. Hovey insisted on saving the precious remnant of a bottle of whiskey until Davidson should come to their room. Hovey could have been comrade to many of these men, particularly the most vigorous and rebellious, but the elegances of Mayfair palled and he longed for simple Bohemia and his old friends. He wrote to Carman the month after he arrived:

I wish you and Tom were over here. I have a large thirst on me and am pining for the vagabonds. The English are very nice but deadly slow—most as slow as Boston.[6]

He was glad to have the season over and give himself wholly to work. Despite all Aïdé's benevolent scheming, Tree would not take *The Marriage of Guenevere*, since Irving had just bought an Arthurian play, and finally decided against *Gandolfo*.

In April Carman, now literary advisor to Stone and Kimball, had asked Hovey to translate four Maeterlinck plays (*The Sightless*, *The Intruder*, *The Seven Princesses*, and *Princess Maleine*), and write an introduction to them. He was sure the book would be prescribed at Harvard and hoped that it would be at other colleges. Since the book would sell at $1.25 the sales would need to be large before the 10 per cent royalty amounted to much, but Hovey was interested in Maeterlinck and agreed to the contract.

Maeterlinck was less than two years older than Hovey. His volume of verse, *Serres Chaudes*, had appeared in 1889, and in that same year he and a friend had set up and printed on a hand press twenty-five or thirty copies of his first play,

[5] Mrs. Hovey, July 10, 1894.
[6] Hovey, June 24, 1894.

La Princesse Maleine, as Hovey and Thomson had printed *Poems.* The other plays mentioned by Carman had appeared in 1890 and 1891, the famous *Pélléas et Mélisande* in 1892, and *Alladine et Palomides, Intérieur,* and *La Mort de Tintagiles* in 1894. Despite their somber qualities, the plays brought quick recognition. In 1891 a translation of *The Blind* and *The Intruder* was issued in Washington and in 1892 a translation of two of the plays appeared in England.[7] In the following two years the editors of the American *Poet-Lore,* Charlotte Porter and Helen A. Clarke, printed in the magazine their own translations of *The Sightless, The Seven Princesses,* and *Pélléas and Mélisande.* Hovey was not the first in the field, then, but no collected set of translations had yet been issued in America in book form.

Hovey set to work both because he needed the money and because he was genuinely interested in the original. Though his wife was angry that he should be forced into translating, she knew that he had "a lot of submission to the inevitable," and he obviously enjoyed the task. The work went quickly, though it took a good deal of time simply to copy the words. He regretted the enforced speed, but the French was relatively easy to translate. Hovey tried hard for the tone of the original. "It is very difficult to keep at the same time the *colloquial* simplicity of the diction, and a certain *poetic* rhythm which he has," he wrote to Carman.[8] This, of course, is the central problem of translating Maeterlinck, and Hovey sought, and successfully, to find an English equivalent which would convey both the naturalistic surface of the dialogue and its symbolic connotations. To carry the naïve from one language to another and to use old and commonplace words so that they gleam with fresh suggestion and yet keep their familiar simplicity is a language problem of real difficulty. The nuances have to be exact without subtlety of expression betraying it-

[7] *Maurice Maeterlinck: The Blind, The Intruder,* translated from the French of Maurice Maeterlinck by Mary Vielé (Washington, 1891).
Gerard Harry, *The Princess Maleine* and *The Intruder,* with a preface by Hall Caine (Turner, 1892).
[8] Hovey, June 24, 1894. Microfilm reproduction of letters in Leland Stanford collection.

self as such, and the narrow line between sublime and ridiculous which Maeterlinck walked precariously is full of danger to the translator. Hovey kept steadily at his task, and by August, 1894, the plays were finished. He was pleased with the translation and thought it had a poetic quality none of the others possessed. In this he was right, and a number of critics agreed with him when *The Plays of Maurice Maeterlinck* appeared early in 1895.

The preface to which he now turned scrutinizes the symbolism in the plays. It begins by stating the familiar position that to the artist "the material universe is a medium through which to express the immaterial realities of thought and feeling."[9] In a narrower sense, any symbolist school which develops this general fact of art must be distinguished from the realists, who see only the concrete thing, and from the poetic, who see all as personality. Those for whom the general idea or principle is most important turn to symbolism, for by the structure of the world and the mind they are forced to invent and use symbols to keep the world of spirit parallel to that of appearance. The too obvious symbolism of allegory and personification is rejected by the present symbolists for a method which, while it presents a complete and palpable action on one level, implies a larger meaning on another, "a lurking universality behind the face of fact and event."

In an effort to bring the common quality of symbolism home to American readers, Hovey included mention of Gilbert Parker, Bliss Carman, and C. G. D. Roberts. This, which might seem log-rolling in the decades when Maeterlinck had reached so far beyond these, was done to free his name from suggestion of imitation and clique, and to demonstrate that the strong young writers were everywhere reasserting imagination and were not limiting themselves to the imitation of nature.

The examination of Maeterlinck is cool and dispassionate. "Two things," he finds, "individualize Maeterlinck from the rest of the school,—the peculiarity of his technique, and the limitations of his emotional range." Maeterlinck's iterations

[9] *Plays of Maurice Maeterlinck*, translated by Richard Hovey (Chicago: Stone and Kimball, 1895).

of phrase had been widely criticized and parodied. They were indeed excessive, as Maeterlinck now realized, and he later gave Hovey permission as translator to cut such as seemed to him to weaken the text or to fall into the bathetic. The other characteristic, the narrowness of emotional range which so strictly limited his tone to terror and fear and restricted his humor to "the grin on the everlasting skull," Hovey accepted without adverse comment, though it was quite foreign to his challenging nature. Obviously, what interested him most was the parallelism of the symbolic method, which was an extension of Delsartean theory into drama. Maeterlinck, he says, was almost if not quite alone among modern writers in using parallelism to express "the shadow land of human emotions."

The little essay of nine pages is a better statement of the symbolic quality of art than it is an analysis of either the Symbolist group or of Maeterlinck himself, and it is rather uncertain and immature, as Hovey realized. He was anxious to rewrite it after more thought, and the revised essay, as published in the *Nineteenth Century* (March, 1895), shows a larger and more capable grasp of the subject and a more consistent direction of thought. The body of the original was included, since Maeterlinck thought the remarks on symbolism the wisest thing yet said on the subject; but the sharper distinctions, the exclusion of Carman, Roberts, and Parker, and the more philosophic approach give it a largeness and authority of judgment the early essay lacked. Also, he more openly challenged the death-ridden gloom of the plays on which Maeterlinck was himself to look back, as Goethe did on *Werther*, and pronounce unhealthy. Hovey was sure that the gruesome was only a phase of the author's work and that he would move out of it, as, indeed, he was already doing in the vigorous rush of his famous love for Georgette Leblanc, the beautiful actress-singer so long to be his mistress.

Though Hovey was critical of the original preface, Maeterlinck accepted both preface and translation with high praise. Apparently, because he was under contract to Stone and Kimball, Hovey waited until he had a printed copy before he presented it to Maeterlinck. He was overjoyed when he received a letter of high commendation.

J'ai lu entièrement la traduction que vous avez bien voulu faire de mes drames et la précieuse préface que vous y avez mise. Ce que vous y dites sur le symbolisme sont les paroles les plus sages et les plus définitives qu'on en a dites jusqu'ici. Et quant à votre traduction, elle est absolument parfaite et admirable, à tel point qu'elle semble même donner en plus je ne sais qu'elle fermeté necessaire que l'original n'avait pas, et cela tout juste dans le sens et dans la mesure ou il eût été souhaitable qu'il la possédât.[10]

This was followed by official appointment of Hovey as American translator.

Hovey was delighted when Maeterlinck came to London in the spring of 1895. The Theatre de l'Oeuvre, under the auspices of the Independent Theatre, put on an Ibsen-Maeterlinck week in late March, playing *Rosmersholm* and *The Master Builder,* and *The Intruder* and *Pélléas and Mélisande.* The company was led by Lugné-Poe, who claimed to have descended from Edgar Allan Poe on his mother's side. Hovey, who attended every performance of the six nights' run, watched him with the most studious and analytic attention and believed him one of the half dozen leading actors of the day. When he talked about putting on *Gandolfo* in Paris, particularly when Maeterlinck said he would translate it for such a production, Hovey's hopes flared.

The most memorable moment remained the meeting with Maeterlinck. The dramatic group had been delayed by a stormy channel crossing and came late to the reception being given for them. Hovey was the first to be introduced to the playwright, whose face had the sensitivity of still waters and whose being was gentle and shy. There was no pose about the man. Despite his gloom-tinctured mind, "he was a good fellow, and a good deal of a man."[11] And Maeterlinck looked at Hovey so that he could never forget him.[12]

At Maeterlinck's written invitation they met at the theater

[10] Maeterlinck, April 10, 1895 (a copy).
[11] Hovey, May 7, 1895.
[12] When Hovey died Maeterlinck wrote to Mrs. Hovey: "I saw you two but an instant. It is years ago. I did not know then the genius of Richard but

the next evening, the Hoveys charmed by his simple ways. When one evening Hovey brought him a copy of the translation in progress, he carried it off to his box and read all through the act. He did not like his own things on the stage, he said, though the praise everywhere in the foyer for "the sheer loveliness" of *Pélléas and Mélisande*, played with low lights behind a green gauze curtain, should have pleased him. *The Intruder* had been rather poorly played; *Pélléas and Mélisande* was an invigorating success which promised a revitalized theater.

The renaissance of the poetic on the stage is a matter of the near future. I look to see M. Maeterlinck followed by many other poet-playwrights,—not imitators, although they will come too,—but like him only in restoring the beautiful where the sordid and ugly have so long been supreme. And I am now sure that the audiences for such playwrights will be forthcoming.[13]

For one who believed so thoroughly in his own potential genius, Hovey continued to show for the Belgian author an astonishingly generous enthusiasm and selflessness. He did everything he could to foster Maeterlinck's work with publisher and public, and Maeterlinck's notes to him are properly grateful. He was most anxious to get out a translation of the essays which appeared as *The Treasure of the Humble*, for which he had a greater admiration than for the plays. The essays, however, were already entangled by commitments to French and English publishers who were opposed to a rival edition.

The translation of a second volume of plays went on. These were *Alladine and Palomides, Pélléas and Mélisande, Home (L'Intérieur)*, and *The Death of Tintagiles*.

In November he sent off the copy. This volume Maeter-

I wonder whether I had not a presentiment of it. Always I have thought of that day and recalled his image, so vivid and so clear.... It was as if some one had said at the moment when I pressed his hand: Open your eyes, do not lose a single detail; you will see him only once and he is one of the three great poets of your generation." From a translation in Mrs. Hovey's hand. The original is reprinted in Barbara Matulka, "Letters of Mallarmé and Maeterlinck to Richard Hovey," *Romantic Review*, XVIII (July-September, 1927), 232-237.
    [13] Hovey, *Poet-Lore*, VII (Aug.-Sept., 1895), 450.

linck found even more satisfying ("de plus en plus parfait"). For it Maeterlinck himself wrote an introduction setting forth his theory of the marionette quality of acting which, he stated, by its suppression of realistic physical action could alone keep poetry alive on the stage. The theater, he claimed, is the place where most masterpieces die.

Whatever truth there is in Maeterlinck's position, the position of a poet and not of a writer for the theater, it was antithetic to Hovey's attempt to wed the poetic and the theatrical. He challenged the statements, and Materlinck admitted that, for the sake of the teaching, he had gone too far. There was danger in such a position, for as realism had killed beauty in the theater, this divorce of beauty from actual representation could kill reality and force drama back into the closet where it had paled for a century. The whole problem of dramatic art was again forced on Hovey by this preoccupation with a somnambulistic drama which could not satisfy his demand for a healthy popular art, however much it lifted art above unredeemed fact.

It would be presumptuous to claim that Materlinck profited from the criticism of Hovey and others, but certainly the change in his own outlook and in his art brought him closer to such critics. For his part, Hovey later stated the constant necessity to change and enlarge one's understanding of Maeterlinck. He found that the poet of terror became in later plays "the greatest living poet of love, if not the greatest who ever lived."[14] He retracted his early statement that Maeterlinck was best in the treatment of evil and claimed that his greatest triumph was his handling of goodness, even saintliness, a much more difficult task, and to Hovey the greatest. One could see now the "combination of spiritual insight with realistic sanity" was always a characteristic of the author, but the realization could come only through the later volumes. Indeed the former prophet of gloomy terror was now revealed as "a prophet of joy." Hovey had not been in error in any particular criticism; he had simply based his findings on evidence not yet complete.

[14] Hovey, "Maeterlinck as a Prophet of Joy," *Bookman*, IX (March, 1899), 64.

As the new material came forth, he publicly withdrew his former charges to include the new disclosure. This he did humbly and frankly. "Time has quickly put me in the wrong and made me repeat with fervour the prayer to be delivered from our own foolishness."[15] It is a prayer one can recommend.

The effect of Hovey's essays and translations in bringing Maeterlinck an American audience is impossible to calculate with nicety. Since Maeterlinck was so debated a playwright, critical comment on the volumes naturally focused on his peculiar style or sought safe evasion by running over the prefaces and using them as a springboard for the reviewer's moral and dramatic ideas. Often the personal material of Hovey's essay in *Poet-Lore* took precedence over all real criticism. Yet however flimsy and even irrelevant such comments were, they provoked an interest in the subject. Certainly the translations pleased the author, the publishers, and those who had any concern for poetry. Harriet Monroe found Hovey a sympathetic translator, even if a little baffled by the ecstatic height of the climaxes, as any translator might well be, and the editor of *Poet-Lore*, herself a translator of some of the plays, was very laudatory. The translations were taken over from the publishers and reprinted in 1906, and certain of them, particularly that of *Pélléas and Mélisande*, are still standard, as one sees by opening the anthologies.

At one time there was a plan for translation of a few of Maeterlinck's songs. He intended to get out a dozen, with designs, and hoped to hold back the French edition until the American translation could be published at the same time. He was at the moment satisfied with only ten, and sent them on to Hovey. The scheme did not materialize, but Hovey translated the songs at various times. Some were published during his life, others only in a posthumous volume. Here, most of all, Hovey felt the difficulty of translation. As he wrote to Carman: "The songs are lovely, but God knows whether I shall be able to translate them."[16] Song, particularly in the

[15] *Ibid.*

[16] Hovey, July 14, 1895. Quoted by Henry Leffert, "Richard Hovey" (unpublished Ph.D. dissertation, New York University, 1929), p. 326.

voice of Maeterlinck, is the supreme challenge. He worked carefully, with the curiosity his phonetic study prompted, and turned out translations which keep the sense within the flow of lyric pattern.

Maeterlinck from the beginning had accepted Hovey's criticisms very generously and was most flattering in his comments on the original work Hovey sent him. He found the love songs of *The Marriage of Guenevere* profound and sweet, and was "tres frappé de l'etrange vie et de la sorte de grande joie panique" of *Songs from Vagabondia*.[17] His respect for the author and his affection for the man did not lessen.[18] When in 1906 publishers wrote about further translation, he suggested that Mrs. Hovey continue "l'oeuvre admirable qu'avait enterprise Richard Hovey—le grande poête dont la mort prematurée a infligé à la litterateur Americaine un perte que je considere comme irreparable."[19]

The early months of 1895 were bitterly cold. Everywhere the pipes froze and a great influenza epidemic swept over England. Hovey bundled himself into a fur coat and went on with the writing of *Taliesin*, which for months had been his greatest desire. When the beer froze he served it with perfect gravity as an ice. The couple had happiness enough to withstand anything. Though the fickle Tree had left for America without renewing his enthusiasm for *Gandolfo*, and although Irving played his Arthurian drama, killing any hope for another such play, the Maeterlinck volume was a success and the congratulations on breaking into the *Nineteenth Century* with the essay made the occasion "like a wedding."

Hovey was becoming a familiar figure, and always an interesting one. Jerome K. Jerome sketched him in an impressionistic way for *To-Day:*

Mr. Hovey is the very type the late Mr. Edwin Long would have chosen for a Pharaoh or for Ehud the Moabitish King—a large, fine

[17] Maeterlinck, April 10, 1895.
[18] For example: "J'ai pu voir par l'inquietude ou m'avait mis votre silence, que vous m'etiez mille fois plus cher que je ne le croyais moi-meme; et cependant nous nous sommes vus si peu d'instants dans la vie exterieure" (written from Oostacker, no date; a copy).
[19] Copy in Mrs. Hovey's handwriting of a letter dated Paris, June 19, 1906.

man, with handsome, majestic Semitic features, flashing dark eyes, jet black hair, and a jet black Semitic-looking beard.[20]

When the famous Alphonse Daudet came to London the resemblance was noticed at once. Though Daudet was older and less striking they were mistaken for each other, which ever after was good for a newspaper quip. It was insignificant in itself, but one of the often repeated comments which made Hovey always somewhat foreign to those who did not know him, a representative of European culture in a civilization which had given its masculine looks to the barber.

The spring that year was very welcome, but it brought the Wilde trial. Mrs. Hovey had never liked Wilde, perhaps sharing the arrogance which he himself had shown the Atlantic and Niagara Falls. They had always fought over the meaning of beauty, as two can whose purposes are sufficiently similar to be confused. She thought he said unprincipled things just to be clever and was "just smart enough to be dangerous." Now the hothouse aestheticism which Hovey had long since come to distrust had faltered to this miserable end. From the Queensbury trial in early April to the day of sentence against Wilde in late May the fetid air was stifling. "One has a longing to get up on a mountain somewhere and take long gulps of sharp clear air, and drink cold water,"[21] Hovey wrote. This "love that dare not speak its name" which Wilde defended was the evil, inverted shadow of the comradeship of the open road.

Hovey wanted to get to France, but he had no money. The publishers did not forward royalties due him, nor pay for small articles he had written for the *Chap Book*. He was angry and desperate. He had not enough even to buy the Maeterlinck books for translation, so he said. Sigurd was sick and money was owed for Radegond. He had to stand off his debts by pleading for time. Finally he could make passage and was "positively capering." He crossed the Channel on June fifteenth, stopped off to see the cathedral at Rouen, and arrived in Giverny literally penniless. Mrs. Hovey had to await the arrival of funds to follow him.

[20] *To-Day*, April 27, 1895.
[21] Hovey, no date [May, 1895].

CHAPTER X

Among the Symbolists

Is there a way, my soul that knows the gall,
To smash the glass insulted by the Lie,
And to escape with my two plumeless wings,
At risk of falling through eternity?
MALLARMÉ, "The Windows," Hovey's translation.

After England the light seemed very strong, and the poppies, thick as daisies, were almost too flamboyant. But at first the people in their quiet retreat seemed dull and behind the times, even in art. It was rather boring after the strenuous intellectual excitement of London, but his friend Barry was there, and McMonnies, and when he relaxed to the slow tempo he found the place very restful and satisfying. It was good to be comfortable and lazy, luxuriating in the warmth and the dry air. The models and painters were working, even if they did not make a lot of talk about it. He threw off his formal English clothes and wore an old pair of white trousers with a red sash around the waist, and a red tie. In the strong light he made a stunning subject and many wanted to paint him. Even without a sou he could be picturesque, and he laughingly suggested having an exhibition of the paintings and sketches done of him.

He liked the village, sometimes playing a few games of billiards, sometimes sitting in the café writing, sometimes rowing on the river, or walking the three miles into Vernon, the nearby town. Since there were thirty Americans in the hotel, he had more chance to practice his French when he got into the village, although he talked a good deal with Ruelle, a poet who later turned some of his verses into French. He was in entire sympathy with the fight against allowing a starch factory to be set up, and when Monet's influence saved the quiet from this intrusion, there was celebration. He wrote a poem which begins:

> Je connais un village,
> Pas trop de Paris,
> Ou personne n'est sage,
> Et tout le monde rit.

He kept working withdrawn in a room under the eaves, all beams and windows, looking out over the Seine valley. The plaster and wood were a tone between pink and terra cotta, the beams were thick with palate scrapings, on the ceiling was a landscape and on the door a Japanese girl. It was a warm gay place to turn Maeterlinck's dark plays into English.

There was still no money. Mrs. Hovey gave a lecture on the expression of the human body in painting, but no one paid her. Tours was not far, but even that distance demanded money. Finally twenty-five dollars for the *Chap Book* articles came, Mrs. Hovey borrowed twenty dollars, and Hovey jumped immediately into the trap for Vernon to buy tickets. If his hopes were high for a tender reunion, they were disappointed. His boy, who had told his foster mother that he would throw stones at the Hoveys, clung to her skirts and yelled. He was quieted with toys, new clothes, and a drum. But he would not speak, and finally fell asleep from sheer exhaustion. For two hours his father stood over him keeping away the flies and looking at the dark-haired child who was still so like him.[1]

The little fellow was terribly shy and sensitive, with a temperament like an aspen tree, laughing and singing, until someone noticed him. He had to be brought to trust slowly and delicately. Hovey walked with him, taught him bean-porridge hot and some words of English, and laughed with him in a language that has no vocabulary. Soon he was pointing out the figures on the cover of *Songs of Vagabondia*, "Tomme, Blees, papa Ové" and going into uproarious laughter over the delightful absurdity. He was interested in everything, and when they set out for Giverny, he in his big straw hat and cor-

[1] Mrs. Hovey, Sept. 12, 1895.

duroy suit with lace collar, he was tremendously excited by the "gros chemin de fer." They decided to call the pretty, self-willed, but tender-hearted lad Julian, and he was introduced to the hotel as the son of a former marriage who had been at nurse in Perpignan.[2] The Hoveys hired a capable English woman, who had followed them over, and she took on herself most of the care, but Hovey found it hard not to draw pictures or make paper boats for the sweet-natured child and so fall behind in his work.

The primary purpose of their trip was accomplished. They were united with their child. This freed them to pursue their other desire—to get the temper of the new literature and to know its producers. So late in November, 1895, they went up to Paris, staying for a while in the Latin Quarter and then subletting an apartment on the west border of the city close to the edge of the Bois de Boulogne (127 rue de Ranelagh, Passy). The apartment was large, pleasantly furnished, and had the light, uncluttered openness of a studio. It had an air of prosperity which denied their real poverty, but they wanted a place where they might bring Sigurd and Julian and his English nurse, and their only hope of money was through Mrs. Hovey's connections. So once again they put up the brave front behind which they hid their very real want. There were friends like the enthusiastic Fullerton, the poet Ruelle, and former pupils. Through invitations, receptions, or exhibitions, new acquaintances were added constantly, particularly among the literary and theatrical people.

Paris was as excited as usual by new manifestos, new schools, new reviews. Seminal ideas from abroad, from German thought and Russian novels and translations from every literature, grew lushly in the fertile soil of Paris. The most obvious literary fact was that Symbolism was now established and triumphant, and already the Symbolists were moving out from common ground toward more individual qualities. The men grouped under that name were those Hovey most wanted to meet and with whom he felt most kinship. In the essay on

[2] Hovey, Sept. 3, Sept. 17, and Sept. 22, 1895.

Maeterlinck he had already claimed his friends as Symbolists; but as poet and as investigator of verse he was far more conscious than they of the technical methods the French were employing.

There is no need here for more than an outline of the development of Symbolism as a school. All art is symbolic, but in France, where aesthetics is taken seriously, a loosely bound group had reacted from the sonorous rhetoric of the Romantics and from the cold impersonality of the Parnassians. The lives and attitudes of certain intermediate figures like Verlaine have confused the central artistic purpose with "decadence," a name hurled by the outraged and worn with proud bravado by the accused. Unless in the technical stylistic sense of that which has gone beyond the clear and healthy balance of all elements, the name was no longer applicable. Hovey thought it should be used only for "imitation of effete formulas." Even though Symbolism owed something to the subtle, suggestive music of Verlaine's sensitive verse and to his desire to twist the neck of rhetoric, it had gone beyond him in intention.

Symbolism was never sharply defined in a way which would include all its adherents completely. It was a development of elements present in all art and most of all in Romanticism, but it took form as a protest against the domination of brute fact and the denial of all overtone and mystery in a period given up to science and sociological literature. In Hovey's words: "Symbolism is the reverse of realism. It is interested not so much in fact as in the implication of fact."[3] Such an interest was counter to all the major modes of expression, the clear preciseness of the Parnassians, the factualness and utilitarianism of the scientific realists, and the general rhetorical artificiality the French are prone to. Its concern was not to represent phenomena, but to suggest the reality which holds a mystery incapable of direct representation. To get to the true from the real the Symbolists practiced an intuitive, spontaneous, and re-creative use of language, using symbols to sug-

[3] Bliss Carman, "The Modern Athenian," Boston *Transcript*, Aug. 29, 1896. This is an interview with Hovey.

gest, rather than openly translating by the key of simile. (Mallarmé wanted to get *comme* out of the dictionary.) In a time of naming and classifying whether by science or realistic literature, the Symbolists believed that the simple naming of an object destroyed most of the delight in poetry, since the suggestive evocation of an object or of a state of soul was the very essential of art. As Mallarmé put it: "To name an object is to do away with three-quarters of the enjoyment of the poem which is derived from the satisfaction of guessing little by little: to suggest it, to evoke it—that is what charms the imagination."

The Symbolists asserted that they were not turning from life, as is often said. They were turning from a kind of vision and a kind of literature which to them were incapable of going beyond the phenomena of physical existence. They believed that the end of art was knowledge, a more complete realization of life, but they were idealists, influenced by the thought of the English and of Hegel, and were concerned with that knowledge which is only glimpsed through the veil, forever mystery, and to be suggested only in symbol. They were too serious about life to accept it in the terms of the scientific determinism and social materialism which dictated so much of the thought of their century.

This general agreement on the end and method of poetry held the group in some cohesion, but the other doctrines of their creed fostered free development. They believed in individualism, since so subjective an approximation to the true could come only with individualism. They believed too in freedom of form. This, in fact, meant that they fought the fight for *vers libre*. Laforgue's translations of Whitman and their own reading of him in the original had shown the possibilities of free form, and their experiments in the prose poem of Poe and Baudelaire made them realize the limitations of orthodox verse forms. Taught by Poe and Verlaine, they realized as well the subtle modulations in musical phrasing which were impossible to the quantitative measures of verse forms. They sought an expression between music and the word. Since the poets were men of high culture, their knowledge of music, as of art, was far in advance of the musically uneducated poets of America, with the exception of Hovey's admired singer, Lanier.

First among the Symbolists and first of those Hovey wished to know in France was Mallarmé, whom he had called in the essay on Maeterlinck "probably the greatest French poet since Hugo," and who was to be declared "poet of poets" by the unacademic. He had written to him from London suggesting the translation of some poems and making some comments on the theory of poetry and the possibility of clarifying the Hegelian approach by study in the Delsarte manner. Mallarmé was interested and replied, provoking another long letter from Hovey, who had found no American sufficiently advanced for such an interchange of ideas. He sent him a presentation copy of *Songs from Vagabondia* inscribed "To Stephen Mallarmé, with admiration deep and sincere, these songs of the joy of life" followed by a quotation from the French poet "Le vierge le vivace et le bel aujourdhui." Mallarmé thought the poems "exquis et beaux . . . si primesautiers aussitant que certains."[4] A partial translation of one of his most famous poems, "Hérodiade," won praise, and later he invited Hovey to his summer home at Fontainebleau.

No place was so much revered as Mallarmé's home in the rue de Rome. Though many might go to the Café François Premier with the hope that Verlaine might still limp to his absinthe, men climbed the four flights to Mallarmé's quarters almost with awe. Now fifty-three, the well-born, well-educated, highly intelligent man had achieved the status of a secular saint. He was the master, loved and revered. To him came not only the young French, Valéry, Gide, Louÿs, de Regnier, but those fortunate English and Americans who gained introduction. On his famous Tuesday evenings he received in the dining room with its eighteenth-century furniture and the paintings by Whistler, Manet, and Monet. No women except Mme Mallarmé were present, though, as Ho-

[4] Quoted by Hovey in a letter to Carman, Dec. 20, 1894.

vey wrote, one might catch a "fleeting vision of Mlle. Mallarmé, beautiful as an early Raffaelle or a Perugino."[5] The china tobacco jar stood open and the drink was rum and water. Sitting in his rocker or leaning against the mantel the master talked, always with quiet dignity and an authority which came only from his brilliant and subtle mind. If he had the ears of a faun, as Max Nordau had said, he had also the eyebrows of a madonna, as Hovey said, and something of that strange combination was in his talk. Maeterlinck had told Hovey that his conversation was "the most wonderful in the world" and Moore in his proud confessions to a Philistine world admitted he had met none whose conversation was more fruitful. Though the conversation approached monologue, by agreement of all guests, it was an exploration of the philosophy and being of art, never an ex cathedra lecture, and certainly never idle gossip about this or that book or author. It was conversation such as Hovey could never before have listened to, for it did not exist in England or America, and perhaps existed in no other place in France. It was also for the stranger an opportunity to meet some of the most interesting writers in France. How often Hovey went to the Tuesday evenings one does not know, but on the day after the first visit he received Mallarmé's card in its small mauve envelope expressing his pleasure at having seen him, so that he need have felt no hesitation in repeating the visit.

His closest association among other writers was with Vielé-Griffin, the American-born poet of exactly the same age and, like him, son of a Civil War general. Vielé-Griffin was not only one of the leading young poets whose collected poems appeared that year but was also an editor and influential theorist. As such he was important in "the movement for freedom in technique and a truth more than skin-deep in the interpretation of life."[6] He must have reminded Hovey of Carman by his fellowship with nature, for there was joy in his work, a "whiff of the outdoors" and a sweetness "serene with the touch

[5] Hovey, *Tatler*, Nov. 20, 1896.
[6] *Ibid.*

of the morning" which set him off from the others. They
planned to publish a short series of essays by Hovey on the
Americans, and an essay on Hovey for *La Mercure*. These
were never completed, but Vielé-Griffin charged himself with
the publication of five of Hovey's poems translated by Ruelle
and printed in *Le Magazin International*.[7] It was an honor,
but perhaps not so great as being asked through Vielé-Griffin
for a poem on Verlaine to be published in a memorial volume
after that poet's naïve and sinful life had come to its end in the
first week of the new year. Verlaine had been too sick and
weary to meet anyone when Hovey got to Paris. Perhaps the
rotten old body and the bleared eyes would have offended his
idea of the poet, but he who himself was so often to celebrate
both the Christ and the faun accepted the paradoxical life of
the man whose singing had intoxicated him three years before.

> Death which has set the calm of Time upon his song,
> Surely upon his soul has kissed the same repose,
> In some fair heaven the Christ has set apart
>   for Fauns.
>   ("Verlaine" . . . *More Songs from Vagabondia*)

Hovey could respond to the work of the Symbolists in three
ways: as translator, as publicist and critic, and as poet and student of verse technique. He responded in all. As translator he
had already involved himself with the songs of Maeterlinck
as well as the plays, and though Maeterlinck is not held by a
narrow definition of Symbolism, he showed much of the philosophy and manner of the group, as well as being an intimate
of it. Hovey was fascinated by this exacting experience with
another language and the interplay of sound and meaning,
particularly in the songs.

He now turned his hand to Mallarmé's *Hérodiade*, which
he thought to be to French what *Kubla Khan* is to English.
Encouraged by the author's praise, he finished the section on
which he worked (less than half of Scene 1). This was pub-

---

[7] The poems were: "Evening on the Potomac," "The Wander Lovers,"
"The Chant of the Norns" (from *The Quest of Merlin*), and two lyrics from
Taliesin. See note in the *Tatler*, Nov. 16, 1896.

lished in the *Chap Book* for January, 1895, almost two years before Symons' translation appeared in the *Savoy*, and so was one of the earliest translations of the author into a foreign language.

Mallarmé's work is usually thought of as perhaps the most difficult of all poetry to translate, both by reason of its inherent obscurity of meaning and by reason of his expert technique. He was intentionally obscure, since the very method of his art was suggestion and mystery. Reality as such did not interest him. The artist's task was to transpose the actual world into dream, to see it "transfusible en du songe." But the dream world is a very personal, psychic world to which the arbitrary associations of one mind will not communicate themselves to another. The shift and distortion and merging of symbol and allusion are logical and sequential only within the context of the creator's psyche. Added to the difficulty of primary comprehension was Mallarmé's distrust of Romantic verbiage used to decorate a simple prose statement. Hence the compression of the usual step-by-step statement from original perception to aesthetic fulfilment into a speech which omitted clues to the movement of meaning. The result was an elliptical idiom which subjected even syntax to the modulations of sound and symbol.

If it is difficult to understand Mallarmé, it is impossible to translate him. He carried so far the potentialities of language, both in sound and suggestion, that the full charge of meaning and emotion cannot be rendered in another tongue. The most literal translations lose the magic of his tonal range; the more interpretive lose the precision of his choice. It is remarkable that Hovey was as successful as he was at that early date when the mode of such writing was far less accessible than now and the gap between Symbolism and familiar poetry much wider. Comparison between his work and that of others shows true perception of the method and end of the poetry and a constant increase in translating skill. Though Maeterlinck found the early translation of *L'Apparition* absolutely astonishing and to be cited among the most extraordinary *tours de force* of literature,[8] it betrays the softening and sweetening of a translation which attempts to substitute the connotative values of one language for those of another, and so is reminiscent of past art rather than suggestive of the forward reach of Mallarmé's experiment. A later attempt, such as "The Sigh" ("Soupir"), demonstrates a very real advance in subtle rendering. Like this poem, six of the eight Hovey attempted were from Mallarmé's more accessible poetry, but the translations of two of the late sonnets are beautiful in melody, even if somewhat opaque in meaning, a fault not to be laid to the translator.[9]

Hovey was eager to undertake a volume of translations from Mallarmé and suggested it to his publishers while he was still in England. He found that Stuart Merrill, the American-born French poet, had signed a contract to issue such a volume. Indeed it was advertised with Hovey's translations of Maeterlinck in the Green Tree Library. The publisher felt that Merrill had forfeited his contract by not submitting the manuscript on time and suggested that Hovey take over the task. Seemingly Hovey was unwilling to enter such an arrangement for fear of being involved in disagreement with Merrill. Whether or not they met in Paris cannot be determined, but since Merrill kept open house and shared Hovey's desire to introduce knowledge of the French into America, one would suppose that they met, at least at Mallarmé's Tuesday evenings. Whatever the fact, Hovey was distressed at what he felt was a questionable method of dealing with both of them and did not go on with the proposed volume.

Mallarmé, himself a lecturer on English literature and a capable linguist, addressed Hovey as "one who clothes me with splendor." If this borrows too much from the exquisite courtesy for which the master was famous, it is not without some justification. Even if the translations have lost something of

[8] Maeterlinck to Hovey (July, 1895): "Je trouve votre traduction de L'Apparition de Mallarmé absolument étonnante. Cella devra dorevant etre cité parmi les tours de force les plus extraordinaire de la literature."

[9] He translated the following: a part of "Hérodiade," "L'Apparition" (Apparition), "Tristesse d'Été" (Summer Sadness), "Surgi de la croupe" (Sonnet), "Quelle soie aux baumes des temps" (Sonnet), "Soupir" (Sigh), "Les Fleurs" (The Flowers), "Les Fenêtres" (The Windows).

their value, they did the great service in their time of making
known to the American public a part of Mallarmé's very limited production and of giving to unilingual poets a presentable
example of a techinque more refined and more oblique than the
oversimplified rhyming of the popular poets of their country.[10]
Though they had nothing of the spread or influence of the
Maeterlinck translations, they had a share in the general
awakening of the literary world of America to new possibilities within an art which at home could find neither a new
thought nor a new speech.

As a commentator on the Symbolists Hovey served less
as critic than as publicist defending the French and interesting
the Americans. Like our poetry our criticism was still predominantly English in orientation. Hovey had no desire
merely to shift national influences, but wanted to call attention to what he considered sources of vigor in any literature.
By this time literary America was not unaware of the names of
the French and of some of their work. Students at Harvard
were declaring their independence by a proud allegiance to
Gautier and Baudelaire, and the number of those who referred
to Verlaine and Mallarmé surprised Paul Bourget on his visit
in 1893. Critics such as Brownell, Woodberry, Matthews, and
Peck were writing of the French painters and writers, and
when Harry Thurston Peck founded the *Bookman* in 1895, it
became the defender of the new. Verlaine and Maeterlinck
were the chief interests of the day. (Gertrude Hall's translations of Verlaine followed Hovey's Maeterlinck volume in
the Green Tree Library.) The peak of interest came in 1895,
perhaps largely because of the translation of Max Nordau's
Degeneration, a gossipy and uncritical introduction to the Decadents which stirred a meretricious curiosity. The little magazines which followed the *Chap Book* in 1895, most of all *Mlle.
New York*, edited by Vance Thompson and James Huneker,

[10] See René Taupin, *L'Influence du symbolisme français*, p. 45: "Ces traduc-
tions comptent parmi les meilleures de l'époque. C'est un chose rare en Amerique
que cette admiration pour Mallarmé, aussi sincère que celle des disciples français
du poete."

brought out some good writing on the Symbolists and published a large amount of their poetry in the original.[11]

Most of this writing was still to come when Hovey wrote his short articles for the *Tatler*, a literary daily which lived for only two weeks, but which was well spread among those interested in modern art. The scope of this miniature magazine gave room for only small sketches, and his comments on Mallarmé, de Regnier, and Vielé-Griffin are brief, though clear and forceful. His major point, taking the articles as a whole, is that only the Symbolists and the Realists are left to choose between, and his voice is strong for those who stand for "a movement for freedom in technique, and a truth more than skin-deep in the interpretation of life."[12] He hailed the election of Vielé-Griffin as a chevalier of the Legion of Honor because it was "not only a personal triumph but a triumph for all his fellows in that vital and virile movement in letters which the world obstinately persists in calling 'decadent.' "[13] Obviously he was going beyond true criticism to foster an art opposed to deterministic theory and the imitation of nature.

Since he was an eminently newsworthy man, reporters liked to interview him, and exchange editors copied and plagiarized. In such interviews he assumed an even greater freedom to

[11] The *Chap Book* was first published on May 15, 1894, while Herbert Stone and Ingalls Kimball, the youthful publishers, were still undergraduates at Harvard. Bliss Carman was their first editor. The publishers, members of the vivid group of energetic young men in Boston and Cambridge interested in the arts, devised the booklet as an advertising scheme, though it sold for five cents. It was in itself part of their program for boosting young American poets and fostering good book-making. The office on Brattle Street was a gathering-place, and the magazine itself carried the personal quality such magazines taught the large commercial journals. It ran up a circulation of 15,000 but its very success sobered its distinction and it soon became an orthodox house organ.

The *Chap Book* was the first of the innumerable "Dinkey Magazines," modeled on those of Paris. Youthful, widely interested in the novel, gay, and eccentric, they led short merry lives for a few months or years. Their influence lasted longer in the larger ventures which learned from them. They were important in helping the young Americans, and in printing the Europeans, particularly the French, and thus creating an international spirit. For example, the *Chap Book* printed Mallarmé's "Hérodiade" and its translation by Hovey, and Hovey saw his first copy of Gillett Burgess's *Lark*, printed on the West Coast, on Mallarmé's table.

[12] *Tatler*, Nov. 13, 1896.
[13] *Ibid.*

interpret and to express his own hopes. He exaggerated or even distorted certain American kinships with the French to promote ends not in themselves aesthetic. He insisted always on the individualism of the French, that they were not united by a school but by their belief in individualism, "a principle of separation not unity."[14] Their freedom and their opposition to mechanism he saw as a way out of the narrow confines of contemporary art and philosophy. He moved from talk of them to his own great hope for a group of American men devoted not only to art, but to "democracy,—a root and branch democracy—that will be satisfied with nothing less than the complete realization of the brotherhood of the race, and that take the words of Jefferson's declaration for no vain rhetoric, but prophecy."

This "group" did not exist outside his own wishful imagination, but it indicates the double quality of his renewed purpose after the French experience: to promote a more developed poetic art, and to dedicate that art to a large social purpose. He seems not to have suspected that Symbolism and all influences growing from it would increase the distance between creator and public by cultivating a fastidiousness and an alleged unintelligibility from which men would turn to the familiar vulgarities. If so subtle an art could have carried the virile meaning he proposed, the history of poetry in our time might have been very different. He alone in America even attempted the amalgam. The more characteristic social poetry was that of a Markham or later of a Sandburg. When finally in the 1930's young Americans followed the British in creating such a poetry, their splendid product found the popular ear deaf. Hovey was facing one of the major problems of our civilization, the tragic divorce between artist and people.

Strangely this flurry of excitement over the Symbolists made little impression on American poetry. Most of our self-conscious art derived from the French came through the medium of the English and gave us little that was different from the adaptation of the Pre-Raphaelites and Wilde. Certainly

[14] Boston *Evening Record*, Sept. 1, 1898.

the trial of Wilde in 1895 frightened many from any art which
might be called decadent or be accused of existing for the sole
purpose of its own being. It was not until after the Imagists
under Pound took over much of the program of the Symbolists
that America had a school of writers attempting free verse, the
musical phrase, and the symbol. It was still later before the
Symbolists were subjected to eager scrutiny by such men as
Eliot, MacLeish, and Hart Crane. Through such disciples
their influence became paramount in the poetry of the 1920's
and 1930's, but not until then was even a small American public ready for such a poetry.

It is difficult to estimate the influence of the French on
Hovey's poetry. Certainly there is no effect of the mood of
decadence strong in France and England, nothing of the per-
verse, no blasé and bored attitudinizing, and little of the search
for the precise nomenclature of refined sensation. Though he
wrote a poem on Verlaine and translated *The Faun,* he was
attracted only by the technical method of that old world "vagabond." On his first trip he had been intoxicated by the verse
effects of the line later to be appropriated by Eliot;

"et o ces voix d'enfants chantant dans la coupole"
with its play of vowels and nasals. It was something he had
not supposed the French language could do, he told Carman.
His translation of *The Faun* when the two were together again
four years later shows the conscious effort to transpose into another tongue the musical iteration, the syzygy, the attraction
of parallelism and alliteration he enjoyed in such carefully
wrought verse.[15] Yet these are the qualities with which he had

[15] Because of its brevity and its care for the range and harmony of vowel
sound the following makes an interesting study of Hovey's method as translator.

Le Faune

Un vieux faune de terre cuite
Rit, au centre des boulingrins
Présageant sans doute une suite
Mauvaise a ces instants sereins

Qui m'ont conduit et t'ont conduite
Mélancoliques pèlerins
Jusqu'a cette heure dont la fuite
Tournoie au son des tambourins.

already experimented and which he had considered in his technical essays as far back as 1892.

So also of similarities between his theory and that of the Symbolists. They shared the same eclectic enthusiasm for Poe, Emerson, Whitman, Swinburne, Rossetti, and Browning. Indeed, the shock of newness in their art must have been greatly reduced by such knowledge of the very sources from which the French drew so much of their method. They were attempting in a formal literature effects which had always existed in English literature. They desired the same overtone of idealism, they shared the same search for technical knowledge, the same desire for the musical phrase, the same exploration of sound effect, the same seriousness about art. Their differences were in degree and preference. Hovey was drawn to the group by sympathy with their central tenets, not by conversion. He discovered a common ground to which he had come by way of Delsarte and his own investigation, and the substantiation of his findings by artists whom he respected highly encouraged his trust in those findings.

The most noteworthy definite influence left on him was the use of *vers libre*. From this time on he wrote much in that freer form. He thought the freedom of unrhymed verse of irregular line length well suited to the English tongue, particularly in occasional verse of dramatic force. "Spring," written immediately after his weeks in Paris, demonstrates how superbly he could handle the form twenty years before it became a *cause célèbre* in America.

For all his technician's interest, Hovey was primarily concerned with a virile and social art, as his self-revealing comments on the Symbolists show. Though he agreed with the

------

The Faun
An old terra-cotta Faun
Grins in the middle of the green,
Boding, no doubt, some ill to blast
The moments that with steps serene

Have led me on, and led thee on,
Pilgrims of melancholy mien,
Up to this hour whose flying past
Twirls to the sound of the tambourine.

basic method of symbolic interpretation, he would not follow it to the creation of an art which was too exquisite and subtle for open statement. One may by idealism flee the evil of life or one may seek to remake it. One may be serious about art because it is "the one clean thing on earth," or he may be serious about it because it can cleanse the earth. Such differences are very real in temperament and practice. The Symbolists were too close to the tower, Hovey too close to the platform, for ultimate agreement. Their aesthetic could not support his militant ethic. Ideally he wanted neither the form or the content to take control of art. He was too much an artist to be satisfied with elementary verse methods, too much an American to care for an art which was not for man's sake. M. Taupin in *L'Influence du symbolisme français* gives more attention to Hovey than any comparable historian of American literature has given, but he regrets that Hovey allowed half measures and preference for philosophic meaning over technique to limit one who, he says, might have had a rôle like that of Verlaine in rejuvenating verse. That he did not play such a rôle is to be regretted, of course; but no one could have played it in the America of the nineties, and certainly if Hovey had attempted such a part it could have been only by denial of his most cherished dream and his poet's creed. He adopted what was usable to his own temperament and to an American art. He translated, explained, defended the Symbolists, but it was a New World faith he wanted to utter.

Through these months in which the new literature was his chief critical interest and the writing of *Taliesin* his great creative work, his social life was varied and crowded. As usual he met and visited all sorts of people: Jules Bois, lecturer on black magic living in Robespierre's rooms, Mme Dorien, the "angel" of the Théâtre Libre, Leon Balzalgette, the Symbolists, Mrs. Vielé-Griffin, senior, sprawled on a Turkish couch smoking. Everywhere he and his wife met courtesy and friendship. Mallarmé himself attended one of Henriette's lectures and spoke highly of it. He told Hovey he had the least accent of any American he had heard and prophesied a success in Paris.

Socially the success was a reality, but they were still desperately poor. They could give no presents to the children on Christmas, when Sigurd joined them. They had no carfare, but the walking kept Hovey thin and well. He had been drinking only water for a year, though he thought his friends would not believe it. Now there was no meat and little of anything else. When a draft from Washington arrived his hands shook as he opened the letter. The poverty bore on him heavily, and there seemed no way out. Though Henriette lectured to singers and actors at the theaters and before the professors of a lycée, there were no private pupils. Americans confessed that they were "shopping poor," and the French were hesitant to take up anything new. Even if all the schemes for boosting Carman, Roberts, Crane, and others by essays in French journals had materialized, they would have brought in almost no money. Though royalties on *The Marriage of Guenevere* were due, they amounted only to seventy-eight dollars and thirty-seven cents, far from what they needed to return to America. Still Mrs. Hovey insisted that it was better to live on cabbages and potatoes than to drop the writing of *Taliesin*.

Then came an offer from Ann Arbor proposing that for a remuneration he return to read a poem at the Psi Upsilon national convention. Hovey replied that he would deliver the poem if his fare were paid from England to Detroit and back to Washington. The offer was accepted and all was excitement. The problem now was how to get clear of bills and make passage for one cover passage for four. M. Baudy, "a brick," was satisfied by a royalty check in partial fulfillment of the Giverny debt. But it seemed impossible to transport the whole menage even if Hovey sailed in steerage. Moreover, even in the final days no check had come. At the last moment the puzzle fitted together happily and the Hoveys, with Julian and Allen, the English nurse, sailed second class on the *Saint Louis* on the first day of spring. It was a good enough steamer, but hardly the ship or class for a returning conquerer; so Hovey sailed under the name of R. Harry. It was another of the irritating devices forced by necessity upon one who lived upon two levels at one time. As the newspapers everywhere proclaimed, Hovey was the first poet in the world to be transported from continent to continent to deliver a fraternity poem; yet in his desperation he had to resort to this petty trick by which a poet could assume the responsibilities of a husband and a father. At any rate, the arrangement brought him again to America and the poem that worked his passage was more than the fraternity could ever have hoped—the greatest fraternity poem ever written.

CHAPTER XI

At War

Blow, bugles!
Over the rumbling drum and marching feet
Sound your high, sweet defiance to the air!
Great is war—great and fair!
The terrors of his face are grand and sweet,
And to the wise the calm of God is there.
                    HOVEY, "The Call of the Bugles," 1898

As Henry James said, being an American is a complex fate, and "one of the responsibilities it entails is fighting against a superstitious valuation of Europe." Hovey met this problem in the most straightforward way. He had none of the self-protective scorn of the uncultivated, none of the nostalgic sentiment of the resident of Boston or Cambridge, none of the conceit of the wealthy tourist disguised as a cultured cosmopolitan. Nor was he a permanent expatriate seeking a sympathetic culture more provocative than the "commonplace prosperity, in broad and simple daylight," as Hawthorne once defined the American scene. He was, indeed, closer to the tradition of travelers like Jefferson or Emerson who went to discover and learn and bring home to plant. He realized the lack of cohesion and culture in our society, but he was not so narrowly an artist that he could accept the social and political institutions upon which European art had rested. He spoke strongly against London, and more strongly against the Paris of the boulevards preoccupied by money, speculation, and shops. "The population fairly reeks with the sordid money-grubbing spirit," he declared. He told reporters:

I am come home with a deeper admiration for America than I felt before making this second somewhat prolonged stay abroad. I am con-

vinced that in the not distant future this will be the country of the best
literature and of the highest art.[1]

And again:

There is no more poetical people than the Americans; we hear so
much about the American being the worshipper of the almighty dollar,
but the truth is a Frenchman will chase the dollar ten miles where
an American will quit after the first mile.[2]

As always, Hovey's dramatic presence and his unsettled
living spread his comments and judgments. He was met by
reporters and quoted by journalists in city after city. As a
Washington paper said, there was an active curiosity about
"two of the most remarkable individuals one can meet with in
any earthly society in this period of grace." Personalities
were the vogue, and the papers made the most of this extraordinary pair. Mrs. Hovey's ideas might capture the ladies
of the local society, but the reporters assigned to her lectures
thought her fair game.

She looked like a composite colored photograph of burning Sappho,
Mona Lisa, and the Blessed Damozel, touched up with a pinch of
zeitgeist, a spice of most Parisian fin de sieclism, and a dash of shrewd
Yankee hustle.[3]

In the confusion of the early spring of 1896 and the journey
to America, there had been no time for composing the promised
poem. Once settled in Washington Hovey turned to the task.
He had no definite contract, no stated length, and he might
have turned out a perfunctory performance. He did not; and
the qualities which made him one of America's very greatest
occasional poets can be studied in the work which was to be
entitled "Spring." As he wrote to E. C. Stedman:

The muse was rebellious, not to say balky, at the start, but by dint
of persuading her that we were not bound for Ann Arbor at all
but only for an old-time ramble in the woods at our own sweet will,
I got her to begin,—and afterward decoyed her by devious paths

[1] Washington *Post*, April 26, 1896.
[2] Cleveland *Plain Dealer*, May 11, 1896.
[3] Worcester *Daily Spy*, June 10, 1896.

Psi-ward. It took some time, however, and the poem was hardly done when I started for Ann Arbor. They gave it a royal welcome.[4]

The poem begins almost in the cadence of speech, but speech slowed and made musical by the insistence of repeated long vowels which serve as a more complicated rhyme than the irregular lines show at first sight. They are written to be spoken by a voice that has feeling for time and tone.

> I said in my heart, "I am sick of four walls and a ceiling,
> I have need of the sky.
> I have business with the grass.
> I will up and get me away where the hawk is wheeling
> Low and high
> And the slow clouds go by.

The tempo quickens as more and more lines shorten and the rhymes come faster on each other's heels. The deliberate beat speeds from thinking to ecstasy, from the general to the immediate. And Spring, fresh and gleeful, goes over into the gladness of comradeship and the song of men.

> *Give a rouse, then, in the Maytime*
> *For a life that knows no fear!*
> *Turn night-time into day-time*
> *With the sunlight of good cheer!*
> *For it's always fair weather*
> *When good fellows get together*
> *With a stein on the table and a good song ringing clear.*

Out of the present run the roads East and West, an East and West which will not continue an unmeeting twain if they hear the work of Spring in the cosmic year.

> For surely in the blind deep-buried roots
> Of all men's souls today
> A secret quiver shoots.
> An underground compulsion of new birth
> Lays hold upon the dark core of our being,
> And unborn blossoms urge their uncomprehended way
> Toward the outer day.

[4] Hovey, May 14, 1896.

Unconscious, dumb, unseeing,
The darkness in us is aware
  Of something potent burning through the earth
  Of something vital in the procreant air.

This more thoughtful rhetoric carries to the end, insisting on the final fruition of this common rapture, whatever delay of frost and old bonds.

For the ages fret not over a day,
And the greater tomorrow is on its way.

The metaphorical use of Spring is an ancient device, to be sure, but Hovey was utterly sincere in transmuting the stir of sap in Rock Creek Park into the quickening of a new civilization. It was his increasing faith that such a renewal could be. In that new world the fellowship of men of good will was the binding power. So, though he wrote a poem for a specific occasion, he made it true to himself and his faith, and kept it alive through its considerable length by his skill in shifting beat and measure and tone to the need of mood and thought. It is a skilful blending of Whitman's dramatic recitative, Symbolist care for tone-color and symbol, and Hovey's technical skill. Characteristically the world has adopted the incidental "Stein Song" to maudlin fellowship which has little to do with Hovey's high sense of comradeship. His most famous lines are roared or stammered the globe over, as they deserve to be, but the lyric exultance and high goal are unsung, as they do not deserve to be.

On May 7 a thousand people attended the public literary exercises of the sixty-third national convention of Psi Upsilon Fraternity in University Hall at the University of Michigan. After President James B. Angell of Brown University and Bishop Perry of Iowa and others had made their symposium on university education, Hovey rose and his rich, controlled voice carried the audience through the poem to their enthusiastic acclaim. The next day the delegates and their guest took a special train to Detroit and made an upriver excursion on the ferry *Promise*. Though there was an orchestra and a holiday spirit of simple pleasure, Hovey was asked to deliver the poem again.   Standing on the upper deck where the spring sunshine and the wind seemed players in the piece, he responded with grateful joy.   He had not failed the trust which had brought him from Paris to Michigan.

The poem had solved the transportation problem, but Hovey had little in his pocket but his ticket to Washington. Again he thought of teaching as a part-time activity which would give him a chance to exist as both experimental scholar and poet.   His former classmate Fuller was now Dean and Professor of Greek at Adelbert College in Cleveland, and Hovey stopped there to further the scheme they contemplated—a modest chair in comparative literature which might be an experiment in teaching.   The project is interesting as an example of what he desired for himself and for education.

I am not to be restricted to English, nor am I to be burdened with anything philological or otherwise apart from the aesthetic ideal or spiritual function of poetry and letters.   In other words, as I understand it, they want me to teach *Poetry,* not grammar nor historical anecdotes nor any other unessentials.[5]

Though it would be half-work on small pay, the trustees could not find the money for the position.   Hovey was "cruelly disappointed."

Yet, though he had no way of support, his name was becoming familiar.   "Spring" was widely quoted and in the next month "Men of Dartmouth," another poem with a wide appeal and interesting background, won the Baker Prize offered for a Dartmouth song.   In the same month the second volume of Maeterlinck's plays appeared.   The strangeness of Maeterlinck's work had lessened with familiarity, and so there was little of the ignorant facetiousness and evasion of critical judgment which the first volume met. The book was well received and the translator served as a public interpreter, talking of the author and the work.   Obviously, from what he said, he still intended to translate *The Treasure of the Humble,* which

[5] Hovey to E. C. Stedman, May 14, 1896.

he constantly praised. Since he had Maeterlinck's approval as American translator, he felt the American issue of an English translation of the essays soon out was no better than piratical and that his own publisher had failed in competence. He urged another volume of plays on Small and Maynard. "I am not urging my own interest now. I will make almost any personal sacrifice to see Maeterlinck well taken care of."[6]

The next large task before him was to put a second *Vagabondia* volume in order, and so when mid-August and the hay-fever season came, he sailed for Nova Scotia from Boston, where he had been staying for a fortnight. Carman was at Wolfville, which Hovey found more beautiful than Windsor, and they settled in that charming town. Roberts had left Windsor the year before, and Carman had an old fondness for this town between the apple orchards of the valley and the marshy meadows of Grand Pré. So the three met there. The veranda of the house looked away across a garden of scarlet and yellow flowers, across the marshes with their purple inlets, to Blomidon rising beside the lilac and blue waters of Minas Bay, its spruce growth deep and cool against the warm red of its clay cliffs.[7]

Carman and Hovey put the finishing touches to the poems and finally read the proof. Though the songs were not part of the great purpose of either, they wanted them to be as good as possible of their own kind.

In October the weeks of country living came to an end and Hovey joined his wife in a combined attack on New York. They took rooms 847 and 848 in Carnegie Hall Studios where they might teach, give readings, hold receptions, and be close to the center of creative activity. The studio was decorated in the taste they advocated. The bare walls were stained a quiet greenish-gray. A couch in black and gold, a few ornate

[6]Hovey to Herbert Small, no date [1896].

[7] Carman, "The Modern Athenian," Boston *Transcript*, Aug. 29, 1896. This is an interview with Hovey under the title of Carman's signed weekly column for the newspaper. Hovey wrote that they spent two days on it and that he practically dictated it. "This northern garden" gave title to one of Carman's later volumes.

chairs, and an oriental screen were the only accessories. Men and women, graceful and decoratively dressed, were to be the dominant facts, not to be intruders into an already overcrowded museum. They had living quarters in Chelsea Square, for which Hovey had had an affection since his days as a theological student.

The first venture came with the *Daily Tatler*, short-lived but long-remembered. Stone and Kimball Company issued the miniature magazine of eight pages, but Kimball was alone responsible for this, the only exclusively literary and artistic daily ever issued in the United States. The gay spirit of the paper is caught by Carolyn Wells's reminiscence.

The office [of Stone and Kimball] was beautiful, with real stained glass windows and aesthetic furnishings that gave real joy to the visitor.

One day when I was there Mr. Kimball and I were lamenting the lack of really original sin in the imitative periodicals of the day, and we concluded that the only completely unbeaten track was that of a literary daily.

The impossibility of the thing attracted us; the increasing difficulties lured us on, and by some superhuman effort on our part *The Daily Tatler* appeared on the following Saturday. It was a small eight-page affair, entirely literary, and delightful in every way.

Now literary periodicals are usually weeklies or monthlies, and few editors of such know anything of the soul-harrowing rush of a daily. For two weeks we lived by the instantaneous process and then gave up the ghost.

The nicest thing about *The Tatler* was its staff, a mob of gentlemen who wrote with ease, while I occupied the early English editorial chair and giggled at the funny things that were said. It was all in the magic Nineties, and everybody was clever and quick of understanding.

Richard Hovey, of blessed memory, was the jibe maker, and he stalked the floor and out-whistled Whistler in his gentle art. All the books sent in for review were marked with the official stamp, which was the paw of the office kitten and a purple ink pad. Our deepest perplexity each morning was whether to sell that day's issue as a paperweight or to sell a paperweight with it—the decision resting on the voice of the New York press of the day before.[8]

[8] Carolyn Wells, *The Rest of My Life* (Philadelphia and New York: J. B. Lippincott, 1937), pp. 174-175.

The gibes were nursery rhyme attacks on the academic, the pompous, the defenders of tradition. Hovey and Carman had begun the series almost four years before in Washington. Now Hovey took up the jingles again. They were part of the wilful naughtiness of a review which flattered no one. It laughed at the fig leaves on George Gray Barnard's sculpture and made fun of the Boston tempest over McMonnies's simpering Bacchante. It was vigorously concerned with art, not flattery; so that, as Thomas Beer says in *The Mauve Decade*, it represented the animation of its time more fully than the larger magazines. Since Hovey was declared by all his friends to be the most courteous, forgiving, and equable of men, one must suppose that the sport of writing nonsense in company strengthened the acid of his pen.[9] The lampoons on Woodberry, Aldrich, Smith, Matthews, Sherman, and Gilder, editors and academic critics, even if deserved, do not rise to the level of criticism. Yet it would be a mistake to dismiss them as the bitter revenge of wounded vanity. Not only Hovey, but also his friends and those he admired, were kept unpublished by the powerful coterie which controlled criticism and magazines, and so he attacked for all.

Since he believed that the present and future of American poetry were in the hands of the excluded, he was properly angry at the namby-pamby policy which feared the vigorous and sincere and gave them no chance. The powerful magazines, the *Atlantic* ("The Pedantic"), *Harper's* ("Sharper's"), and the *Century* ("The Cinchery"), were closed unless one would harness Pegasus to a moral dray, goad him over the commonplace, break his spirit, and "stable him in *The Pedantic.*"

> When shall the Golden Age of Song
>   Return to earth again?
> When all the dilettante throng
>   Is silenced or is slain.

[9] "Hovey's friends were sometimes angry for him, but he was not angry, or often discontented, ever, for himself. He was too big a man" (Herbert Small, *Conservator*, Philadelphia, March, 1900).

The gibes, which are both laughable and unpleasant, were the crackling skirmish of Hovey's campaign for an American art. Before the year was over he would state positive ideals which give reasonable purpose to this preliminary sniping.

The *Tatler* sold so quickly the uptown stands received no copies. The harassed editors were exhausted by this obstreperous offspring of a reckless hour, and on the thirteenth day, unable to keep up the pace success was demanding, they let it die. The paper had published six poems by Hovey, among them the best of those in the new *Vagabondia* volume, as well as his thumbnail sketches of the Symbolists, but the flippant jingles brought down the wrath of the proper. Those who did not know the true reason for the demise of this *enfant terrible* saw it as a just retribution and blamed the author of the saucy pasquinades.

That brilliant and eccentric poet, Richard Hovey, was its editor, and also one fears its murderer, as he used the *Tatler* largely for purposes of revenge, a something which palls upon readers more quickly than turkey réchauffée on the day following Thanksgiving.[10]

Hovey was much in the public print at this time. Despite his seriousness about art, he never objected to satirical comment about himself. He even joined in the fun-making. Stone and Kimball issued publicity for the Maeterlinck volume which reported Hovey's one-time resemblance to Dante but present likeness to Daudet, for whom he had been mistaken in London. In *Town Topics* appeared an amused paragraph.

Now Mr. Daudet is an interesting person, but it will occur to some people that it was a distinct condescension, if not a loss, for Mr. Hovey to resemble him after having resembled Dante. It seems almost like taking an undue advantage of Dante to have made this change. Even now Dante may be walking, erect and triumphant, in the thymy plots of Paradise explaining to all comers that he is the man who looks like Richard Hovey.[11]

This was widely copied in the newspapers and caused an amused chuckle, but the chuckle turned to an astonished gasp

[10] Boston *Home Journal*, Dec. 5, 1896.
[11] *Town Topics*, Boston, Oct. 1, 1896.

when Hovey announced that he had written both the publicity and the ironic comment on it.[12]

His full-faced beard was the easiest object for jokes. According to the Boston *Transcript* he put it off or on as he wished, but "had directed by codicil to his will that he shall be shaven before he is buried."[13] The public chaffing was good-humored and so fantastically exaggerated that it amused without hurting: Indeed, it was Hovey's imperturbability and indifferent individualism in a shaven and conventional day which provoked the cartooning. One sometimes suspects a mixture of jealous admiration and self-protecting depreciation in the writers, at other times the mere pleasure of the ridiculous.

Town Topics reported that there was a constant parade of authors on Tremont Street. A dozen or so were counted at one time.

Number four is Mr. Richard Hovey of Ghent, the greatest living poet among the graduates of Dartmouth College. Formerly he looked like Dante, but now prefers to look like M. Alphonse Daudet. Wears a robe of blue and green serge, buttoned with miniatures of Mr. Maurice Maeterlinck—please pronounce Mah-ter-lingk. Wears a Spanish hat and feather; also rubbers for the purpose of stemming the tides of song without getting his feet wet. Is preceded by a gigantic Nubian slave in green livery, who continually observes, "My God! My God! My God!"[14]

Authors were at least news and entertainment.

There is little to show how Hovey spent the winter of 1896-97, except for work on *The Birth of Galahad*. No new poem was printed after the demise of the *Tatler*. Though two volumes had appeared on the market since his return, the royalties were small. When he went to Washington in the spring to see his sick father, he applied for a teaching position in the Central High School. Once more he was refused, greatly to the anger of the Washington *Post* at the loss of opportunity to the school to become famous by having, as it put it, one of the best known of modern poets numbered as a member of the staff, rather than some safe person unknown outside Baltimore.

[12] New York *Journal*, Oct. 11, 1896.   [13] *Transcript*, Sept. 29, 1896.
[14] *Town Topics*, Nov. 5, 1896.

With the coming of summer Hovey entered again on an extended holiday. First he camped with his wife and others at Rockaway Beach on Long Island, where he rose at eight and made coffee with all proper solemnity. In late August he moved on to West Gouldsboro, Maine, a place which had everything he wanted: sea, fresh water, mountains, and woods. His garret room looked across Frenchmen's Bay to the Japanese effect of the sunset. The less attractive "rusticators" left with the end of the season, the picnics and the talks and readings to summer people and natives which had kept his working hours limited to the night were over, and he divided his time between work and his friendship with Henry Sandham. Sandham was a Boston painter, "a very good fellow" of about fifty and "pleasantly vagabond," who had a canoe and a little sailboat on the lake and a sloop on the bay. They sailed together many days in the fresh September breeze. More than at any other time he felt the exultant thrill and bold defiance which are so frequent in the poems. In the last days Sandham made a portrait, shown at the Pennsylvania Academy later in the year, posing Hovey in broad-brimmed hat and open collar against a rough polychrome background suggestive of waves. Hovey liked it, as well he might. "*I* think it very good. Monet-ish in scheme of color—open-air quality—very breezy in handling and pose of figure, very manly and leader-like in expression."[15]

Before he began the period of concentrated work on *The Birth of Galahad,* he read through the books he had brought from Boston on Thomas Morton's gay experiment at Wollaston, or Merrymount, as it has come to be called. He had the idea for a slight comedy, but the material was much more suggestive than he had supposed and the projected play bigger and more difficult. So he went through the books and realized that the action should mellow. The play never got beyond the dramatis personae, which included three of his ancestors, Allerton, Cushman, and Standish, but the conflict between the Puritan and the expansive Renaissance man fascinated him, as

[15] Hovey, no date [Oct., 1897].

did all oppositions of culture. He never gave up the intention of writing the play.

After six weeks in Maine he made visits to Tom Meteyard in Scituate and to Herbert Small and Sandham in Boston. He was in New York for only a short time when the serious ill-ness of his father called him to Washington. The General had spent the summer with his brother-in-law, John Cook, now president of Illinois State Normal College, as he once had been. When the sick old man arrived they were celebrating the fortieth anniversary of the institution he had fathered. He had now returned home to die, but his tremendous vitality would not let him go. He remained bright and cheerful, though he knew he would not live and his body was wracked with cramps and fierce coughing. Hovey took the place of the night nurse, tending him, massaging him for hours, sadly witnessing the break-up of the resistant body. There was no privacy, no place to think, no way to work except by robbing his sleep. He was tired when at last death came, though he had still all the arrangements for burial and pension to make. They buried the General in Arlington Cemetery with the nation's old soldiers.

> There rests my old friend in his soldier's grave, . . .
> Old grim idealist with the tender heart,
> The grizzled head, grey eye, and scanty speech,
> And hand that never faltered in the fight
> Through all the rough work of a long campaign,
> God keep you, General, with the heroes gone!
> ("Decoration Day," Bliss Carman)

Except for a few days the Hoveys had been separated for three months. In New York Mrs. Hovey was discouraged in her effort to find money even for meals and gas bills. She was too tired and lonely. They began a correspondence which might better be left untouched were it not that many have doubted the fullness and continuity of their love and that Hovey was always put forward by her and his friends as the exponent of a richer and more complete relationship between the sexes than commonly existed at that time. Hovey was a public propagandist for such a relationship and demanded acceptance of it from those he would admit to fellowship in any school calling itself new. He wrote of the new writers, denying that they were decadent and insisting that they were renascent. One of their notes, as he called their agreements, was freedom, and freedom to be worth the name included freedom for woman.

It is generally speaking characteristic of the younger poets to find the conventional standards at once narrower and more exacting than the true psychology and ethics of love. They have a tendency to look upon the current conception of marriage as a fetish instead of a sacrament, to believe that the woman should submerge only so much and no more of her personality than the man, and to refuse to think evil of God's way of making life. This is, of course, dreadful—worse even than anarchism—but there seems to be no way to stop it.[16]

Though others of the "group," such as Carman, Roberts, Verhaeren, and Davidson, granted woman spiritual equality out of natural generosity, Hovey from beginning to end of his literary life studied the relationship of woman and society and woman and man, both as critic of society and as psychological poet. With his strong religious nature it was necessary to him to see love as a sacrament. The word comes into his writing over and over again. At first reading it may seem a pseudo-religious sentimentality, but it is one of the key words of his work. No one in modern times except Browning has so constantly merged physical passion with spiritual meaning. Carman once said that the Marna poems reminded him always of the line in the marriage service: "With my body I thee wed." Hovey's whole intent was exactly that of the church service, but, of course, he elaborated the sacramental principle with all the knowledge at his command. Here was the ultimate expression of his constant concern, the trained and sensitized use of the body to the glory of man and God.

In the separation of the Hoveys things were written out of their desire which cooler moments distrusted. She feared

[16] Richard Hovey, "Decadence or Renascence," *Time and the Hour*, Dec. 4, 1897.

they were getting sensual, though she would rather enter a convent than succumb to sensuality. He too feared any imbalance in the wholeness of love, but because he saw life as good and the senses and soul one in true love, he accepted his body.

If my senses gave me no delight, if I did not enjoy my senses to the uttermost—all, sight, sex, hearing, taste, smell and touch—I should be very unhappy. I should feel that part of me was dead; that I was only half a man. I want the faun in my soul as much as the poet or the angel.[17]

Like Lawrence later, Hovey tried to find a vocabulary for love which might be neither academically medical nor evasively sentimental. Like other men he was forced to accept the Anglo-Saxon words degraded by men and to rescue them. He traced them back to the old roots lost in the antiquity of Sanskrit or Greek and found them related to life symbols and processes. The discovery of their rich symbolic connotations delighted him. They needed only to be washed free of prurience and they might unfold the long process of man's love as well as release the poetic sound-values of the words themselves. Here, in little, Hovey achieved what he tried in larger ways, the lifting of the natural sensuous life to a poetic and religious level.

The separation, seven years after they first met, gave him opportunity also to assess the quality of their individual love. Like Launcelot and Guenevere they had defied the ways of their society, breaking the old fidelities to come to a new relationship which by its greater synthesis could alone excuse the breach with the old. As very few ever do, they had lived together in hourly intimacy, studying and talking as professional students about those common ends and methods where tension can most easily develop. They had lived through the most irritating sort of poverty for which each might have been blamed. Moreover, there was behind her the shadow of two other husbands. Yet out of frankness and honesty and ability

[17] Hovey to Henriette Hovey [Nov. (no date), 1897].

to rise from the particular to general understanding, they had created a modern love, sensuous, intellectual, and spiritual. They had proved that two who care greatly may win through to the high goal Hovey declared possible to modern men and women. They were free, independent entities; and yet they were inseparably one.

The reason why I have never loved as I love you, the reason why I shall never love as I love you, is this capability for absolute each-other-knowledge. That never happened before: that will never happen again. It is not possible that another woman could be, to whom I could so wish to reveal all—of whom I could so long to know all. Union with another would be like a mechanical mixture: union with you is chemical, a new One.[18]

An author's life must not be confused with judgment of his art, but as so often with Hovey one is struck by the close relationship he made between living and writing. Art proceeded out of life discovered and was itself in turn a discovery of life. No healthier aesthetic could be devised. Moreover, the search for ultimate synthesis of man's whole nature was an experiment which asked the creator's very existence as material and all his honesty as method. Hovey lived out his part of his experimental life with extraordinary success.

Hovey's most influential and his most constantly attacked poems come from the period of the Spanish War. Since they are the only memorable product of a frenzy which swept the country, they are useful to social historians as a brief statement of a popular temper of mind later repudiated. Since they are the product of a high-minded poet who had no economic stake in territorial expansion, they help one to respect a position later vilified as mere jingoism. It is the part of a biography not to excuse but to explain. This can best be done by setting Hovey's "jingoist" poems into the context of his Americanism. This nationalism is surprisingly strong for one with a classical culture, an aristocratic manner, and European interests. He was immensely proud of his heritage as an in-

[18] Hovey to Henriette Hovey [Nov. (no date), 1897].

dividual, and he was equally proud of the social heritage of democratic ideas. One remembers that his college thesis was devoted to tracing the growth of the democratic tradition. The fragments of what he intended as a trilogy of plays dealing with Columbus suggest that America was more than a geographical discovery; America was the dream of the future.

He was the finest type of literary radical in America. Like Emerson and Thoreau and even Whitman, who was more cosmopolitan than he admitted, he desired to effect change in American culture by bringing the best of man's thought to expression in modern and American terms. Like them he saw the universal laws working through the present to a greater future, but obstructed and perverted by man's greed and materialism and godlessness. He was not that type of nationalist we have lately glorified for setting down the crude reality of a frontier culture. The justification of our culture was for him, as for Whitman, in the future, and that culture would be great not because it was different from everything before, but because it would be the ultimate and most beautiful expression of modern history. It would not be enough to be American, or use American materials, but the way forward led through America.

Some people think originality in American art means aboriginality. If an American painter paints a Sioux Indian, he does it as much from the outside as an Englishman or a Frenchman would. Neither did American literature come out of the picture-writing of Lake Superior nor will American architecture be an efflorescence of the wigwam.[19]

As he said, Hovey returned to this country with greater admiration than before and more than ever convinced that it was the country of the future. He saw us already the only country producing anything worthy of the name of architecture. He said that our people liked good poetry more than the English.

There is in America a far greater proportion of intelligent people who know what is good and what is poor. The average of intelligence

[19] Manuscript notes, DCA.

here is higher than in England, and the average quality of our verse is purer in style and technique.[20]

We had, in fact, reached a cultural level equal to that of Europe, and he anticipated that the French and English would soon be coming to New York to study in the new artistic center of the world. "The Americans are the Greeks of today."

His most widely quoted statements were concerned with the new writers in France, England, and America. While not a school, these writers, it seemed to him, share certain principles of faith and action, though so individual that their similarities can only be called "notes." His elaboration of these common notes is less a solid judgment on such incomparable men than an outline of his own belief and of his program for a truly American and modern school of writing. The "notes" are a "root-and-branch democracy," veritable freedom for man and woman alike, an "Hellenic note of joy," virility, philosophic idealism, religious awareness (not necessarily faith), and spontaneity and freedom of technique. Obviously these seven notes have the freshness and energy one associates with the typically American at its best. They preclude the worship of sorrow, an effeminate sentimentalism, and a philistine and materialist blindness to meaning in the universe. They were also the qualities he sought and achieved in his own work.

Such notes, if united in a sincerely held program, would put a poet left of the political center. Hovey had been there from the beginning of his mature life. Though he had the manners and the indifference to opinion of the aristocrat, he had spoken steadily for the people. This was, in a sense, incidental to his central purpose, for he did not think primarily in economic and political terms. As with Morris and Ruskin, his radicalism started from art and social culture. He was concerned with healthy and high-minded living, not with political equality, with the whole problem of man in society rather than

[20] Hovey, "Decadence or Renascence," *Time and the Hour, loc. cit.* The material of this brief essay was incorporated verbatim in what posed as interviews (Boston *Evening Record,* Sept. 1, 1898, Boston *Sunday Herald,* Oct. 30, 1898), and in a lengthy notice in the *Bookman,* Dec., 1898. It thus had considerable spread.

with any particular aspect of it. The doctrinaire ideologies such as Marxism are based upon material determinism, and this he opposed as an explanation of life unworthy the dignity of man. He was closer to "The Fellowship of the Good Life" than to any group, thinking in terms of the end to be achieved rather than the method of reaching that end. He was not, then, a political or economic philosopher representative of a group or platform, but like the vigorous English poets of the later nineteenth century the sworn enemy of philistinism, the profit motive, and theories of life which robbed man of rational purpose within a meaningful universe. Any way forward demanded enmity to the capitalist economics and industrialism which were reducing more and more of the population to a proletariat presided over by a philistine plutocracy. In this he was simply one of countless middle-class intellectuals of the time who were everywhere responding to a situation which insulted the Christian and libertarian principles under which they had been educated. Writers were prominent because they were articulate and because, having little to lose, their eyes were clearer to the degradation of man, but in America the nationalist movement, following Bellamy's *Looking Backward*, Christian Socialism, Marxian Socialism, the Populist Movement leading up to the presidential campaign of 1896 were grouping nameless thousands against entrenched privilege.

Hovey accepted the single-tax program of Henry George as the first experiment to be tried.

> In politics I am a radical. The most pressing question of the day is the question of starvation. I believe the enslavement of men through their necessities is the peril of our civilization. I think there is a truth in socialism, though socialism be impractical immediately, as a sudden change, whatever it may or may not be in the future. What is entirely practical and suitable for immediate adoption is the single tax. The sooner we put that in force the better. It may prove the sufficient solution for the problem of poverty.[21]

After George's death Hovey was asked to write a poem for the unveiling of a bust in "The People's Club."

[21] *National Single Taxer*, IX, no. 4 (April, 1900).

Oh, be his death a clarion
To hearten, not dismay!
Fight on!
We have not lost the day. . . .[22]

Despite the call to fighters in a common cause, Hovey was not a single and unskeptical party man. Carman, who saw him often at this time, said later:

Richard Hovey had thought on many subjects. The single-tax theory, for instance, had no more firm adherent than he. And while he had all the uncompromising logic of a reformer, he had none of the bitterness of the zealot. He saw that there are tremendous wrongs to be set right; he saw that it is our business to set our hand to the undertaking. But he saw also how slow progress is, and how sweet life is, and how good love is. I fancy that doubt of the ultimate benignity of nature never entered Richard Hovey's mind. Perhaps it was this that made him such a fortress for his friends—this and his gentle quietude of nature.[23]

It was only because people had not seen through to the problems he posed in symbolic form that Hovey had ever seemed less than passionately concerned with the good life for all men. He believed whole-heartedly in the artist's identification with his society. As he had written a decade before:

Whenever the artist withdraws from the religion, hopes and aspiration of his fellows and from their mutual sufferings and wrongs, he becomes a mere dilettante. He turns his calling into a foppery. . . . It is the duty of every man to live in an atmosphere of political study, of religious aspiration and the love of beauty, that the life of the nation as well as his own be made nobler and sweeter. This is the only "culture" worthy of the name.[24]

It was this Anglo-Saxon cast of mind, refusing to isolate itself from men and society, which had been uneasy over the excessive privacy and dreaminess of the Symbolists. More and more he expressed admiration for the courage and noisy man-

[22] Hovey, "Henry George," *Along the Trail.*
[23] Bliss Carman, "Richard Hovey, My Friend," *Criterion*, XXIII (April, 1900), 527.
[24] Hovey, "The Dying Century," *loc. cit.*

liness of Henley and Kipling, though he deprecated the latter's reactionary Toryism. The virility which was one of the "notes" he praised implied a stand in the clash of forces.

Poetry is thought to have something to say to strong men in the midst of the battle of life, and not to be an elegant amusement for school-girls and dilettanti. More stress is laid on the masculine element in thought and life and the effort is to be downright and muscular.

This flexing of muscle, characteristic of the rejection of the ennui and effeminacy of aestheticism, had a deep root. One might trace it back to the Hegelian principle of opposition, from which Hovey said he learned much, or to Whitman's "call to battle," or even to Emerson's serenity founded on the acceptance of struggle and the necessity of evil to the emergence of goodness. Hovey's deep belief in the gradual realization of spirit was good transcendental doctrine, but he felt with passionate conviction that only the modern creative man who dared to accept evil and passion and paradox as the materials of fuller development could win the final revelation of life's wholeness. He showed his postevolutionary cast of mind by accepting strife as the law of life in a more physical way than his predecessors. The constant doctrine of the dramas and of poem after poem emerged from the quietness of philosophic thought into the arena of politics and social action, and Hovey declared that God "works through battles to his ends." He was in the mood to play the bugler to some great crusade. That for him was the Spanish War.

It is possible to understand the psychological motivation of men in time of war only by putting one's self in the con-temporary mood. This is very difficult, particularly for this time, since subsequent history and the growth of economic realism after World War I have so deeply colored our con-ceptions. We look back upon ruthless dealings in Cuba and the Philippines and upon the extension of markets of trade and find it almost impossible to recover the naïve optimism and unselfish militarism of the earlier day. Certainly business and banking did not want war. They were still uneasy after five years of depression and fear. The momentum of prosperity was only beginning to gather force. Every war scare brought a drop in the stock market. Though business interests in Hawaii and Cuba desired the protection of the United States, businesses in the states were opposed to them as competitors who might be too advantageously placed by the lowering of duties. Men such as Mark Hanna, Andrew Carnegie, and James Hill, the business journals, chambers of commerce, and associations of manufacturers were vigorously opposed to any part in the Cuban revolution.[25]   Indeed, the outcry against both Cleveland and McKinley was that they listened to business interests rather than the excited citizenry and the voice of conscience. War, up to Dewey's success at Manila, provoked fear of loss of trade and prosperity, of the unsettling of the monetary system which had just weathered Bryan's silver-tongued oratory, and of decline in imports. Business and banking fought the movement toward war as the irresponsible product of reckless jingoists.

Hovey himself felt that a war would be in defiance of all economic caution. It would prove America's ability to rise above money-making and to undertake for no gain a cause expensive in money and blood. When the declaration finally came he said just this.

Abroad we have the reputation of being soulless money-getters, hunters for the almighty dollar. But that notion has been exploded by the war. The almighty dollar has been proved a myth and we have shown that we have as keen a sense of honor and quite as much sentiment as any nation in the world.[26]

Other nations were deaf to the cause of independence, tied by economic bonds and outworn allegiances, but America dared strike for the right.

> Who now are they whose God is gain?
> Let Rothschild-ridden Europe hold her peace!
> Her jest is proved a lie.
> They and not we refrain

[25] Julius W. Pratt, *Expansionists of 1898* (Baltimore: Johns Hopkins Press, 1936), pp. 230 ff.
[26] Boston *Sunday Herald*, Oct. 30, 1898.

From all things high
At the money-changer's cry;
They and not we have sold
Their flags for gold;
They and not we yield honor to increase.[27]

Like many idealists Hovey responded to war because a "trades-man's peace," as Tennyson once called it, was so unsatisfying to all idealism. Peace that is no more than the bartering of goods and profits always leaves a vacuum into which rushes the high and selfless excitement of war. The next war was to find hundreds of the best English and German young men anxious to serve a purpose higher and more sacrificial than a shoddy absence of war.

For men in peace,
Lacking brave emulation and the zeal
Of a great cause, fall to their petty ends
And, letting their high virtues atrophy,
Wallow in lust and avarice, till the heart
And nobler functions rot away and leave
A people like an oyster, all stomach.[28]

Of all those who spoke out, the papers and journals of the Protestant Church were closest to Hovey in understanding and vocabulary. Except for the Society of Friends and the Unitarians, the organs of Protestant opinion saw the struggle as a war for humanity. Here was Providential guidance to a great missionary work which might Christianize and civilize the backward areas of the world, where, incidentally, the Catholics had been strong under Spain. The Lord of Hosts, to whom they were fond of referring, was leading this great Christian and Anglo-Saxon liberation, and they could not shirk their responsibilities. The very phraseology, with its Biblical rhythms and symbols, was the same in Hovey and the church-men.[29]

Taken at the idealistic level the Spanish War was aid to

[27] Hovey, "The Call of the Bugles."
[28] Hovey, *Marriage of Guenevere*, Act IV, sc. i.
[29] See Pratt, *op. cit.*, pp. 279 ff.

a revolutionary government struggling against a narrow imperialist policy. The people were predominantly behind the cause of Cuban independence, and quite properly so. The very history of America dictated their republican position and dim memories awoke an Elizabethan hatred of Spanish monarchy. The appalling conditions in Cuba called for emancipation. Both party platforms in 1896 declared for Cuban independence. To enter a state of war to free another country from tyranny could be only the act of the unselfish or that of the scheming. The ingenuous and the idealistic could see only one way of action.

These ordinary good men were not expansionists, at least at first. The true promoters of manifest destiny were the politicians, such as Roosevelt and Lodge, and the philosophers of history such as Fiske and Mahan. Whether like Fiske one saw an evolutionary selection working toward dominant nations or like Mahan saw that sea power gave such dominance, the future of America was inescapable. But even Roosevelt was timid compared with the "new journalism," which was having its first great moment. Since Hearst had opened war on Pulitzer's *World* in 1895, a lusty type of journalism—sensational, personal, biased—had entered the field of public opinion. "The new journalism prints what is new and prints it first," boasted Hearst's *Journal*. Since the only criterion was circulation, the newness and the sensationalism sometimes outstripped fact. Hearst is reported to have said to Frederic Remington, his field artist, "You get the pictures, I'll make the war." Even if it was not "Mr. Hearst's war," as it is sometimes called, circulation boomed from seventy-seven thousand to over a million. The paper fed itself fat on the excitement and idealism of the people.

When on February 15 the *Maine* blew up with loss of two-thirds of its crew, Hovey wrote off in hot anger "The Word of the Lord from Havana." A violent Jehovah denounces his people for their deafness to the oppressed. "Drunk with gain" and fawning on Spain, they have been smitten in judgment. He calls them once more:

Ye who remembered the Alamo,
Remember the Maine!
Ye who unfettered the slave,
Break a free people's chain!

He sent the poem to the New York *Journal,* but its editor, Merle Goddard, dared not print it because of its license in using the name of the Lord, even though the *Journal* now declared that "intervention is a plain imperative duty" (February 18). Many have claimed the first use of the slogan of the war for Hovey. He was indifferent to such a distinction.[30] But he was jealous now of national honor as well as distressed over the Cubans. He sat at home with his anger boiling over into what his wife called "sassy sonnets" to McKinley.

Oh for an hour of Jackson, lest we rot,
And this fair land become a stench to Time.

He was bitterly indignant at what he felt was the kinglike indifference to the wish of the people on the part of

The sceptered waverer at Washington
Who waits on Wall Street to declare its will.

Though I am a radical, I am also an imperialist. So was Julius Caesar, and he was the greatest political mind the world ever knew. The world unified under one government—that is one necessity of political thought. The individual and local community free—that is the other. Caesar was an imperialist; he was also a labor leader. Had the aristocrats not killed him, he might have solved the problems which, unsolved, destroyed Rome—which again now, unsolved, will destroy us.

[30] " 'The Word of the Lord from Havana,' was written long before the declaration of war. At that time a spirit was abroad in the papers of the land that for some time after it was written prevented the publication. Even the New York Journal wrote me that it was *afraid* to print it. So that the date of its appearance in the New York World (March 20) is not to be taken as even approximately the date of its composition. I say this, because there has been a question raised as to the priority of use of the phrase 'Remember the Maine!' which occurs in the poem and which has become the battle cry of the nation. The poem was written immediately after the blowing up of the battleship and before anything but the bare news had appeared in print. The phrase 'Remember the Maine!' sprang to my thought, as it appears in the poem, as an echo of the old war-cry 'Remember the Alamo!' But it would be foolish for me, or any man, to claim its origination, for it must have leaped to the lips of thousands, as it did to mine" (undated note in Hovey's handwriting, DCA).

Despite a somewhat eccentric reading of history, the obvious faith is in the kind of world men hope to build in the future, a world both of unity and of freedom.

Hovey's stand in the Spanish War has been unfortunate for his reputation. No one can impugn his intentions, whatever they may think of his methods. He has suffered the fate of those who lead the people in a popular crusade when later action nullifies or denigrates original intent. Men like William James who told his classes not to yelp with the pack come to esteem on the backwash of disillusioned faith; but Hovey had no sympathy for the academics who could not see the agony of the thousands who suffered and starved under an intolerable situation.

> Ye pompous prattlers, cease
> Your idle platitudes of peace
> When there is no peace!
> Back to your world of books, and leave the world of men
> To them that have the habit of the real,
> Nor longer with a mask of fair ideal
> Hide your indifference to the facts of pain!
> "The Call of the Bugles"

He remains a most interesting study in a time which has lost its moral credit, though now we face a world in which even the plotting of the extreme expansionists must, at least to some degree, be accepted as shrewd. As Cleveland held, the mission of this nation was to build up a great country out of what we had, not to annex territory. Yet a modern world power found itself facing a situation in which England, France, Germany, and Italy were building colonial empires in a day when distance was being abbreviated in time. America felt forced into annexing Hawaii to keep it free of Japan in what the Senate, following Mahan, saw as the first skirmish in the coming struggle between the West and the awakening East. The problems of Hawaii, the Caribbean, and the Canal had to be solved if the United States was to have any strategic defense. Within a half century, and with no desire for empire, the country was again to be fighting for the outposts and bases which alone can protect it.

The idealist seldom supports war with impunity. Neither those who write nor those who fight make peace or policies of trade. It is only justice that we try to understand them in their time. Other men, by the sheer logic of history, are proved right for the wrong reasons. They were wrong for the right reasons.

CHAPTER XII

At Peace

> Under the teeth that clench and the eyes that weep,
> Deeper than discord or doubt or desire or wrong,
> One with the wills that sow and the Fates that reap,
> Joy in the heart of the world like a peal of song.
> HOVEY, *Taliesin*, 1899

The problem of income was still unsolved. An article like that he wrote on Maeterlinck with the knowledge of friend, critic, and translator sold for only fifteen dollars, and the shorter poems he placed for an average of five dollars. He thought he might solve his difficulty by tackling the larger problem of literary criticism. He felt that the critical writing in most magazines was "perfectly rotten," as he told an interviewer, and far below the level of both the newspaper and the popular taste. The *Daily Tatler* had proved that vigorous encouragement of the new and judgments beyond the conventional would find readers. His friend Stedman was urging him to start a literary weekly. Now he heard that the *Literary World*, a Boston magazine, was failing and could be bought for about $3,000. Barry, always his good friend, was eager to edit it with him, and Small, Maynard, and Company would help it along for a promise of future advertising. He needed $1500 for his share, and tried to get three loans of $500. His uncle, Aaron Gove, had expressed confidence in his future, and Hovey wrote to him for help saying:

> I have waited so long for my opportunity, I have undergone so many buffets and stuck to my guns just the same, that I feel almost as if I had a right to expect of Fate that this should not slip through my hands now.[1]

But the opportunity did slip through his hands and with it

[1] Hovey, Aug. 8, 1898.

the chance to undertake a refashioning of the literary magazine.

During these days he was in Boston, "as picturesque and poetical a figure as ever," as the papers said. In his Norfolk and knickerbockers, his pale green stockings, his campaign hat jauntily worn over his heavy dark beard, he was a striking figure. A dozen news boys gave him a spontaneous ovation under the delusion that he was a returned Rough Rider, but other passers hissed him as a Spaniard. Boston was particularly sensitive to his unconventional dress. It was noticeable there for the simple reason that he was usually in unseasonal transit from summer vacation to the city, and his more formal clothes were elsewhere, perhaps in pawn. So the autumnal visits got to be something of a newspaper event. Though Hovey had never greatly cared for Boston, his capacity to hold his friends made him always welcome. He was guest of honor at "The Pewter Mugs," an association of capable and productive "vagabonds," and guest of honor at the Press Club, where his songs were sung by a quartet including Bullard, the most successful composer to his lyrics.

Though the plan for the literary magazine fell through and the colleges had already begun the year, suddenly there came a telegram from Miss Smith (later Mrs. Putnam), Dean of Barnard, asking him if he would give two lecture courses at the college. Curtis Hidden Page, on the staff at Columbia, had suggested the lectures. Miss Smith wanted to get away from the teaching of literature as a pseudo science and believed that Hovey's spontaneity and creative vigor would give her students more than the usual course. Since there was no formal work in English literature which demanded a set body of information, she could go after the important thing. As she later wrote:

I believed that I was securing for our students at Barnard an almost unique advantage; the advantage of hearing English literature discussed by a man who had not merely walked around it and looked at it as a connoisseur but who understood the laws of its being, who added to a profound and delicate critical sense the gift of exquisite expression, and who could bring home to a student intelligent enough to receive it the consciousness that our great literature, the only art in which the English race is eminent, is the obvious means appointed by providence for our intellectual salvation.[2]

Hovey wired acceptance, and although classes had been running several weeks forty-three students managed to remake their schedules to include one or the other of the new courses.[3] Hovey had never taught; he had made no formal studies in the older literature since college days. He had less than a week to prepare himself, and that week was largely devoted to clearing up affairs in Boston and setting up a new home (The Castle, 202 West 103rd Street). Teaching is so imponderable an activity and so much made by the relation of teacher and student within an evanescent present that it is difficult to gauge success. Certainly Hovey's notes for the lectures are scanty and unprofessional, a series of complete sentences which are broad statements without transitional filling. They are fresh and critical, without apparent borrowing, but woefully scant. A half to a full page of such sentences per lecture was the rule, but one has always to remember his brilliance as a talker and his moving power as a reader. Yet even with these gifts he came to class late and left early, the impact of feeling and discovery substituted for the usual money's worth of historical and pirated information.

Hovey was always concerned with education and he and his wife planned to write a book on the subject in collaboration. He came at that time when the older classical education was breaking down and the new elective and anarchic curriculum replacing it. As one concerned with the ultimate purpose of the old but always interested in the new and the scientific, so that he could not reject them, he thought it important to preserve a particular function for the arts. As he wrote in a penciled note for the future book:

Education physical and mental we see our way to more or less

[2] Mrs. Emily James Putnam to Mrs. Richard Hovey, March 15, 1912.
[3] His courses in 1898-99 were English I, The General History of Literature; English XI, History of English Literature from 1789 to the Death of Tennyson. In 1899 his courses were English LI, Shakespeare; English LXI, English Literature in the 19th Century.

clearly. But the education of the moral nature we are still groping and fumbling about. Art, which is the expression of this is also its education.

The two objects in all art education, he thought, were the creative expression of the self and enjoyment. The stress on enjoyment is typical of him. He told his students:

> If you don't like Shakespeare, say so. It will be the first step to liking him. Trying will never bring you to it. Like the thing you like. Give yourself up to it. There is nothing so educative as joy—so developing as happiness. Poetry should educate the soul through its delight. Like heartily what you like and you cultivate at least liking itself, and prepare the soul to be able to like other things hereafter—when it chooses. . . . Teaching is not a teaching of the mind but of the soul— and its method is by giving enjoyment to the soul.[4]

The swiftest way to bring enjoyment to the soul, and incidentally, the easiest for him, was by reading, and much of the class time was given to this. The result is still remembered gratefully by some of his students.[5] Undoubtedly his methods were perfected by the second year of his teaching and his enthusiasm for Shakespeare and for the nineteenth-century poets gave more body to his work.

As a result of this gathering of ideas about certain figures he gave a series of semipublic lectures, a course of six lectures in the drawing room of his friend Mrs. King, concerned with Blake, Shelley, Whitman, Maeterlinck, and the "new drift" in French and English poetry. Carman said he had never heard literary topics treated with such ease and mastery. "For myself, I must say that one sentence of Richard's would do more to illumine a topic than a score of current magazine

---

[4] Notes in a class notebook, DCA.

[5] His most brilliant pupil then and afterward, Dean Virginia Gildersleeve, wrote to the author (Feb. 16, 1943): "I remember him very well and am indebted to him for what he taught me about poetry. His method was to read poetry aloud, and I know of no better one, if the teacher can read as well as he could. Mr. Hovey was entirely unlike the usual college teacher. He was artistic and temperamental. He generally arrived at class very late and left before the period was over. If my memory is correct, he generally wore a soft black felt hat, a frock coat and pumps, and the sight of him riding a bicycle in this garb was rather striking."

articles."[6]   This power of illumination, often remarked, was
not the result of momentary intuition, but of long research into
principles of poetic structure and philosophy.   The freshness
of opinion sometimes made it seem more impressionistic than
it actually was, whether it was concerned with the technical
mastery of poetic form or with judgment on Shelley's love life
or Ruskin's economics.   His work was honest and free in its
statement of his own beliefs, "with no swagger and no flinch,"
as his wife said.   One wishes he might have given a course of
lectures at his own college, even if it was not yet bold enough
to place him on the faculty.   Long after his death President
Tucker said, "We made an irretrievable mistake."[7]

Hovey's chief aesthetic interest during 1898 was the sonnet.
He had solved the problems of the free, declarative occasional
poem.   None could touch his ability in that.   He began to
experiment with a strictly ordered form.   His interest came
almost accidentally, for though he had always written sonnets,
particularly in college and soon after, he chanced to pack his
anger against McKinley into a form usually reserved for a
more contemplative expression.   His wife objected to the use
of the form for such a subject matter.   This led to a study
of the strongest sonnets of Shakespeare and Milton and to
Hovey's reinforced belief that the sonnet could carry a much
heavier charge of emotion than contemporary use sanctified.
He also wanted to write a love sonnet which would be en-
livened by an out-of-door quality such as "the Marna poems"
had, a sonnet that would be distinctly American in vigor.   So
with words and symbols from sea, battle, riding, and storm he
fashioned several energetic sonnets, strongly accented and punc-
tuated with dominant sounds.   They are too muscular and
nervous, if judged by comparison with more reflective sonnets,
and they do not carry the sense of love so much as a kind of
free-for-all against the natural forces and against fate.   He felt

[6] Carman, "Richard Hovey, My Friend," *loc. cit.*
[7] A note attached to a letter from President Tucker, written in Mrs. Hovey's
hand, says: "This reminds me of the deadly pallor of President Tucker's face
when he said to me at Dartmouth, long after Richard's death, 'we made an irretrievable mistake'."

he had succeeded best in "Two and Fate" ("The ship we ride in sniffs the storm"). Whitman's dream of a sunburned and athletic womanhood and of love close to earth is pushed to its limit. One feels that only a highly civilized man could have been so self-consciously strenuous and that such a man would respond in this way only momentarily. The intention forces the poems too far, and yet, before the turn of the century, they caught a kind of vigorous and exultant companionship which was to be an accepted and valuable part of love in a few decades. Nature was not a pastoral backdrop for picturesque lovers, but a setting into which woman came out of the house and out of gentility to a shared experience of "love in the winds." The new woman was for Hovey the capable and active comrade, out-of-doors as well as within.

> Ho, love, I laugh aloud for love of you,
> Glad that our love is fellow to rough weather,—
> No fretful orchid hothoused from the dew,
> But hale and hearty as the highland heather,
> Rejoicing in the wind that stings and thrills,
> Comrade of ocean, playmate of the hills.
>
> "Love in the Winds"

He was encouraged to go on with the sonnets by Bertram Goodhue, who had designed borders and initial letters for a sonnet series Copeland and Day were issuing. Goodhue, who designed the handsome edition of *The Birth of Galahad* in this same year, was anxious that Hovey bring out a volume of sonnets with the same high publishing standards and with the esteem publication in the series would give. Hovey liked the idea, since it fell in with his own interest. The nine sonnets published after his death in *To the End of the Trail* are there designated by his wife as part of a dramatic series he projected. They happen also to be, with no intention of the author, those sonnets which had not before seen book publication. It is impossible, therefore, to determine whether they should stand alone or should be grouped with the other sonnets of the same period. If one collects from *Along the Trail* and *To the End of the Trail* all the sonnets written at one time, he finds that

fourteen were composed in the one year 1898. If they are
brought together, even without being forced into position as
possible members of an abortive dramatic series, they empha-
size the experiment Hovey was attempting. They fall into the
general philosophy of composition he was stating and working
within, and give both unity and spread to his purpose of creating a virile, modern, and American poetry. The long tradition
and formal design of the sonnet presented a definite wall of
defense against conscious attack. Success would prove that
even this Old World form might be infused with a new
American strength.

If one looks at the poems simply as a challenge to the form
and even if he excludes the rather chest-thumping masculinity
of those mentioned above, he must acknowledge immediately
the energy of utterance. The training in musical structure now
hides itself from obviousness and maintains a tone of controlled
beauty that seldom lapses into mere sweetness. The long study
of vowel and consonant sounds asserts itself without over-
consciousness. Poems of jealousy and torment are easier mani-
festations of experiment, for the jangled spirit speaks naturally
in broken and discordant tones, but even the evocation of quiet,
spiritual love emerges from the harshness of daily work without a too obvious resolution into harmony.

After Business Hours

When I sit down with thee at last alone,
    Shut out the wrangle of the clashing day,
    The scrape of petty jars that fret and fray,
    The snarl and yelp of brute beasts for a bone;
When thou and I sit down at last alone,
    And through the dusk of rooms divinely gray
    Spirit to spirit finds its voiceless way,
    As tone melts meeting in accordant tone,—
Oh, then our souls, far in the vast of sky,
    Look from a tower, too high for sound of strife
    Or any violation of the town,
Where the great vacant winds of God go by,
    And over the huge misshapen city of life
    Love pours his silence and his moonlight down.

There is no dramatic thread of story, even in those sonnets published together. They are simply statements of a lover in moments of doubt, jealously, and certainty. They are not written out of Hovey's personal situation, except in the poems of sure love inscribed to Marna, but are imagined states of feeling. They carry on his investigation of the relationship between man and woman. They are not the poems of a young wooer, but of the man of long-consummated and familiar love who realized the truancy of the human heart. The beloved is not a young and timid girl, but a woman of experience and free determination. Rossetti, Elizabeth Barrett Browning, and Meredith had reanimated this earlier use of the sonnet as vehicle for the examined love relationship, as he was aware. It is natural that a mature lover should adopt it for the intellectual and self-conscious evaluation foreign to the single-spirited lyric. Accepting the fact that "love has no rights," the lover is all the more tortured by the evil promptings of his imagination, suspecting that love will betray itself to less than love, most of all to pity, that love will be "too tender-hearted to be true" and play the Cressid. This is the chief fear, as perhaps it is of all lovers who respect and fear the compassion of the beloved.

In the whole body of the poems, however, this possibility of infidelity is accepted and overreached by the sonnets of assured love which welcome the storms of nature and of the heart. To see them whole one should incorporate the three written in 1897 and collectively entitled "Love and Change." Three lovers speak; one sees love drop withering away as all things do; another finds love eternal, but lesser loves going out to all things lovable until love finds its peace in God; and still a third accepts mutability, the ancient enemy of love, and lets it serve as guide to new discoveries within the single love of his life.

> My love for you dies many times a year,
>   And a new love is monarch in his place.
> Love must grow weary of the fairest face;
>   The fondest heart must fail to hold him near.

For love is born of wonder, kin to fear—
  Things grown familiar lose the sweet amaze;
  Grown to their measure, love must turn his gaze
  To some new splendor, some diviner sphere.
But in the blue night of your endless soul
  New stars globe ever as the old are scanned;
  Goal where love will, you reach a farther goal
And the new love is ever love of you.
  Love needs a thousand loves, forever new,
  And finds them—in the hollow of your hand.

The conclusion carries the free, questioning, equal relationship to an end consonant with Hovey's trust in man's ability to bring new conditions into spiritual harmony. It is achieved not by exclusion, but by widening the range of life to include struggle and minor disillusion and change as the very necessities of a courageous and developing existence.

Whether or not Hovey intended to go on with the "series" later, or whether he had said what he wished as sonneteer and as lover, he dropped the work when teaching and other matters demanded his time. The poems as a group are the last large piece of work he did in poetry, except for the gay continuation of Byron's *Don Juan*. They deserve more than the complete neglect into which they have fallen. They show him writing of men and women in a dramatic way outside the restraint of the Arthurian legend and in a contemporary setting. The curiosity about men and women and the strong social awareness which had always set his characteristic work apart from Carman's is fully evident. The exuberant lyricism is trimmed to a tauter speech. He was now able to be romantic with far less of romantic vocabulary. If they are not altogether a new type of love sonnet, as Curtis Hidden Page asserted at the time, they were new in his own day, and by virtue of the companionship in nature unlike any ever written before. As Page said: "His love poetry is neither prudish nor prurient, but frank, free, and joyous." Since some of the poems were widely published in a day when women were venturing forth as something sturdier than "weaker vessels," they had their place in provoking an idealism to substitute for the loss of Victorian womanliness.   Both the natural active woman and the educated self-reliant woman were given their dues, but, even more important, they were made one.

During the midyear holiday Hovey went to Washington, where Carman was staying at the house.   He was still tired from a severe attack of grippe, but the respite from teaching opened a chance for writing.   Carrying over his contemporary approach and his concern with the problems of love, woman, and social institutions, he began a modern prose play later called *Vows*.   He tried to see Mrs. Fiske, since the big part would be for a woman, but before he had that chance Mrs. Earle, an old friend and pupil of Mrs. Hovey, had interested Mrs. Patrick Campbell in the play, so that the trip to England seemed not too extravagant a project if the actress should cable an invitation.   For that he waited eagerly.

Meanwhile there were teaching, poems, and the whole cause of literature.   He was emerging more and more as a writer to be reckoned with.   *Ainslee's* had been advertising in the streetcars his contribution ("At the Crossroads") to the January issue.   In December and January the *Bookman* carried his name not only as signed to a poem, but in its comments and in a two-number criticism by Curtis Hidden Page.   The section called "Chronicle and Comment" said: "Mr. Richard Hovey has grown more steadily in the appreciation of the public during the last few years than any of the younger American poets."[8]   Page's critical review of his work was handsome and lengthy.   It praised "a breadth of command in technique unapproached by any among our hordes of good versifiers."   Indeed Page went so far as to declare: "He has ranged wider, and penetrated deeper, in the comparatively unexplored country of rhythmic expression, than any other writer of English."[9]   To this technical capacity the criticism added "creative imagination" and "the constancy and purpose of endeavor" which are

---

[8] *Bookman*, VIII (Dec., 1898), 306.
[9] Curtis Hidden Page, "The Plays and Poems of Richard Hovey," *Bookman*, VIII (Jan., 1899), 449.

the directing force of skill. Faults were admitted, but the conclusion was: "He is master of his art and master of life."

Such a judgment from a critic and scholar in one of the most reputable literary magazines points up the regard in which he was now held. He was still thought of by many as "one of the younger writers." This patronizing advantage irked him, for he felt that at thirty-five he and his friends, all of them older, had won the right to be judged purely as writers. If not, they had failed and there was no use glossing over the fact by pretense of juvenility.[10] There was, however, nothing of the patronizing in William Archer's *Poets of the Younger Generation*, completed in this year although not published until 1902. Because of the death of "that very able writer," Hovey's portrait was used as frontispiece to a volume which gave high praise for everything but his dramas. Archer was very aware of what he called the "American neo-paganism" in much of Hovey's work, and saw him "the wearer of Whitman's mantle. . . bringing the spirit of Whitman into time with the traditions of English poetry."[11]

Because he looked upon himself as primarily a dramatist, the possibility of success for *Vows* made it very important to him critically and financially. When Mrs. Campbell showed her interest, he left for England at the close of the spring term. The play so far had only two of its four acts written out, and so he stayed at work in his cabin on the *Teutonic*, emerging as a surprise to his fellow-passengers at the end of the voyage.

The play, laid in contemporary France, concerned itself with the study of a simple, genuine, ardent woman brought into conflict with the position of the Roman Catholic Church on divorce. Mrs. Vantyne, wife of the American ambassador, is a very recent convert to Catholicism, and ecstatically happy with her husband and children. Suddenly a clumsy plot device introduces her divorced husband, a vulgar fellow who had deserted her. She is forced to realize her position. The

[10] Hovey to Rice, Feb. 4, 1899.
[11] William Archer, *Poets of the Younger Generation* (London and New York, 1902).

priest's statement that such a woman is an adultress and the mother of bastards sends her into insanity, which is climaxed in a scene of melodramatic madness in which she covers the priest with roses and gives herself into his hands with a kiss. The exhaustion of emotion saves her, but she sees no solution but death, for in Heaven she supposes that she will be able to love both husband and God. The priest, however, says that such wilful self-destruction will cause rejection by Church and God and condemnation to Hell. This frees her from the death wish and from her religious fixation.

I do not believe in that God. I believe in a better God. That is a cruel God. He makes life a horror and death a horror. I will have nothing to do with him.[12]

So life and physical love win and she returns happily to the "earth of joy and love."

Hovey had said once again that one of the three major problems which concerned him most was "the enfranchisement of women from her traditional and conventional position."[13] This play could have had no part in his own advance in understanding the problem. It was simply an open social challenge to the Roman Catholic Church in its control of love by insistence on single marriage, and so a dramatic social defense of the rights of women and of love. As he had attacked the law of the state in the Guenevere series, he here attacked the rule of the Church. It was part of his program of clearing the way for a larger freedom.

The play attempted a difficult theatrical problem, and without great success. The necessity of lifting a conflict of abstract ideas to dramatic action forced that action into emotional extremes. The plot, the secondary characters, and the opening acts exist only to make possible the high emotional moments in which conflict is visibly real. Since the opposition of ideas is within one woman, its expression must be psychological. A neurosis is difficult to present dramatically, and was much more difficult at that time. A strange and shadowy figure in the

---

[12] Hovey, *Vows*, MS copy in DCA.
[13] *Bookman*, VIII (Dec., 1898), 306.

play (Dr. Winfield) today might be made an articulate psy-
chiatrist and commentator on its meaning and serve as arbiter
and as foil to the priest. As it is, the play can end only in
insanity or complete victory for one side. That victory is a
declaration of Hovey's position but no satisfying abstract solution to the problem.

He read the play to Mrs. Campbell and Mr. Forbes-
Robertson. They had already made a great success in Shake-
spearean production, both in England and on the continent, but
were, so rumor had it, on the point of breaking their collaboration. The reading was successful, as Hovey's readings always
were. Forbes-Robertson put his hand on Hovey's shoulder
and wished he might see him play Othello. But though Mrs.
Campbell herself liked the plot immensely, they thought the
play too daring. She kept the manuscript for study, but finally
turned it down. "They both agreed it was far and away better
than any other play submitted to them but they were scared,
scared blue at 'the great British public.' "[14] The attack was
too open. Pinero's play *The Gay Lord Quex* Hovey found
dull and vulgar, but it could be advertised as witty and im-
moral. His was too earnest and too moral. He felt the disappointment keenly, for he knew that it was through art that the
great change had to come. "I believe something is going to
happen—in art, not in life. But art is life for us, at this moment, at this stage of the game."[15] He saw other actors but
they shared the same fear of so forthright an attack on the
Church's historic position. The discouragement, the feeling
that the play would never be put to the test of actual production, disheartened him from working.

More than at any other time in his life he needed encouragement. From a variety of obscure causes, he was physically
and mentally sick. Though he hid his disappointment from
his friends, so that they later spoke of how bravely and wisely
he faced things and of how merry he was, they noticed his
nervousness, his inability to keep still. He was, as he said,

[14] Hovey, July 20, 1899.
[15] Hovey, July 4, 1899.

"all tied up with nerves," but the soft climate and a stay at Christchurch in what he thought of as the Shelley country helped to relax him, though not to cure his melancholia. He felt that psychic forces were working against him, " a strange, thwarting, blank, snarled-up condition of the atmosphere," which blackened the summer of 1899.

I feel as if I were no earthly use in the world. Failure in everything I hold most dear to do, useless to the world, to the theater and to *you* and yours, let me say ours rather, what earthly excuse have I for living? Hope is nearly battered out of me. . . . Oh my love, if only I could yet be of some great use to you.[16]

It is painful to probe the misery of one who praised life and love and joy so spiritedly, but the web of his life bore this somber warp at the end. The pathos is deeper because his feeling was so at variance with his faith and his habit of mind. His friends were unanimous in their emphasis upon his quiet courage. Carman, for example, later said:

What one of his friends characterized as his "gentle grandeur" was perhaps his most distinguishing characteristic.

It was this gentle grandeur of character, coupled with great sweetness of nature and great idealism of spirit, that made him so indifferent to circumstance, so superior to fortune.[17]

The high brave mind was clouded over by the body's failure, yet he knew with intense consciousness how far the sustained mood failed the true course of his life.

I am heartily ashamed of my condition—I seem so weak, so pitiful, so little great. If I did not feel that all this was physical in cause, a sickness really, I don't think I could endure the humiliation of it. I do not wish to be pitied nor to be a pitiable object, nor to lean on others. I wish to be strong and useful, and have others lean on me so far as it is good for them. . . . I know well enough that there is to be joy and love and sunshine again, yes and even success and even money. I face the future without a qualm or a doubt. But meanwhile I am suffering horribly in my mood, and in my physical powers.[18]

[16] Hovey, Aug. 16, 1899.
[17] Bliss Carman, "Richard Hovey, My Friend," *loc. cit.*
[18] Hovey, no date [Aug., 1899].

The long chance he had taken had failed, and he was in England without passage money home. As always, absence from America sharpened his longing for it. He thanked God daily that he was an American and could be free of "the unutterable smudge of English life."

I am so anxious to get out of England that if I had my passage money I should be tempted to start at once, hay fever or no hay fever. My impression is the same as when I was here before. There is a sordidness about Europe that is awful. America has bad enough faults, but it is not so depressing. There is hope—and a future. What hope for Europe? Look at the Dreyfus verdict![19]

Finally he got an advance from Small, who was always his good friend in many kindly acts beyond mere business, and took passage on the *Winifredian*.

His college work was waiting, but it wasn't enough for his needs. Poetry was almost without profit; so he turned to criticism and editing. M. A. de Wolfe Howe, editor of the series of Beacon Biographies issued by Small, Maynard, and Company, asked him to write a life of Poe. This appealed to him, but only if he might make of the book a real piece of criticism. Obviously to do this required time and freedom, and he could have these only at the expense of other activity and the income from that activity. Therefore he asked $700 rather than the $550 offered, knowing that his name would help the series and that he could write a book which would remain valuable and standard for years. This was no conceit, and was based upon the most objective of calculations. He was ill, forbidden by the doctor to do any work for six months. But a note was due and necessity forced him to bargain for an immediate payment, though it might be far less than the very fair royalty scheme offered would finally produce. On the other side, he was a critic who probably knew more than any other American about rhythms and musical verse and who was familiar with the European estimate of Poe's foreign admirers. Though Poe had limited himself to a narrow scope, Hovey had sympathy with his aesthetic self-consciousness, however foreign

[19] Hovey, Sept. 12, 1899.

to his thinking Poe's psychopathic moods. No one had yet done justice to Poe within his limits, he felt.

At the same time he foolishly but courageously undertook to edit *Prometheus Unbound* for Silver, Burdett Company. They had asked him to do a Tennyson volume; he asked for Shelley.

Since these undertakings were no more than sketched out in his mind they are noteworthy only as they show his need and suggest his interests. Once necessity had dictated the transfer of time from poetry to criticism, he intended to do more than a competent job and obviously had the capacity to speak freshly and authoritatively on the work of such lyricists.

Still another literary iron in the fire was a continuation of Byron's *Don Juan*. The *Smart Set* was offering a prize of five-hundred dollars and, though he did not want to enter a contest and felt a certain indignity in doing so, the award started him and his own enthusiasm carried him. He intended to go on for twenty cantos, so his wife wrote, but he did only 472 lines. These lines show he had not yet got altogether into the mood nor found direction. Some stanzas are clever, the rhymes are amusingly far-fetched, the logic is unconventionally ordered, but the shifting interest and the confusion of Hovey, Byron, and Don Juan are being resolved only when the manuscript breaks off.

He begins with Don Juan in Atlantic passage on September 30, 1899, surely his own trip from England, and gets him started in an affair with the wife of a self-made, spiritually unborn American business man.

> She was a slight, red-headed type,
> With eyes like sealskin and a cheek like ermine.
> Soft, lush, and deep; her lips were overripe,
> If anything—but who would dare determine?
> She fenced, rode, flirted, smoked—had hit the pipe,
> They say—(but all looked dainty in her mien)—
> For Ellinor (her Christian name was Ellinor),
> Had twenty-seven different kinds of hell in her.[20]

[20] Hovey, *To the End of the Trail* (New York, 1908), p. 116.

This promising source of satire he drops undeveloped to fulfil Byron's promise of an episode in Hades, almost as if he could not control his impatience to exercise himself in play with the epic tradition. So Juan becomes the dead Byron, contested by his good and evil angels who by the process of nineteenth-century feminism have become female. Since the good angel very soon leaves in prudish dismay, the darker and lovelier creature takes him to Hell. The old place has changed and Hell is now clean, philistine, and scientific. It is furnished with laboratories, the Bertillon system, and athletic fields: "All Hell has become one vast Reformatory." Lucifer has turned Dry-as-dust and the devils, scientific criminologists. Still, because of the earth-born population, it is a more interesting place than its rival state.

> Heaven is much more boresome, so they say,—
> A sort of middle class Y.M.C.A.[21]

This jump to the contemporary offered unlimited material for satire, of course.

> ...I
> Must let dead cantos bury their own dead
> And write of what the public wants to buy.
> Southey's forgotten; so is Castlereagh;
> But there are fools and scoundrels still today.[22]

Not enough is written to show whether Hovey understood the moral earnestness and conviction of liberty which steadied Byron's satire and made *Don Juan* what its author believed it —"a moral poem." Whatever the sympathy in ultimate beliefs, great temperamental differences divided the men, and death left it uncertain that either could have gone on to turn "the giggle" and the negative attack to that open affirmation of moral good which Byron finally intended. One suspects, however, that though Hovey might for a time enjoy the exercise of witty castigation, he could not have satisfied himself within this genre. Like all maturing poets he was growing more

[21] *Ibid.*, p. 128.
[22] *Ibid.*, p. 129.

social and analytical in his poetry, but his great purpose was still involved with an explicit and verbal beauty. The social realism and astringent sanity of Byron's purpose called for a paradoxical wit and a reckless attack which Hovey did not command, nor has any other since Byron. Even if at times he could have approximated the brilliance of *Don Juan,* he no longer had the ebullient energy which is the very soul of that masterpiece.

The last year of the century had been very difficult. He had been sick and poor. The turn of the century meant to him a mathematical point for the opening of that great century toward which he always looked with eager and Whitmanesque hope for the future. He was almost millenarian in his faith that men were good enough and wise enough soon to drop the institutions and material desires which held them from a full part in life. As always he cast his horoscope at the beginning of the year. This time it promised good. As he told Roberts, after the first of March everything would be clear sailing. Saturn, who had been afflicting his horoscope for several years, was going to pass from influence with "a hard kick for good-bye at the end of February."[23]

In a month, however, he was told that his contract with Barnard would not be renewed since the departments of Rhetoric and English were to be consolidated and put under the charge of a single professor of more academic training who would be satisfied with a more pedestrian kind of teaching. Dean Putnam wrote that if a lectureship were contemplated she would offer it to him, and spoke handsomely of his work. "I wish to tell you that my personal conviction is that we have never had lectures given in any department in Barnard more adequate, brilliant, and generally valuable than yours."[24] Whether or not because there was enmity from another source, as his indignant mother protested even to President Butler, the position which so satisfied his peculiar needs and abilities was at an end.

[23] Pomeroy, *Sir Charles G. D. Roberts,* p. 48.
[24] Putnam, Jan. 31, 1900, DCA.

Hovey's depression of the last summer and the attendant physical and sexual debility had been at least in part the psychological effect of varicocele of the testicle. In February he entered the New York Postgraduate School and successfully underwent an operation.[25] His roommate in the hospital was a student for the priesthood, twenty-five years old, who showed an almost professional interest in Hovey's soul and ideas. They talked too about literature, and Hovey, who had long since discussed the limitations of realism, defended it and Zola's sincerity against the moral blame of the young ecclesiastic. They talked freely of religion and Hovey declared that he would be a Catholic if he could be a Christian, but that he could not accept as historically true the divinity and resurrection of Jesus. Again they talked about death, of which Hovey was not any more afraid than he would be of "passing from one room to another."[26]

Death must have seemed a long way from him, since he was a man of only thirty-five who posited his whole philosophy of existence on movement toward the fulfilment of man's final possibilities within a world which, properly seen, was one of joy and beauty. When he had imaginatively met death it was always as a final adventure within a scene of natural energy. The brave man met death with a spiritual force equal to nature's physical power. It could even be a moment of supreme joy.

> At last, O death,
> Not with the sick-room fever and weary heart
> And slow subsidence of diminished breath—
> But strong and free
> With the great tumult of the living sea. . . .[27]

On the morning of Saturday, February 24, 1900, he looked bright and well. The nurses made excuses to speak to him, for

[25] His card of admission shows that he was in Room 81, Dr. Dudley in charge.

[26] Father John T. Prout, letter to Mrs. Hovey, no date: "He greatly comforted a young fellow in a nearby ward by saying, 'Death is nothing, my boy. Who's afraid of going into the next room?'"

[27] Hovey, *Bookman* XII (Nov., 1900), 256. A footnote said that this was "believed to have been the last [poem] written by Mr. Hovey."

they liked to enter his room. They said that his warm greeting and smile braced them when they were tired.[28] He sat in a rocking chair by the window wearing his blue dressing gown. Mrs. Hovey had brought him a bunch of narcissus which he caressed. After lunch he was walking up and down when suddenly he felt faint. The nurse helped him to the bed and called the doctor. Nothing eased his difficulty in breathing, for a blood clot had lodged in his heart. Within twenty minutes life was over. "Oh, Henrietta, I am going," he said, and died.

[28] This and the following information comes from a letter by the nurse, Eleanor C. Brown, to Mrs. Hovey, March 7, 1900.

A BIBLIOGRAPHY OF THE FIRST EDITIONS
OF BOOKS BY
RICHARD HOVEY

based on the collection of Hovey's works
in the Dartmouth College Library

Compiled by Edward Connery Lathem

1880 Poems

POEMS | BY | RICHARD HOVEY. | [*ornament*] | WASHING-
TON: | N. B. SMITH, Printer, 615 7th Street, N. W., | 1880.

COLLATION: [Unsigned: 1-5⁶]; 30 leaves; pp. [1-7], 8-59, [60].
Leaf measures $8^{13}\!/_{16}''$ x $5\frac{3}{4}''$, all edges trimmed. Printed on white
wove paper, no watermark.
[Note: A blank binder's leaf is present in front of the first signature,
with a corresponding one at the end of the book following the final
signature.]

PAGINATION: End paper, brown coated on white; binder's leaf;
p. [1], title; p. [2], copyright notice; p. [3], table of contents; p.
[4], blank; p. [5], divisional fly title: PART I.; p. [6], blank; pp.
[7]-44, text; p. [45], divisional fly title: PART II.; p. [46], blank;
pp. [47]-59, text; p. [60], blank; binder's leaf; end paper, brown
coated on white.

BINDING: Green grained cloth, bevelled edges. Front cover has
title in self-cloth within a gilt-stamped ornamental design: POEMS
Spine and back cover blank.

CONTENTS: Part I consists of fourteen poems: Ode to Laughter,
Ode to Melancholy, Song of the Wind, Lilian, Love, To Juliet, To
Edna, Ode—translated from Horace, The Hermit Thrush, Winona,
Ode on Memory, To Shelley, Shakspere, To Thaliarchus—para-
phrased from Horace. Three poems comprise Part II: A Horrible
Tale, To a Fragment of Rock, Reflection.

NOTES: Entered for copyright December 12, 1880; copies received
at Copyright Office January 21, 1881.

Issued also in blue wrappers, pages trimmed to a size 7" x 4⅞". Front cover printed in black using the same type setting as the title page, the whole inclosed within a double-rule border. Spine blank. Back and inside covers blank. Without the binder's leaves front or back noted as present in hard-bound issue described above.

Based on the incidence of the book's appearance in book auctions, it has been asserted that copies in cloth are considerably scarcer than those in wrappers. The Dartmouth collection includes duplicate copies of both forms.

[1883?] Hanover by Gaslight

HANOVER BY GASLIGHT | OR | Ways That Are Dark | BEING | AN EXPOSÉ OF THE SOPHOMORIC CAREER OF '85 | BY | RICHARD HOVEY | [*horizontal rule*] | [*four-line quotation*] | [*horizontal rule*] | IMPRINTED FOR | the class of '85

COLLATION: [1]⁴, 2-7⁴, 8²; 30 leaves; pp. [1-5], 6-44, [45-46], (new paging begins:) [1-3], 4-13, [14]. Leaf measures 9¼" x 5¾", all edges trimmed. Printed on white laid paper (now discolored brown), no watermark.

PAGINATION: P. [1], title; p. [2], blank; p. [3], table of contents; p. [4], blank; pp. [5]-44, text; pp. [45-46], blank; [new paging begins for separate section of text:] p. [1], fly title: HISTORY | OF | SOPHOMORE YEAR, | C. S. D. '85, | BY | MAURICE L. CLARK.; p. [2], blank; pp. [3]-13, text; p. [14], blank. [Note: The section by Clark which is appended to Hovey's history of the sophomore year of the Dartmouth Class of 1885 is a parallel account of the events of the same year for students in the Chandler Scientific Department, at that time a separate branch or associated school of the College.]

BINDING: Terra cotta wrappers. Front cover printed in black: *Hanover | by Gaslight* Spine blank. Back and inside covers blank.

1889 The Laurel

The Laurel; an | Ode. To Mary Day La- | nier. By Richard | Hovey. | [*laurel wreath design*] | Published by the Author, at | Washington, | A. D. MDCCCLXXXIX.

COLLATION: Pamphlet; 18 leaves, except for title page printed on one side only; ff. [1], 2-16, [17-18]. Leaf measures 7⅜" x 5¼", all four edges trimmed. Printed on white wove paper, watermarked: Jos. EICHBAUM | AND CO. | PITTSBURGH

PAGINATION: F. [1], title; verso, copyright notice; ff. 2-[17], text, versos blank; f. [18], blank, verso blank.

BINDING: Pearl gray paper cover stock, embossed with all-over pattern in blind on outside of sheet; one sheet forms front cover and one the back cover; punched at side and tied with green moire ribbon, picot edged. Front cover printed in blue: *THE LAUREL.* Back and inside covers blank.

NOTES: Entered for copyright December 19, 1889; copies received at Copyright Office January 3, 1890.

In addition to several copies as described above, the Dartmouth collection includes one copy which has a sheet of marbleized paper inserted between the front cover and title page, and which is tied with a green satin ribbon. It bears the following annotation by its former owner, Curtis Hidden Page: "Given me by Hovey in New York, about 1897."

[1891] Launcelot and Guenevere

LAUNCELOT AND | GUENEVERE | *A POEM IN DRAMAS* | BY | RICHARD HOVEY | NEW YORK | UNITED STATES BOOK COMPANY | SUCCESSORS TO | JOHN W. LOVELL COMPANY | 142 TO 150 WORTH STREET

COLLATION: [1]⁸, 2-16⁸, 17⁴; 132 leaves; pp. [1-9], 10-263, [264]. Leaf measures 7⅜" x 4⅞", top edge gilt, all edges trimmed. Printed on white laid paper, no watermark.

PAGINATION: End paper; p. [1], false title; p. [2], blank; p. [3], title; p. [4], copyright notice with date 1891; p. [5], table of contents; p. [6], blank; p. [7], divisional fly title: DEDICATION.; p. [8], blank; pp. [9]-263, text; p. [264], blank; end paper. [Note: Divisional fly titles with versos blank also appear on pp. [21] and [89].]

BINDING: Maroon mesh cloth. Front cover has title in self-cloth within a gilt-stamped panel: LAUNCELOT | AND GUENEVERE [*as part of a decorative design showing hearts and a whirlpool, and within the upper of two panels formed by a gilt-stamped, single-rule border and cross-bar; at the bottom of the lower panel is stamped, also in gilt:]* RICHARD HOVEY Spine gilt-stamped: LAUNCELOT | AND | GUENEVERE | [*horizontal rule*] | *RICHARD* | *HOVEY* | *LOVELL* Back cover blank.

CONTENTS: The text has three parts, entitled as follows: Dedication, The Quest of Merlin: A Prelude, The Marriage of Guenevere: A Tragedy.

NOTES: Entered for copyright August 13, 1891; copies received at Copyright Office December 26, 1891.

The earliest dated author's inscription among the first editions in the Dartmouth collection is December 25, 1891.

Reviewed in the Washington *Post*, December 20, 1891.

"The Quest of Merlin" and "The Marriage of Guenevere," which comprise the two poetic dramas of this volume, were subsequently published as separate books in 1898 and 1895 respectively.

1893 Seaward

SEAWARD [*in orange*] | *AN ELEGY ON THE DEATH OF* | *THOMAS WILLIAM PARSONS* | BY RICHARD HOVEY | [*ornament in orange*] | BOSTON | D. LOTHROP COMPANY | 1893

COLLATION: [Unsigned: 1-7⁴]; 28 leaves; unnumbered. Leaf measures $7^{15}/_{16}''$ x $5^{13}/_{16}''$, top edge gilt, other edges untrimmed. Printed on white laid paper, no watermark.

PAGINATION: End paper; pp. [1-2], blank; frontispiece portrait of T. W. Parsons, with tissue guard, *inserted;* p. [3], title; p. [4], copyright notice; p. [5], one-line quotation from Dante; p. [6], blank; p. [7], three-line quotation from Emerson and four-line quotation from Parsons; p. [8], blank; p. [9], decorative half title; p. [10], blank; pp. [11-33], text; p. [34], blank; p. [35], fly title: NOTES; p. [36], blank; pp. [37-42], text of notes; p. [43], fly title: A STUDY; p. [44], blank; pp. [45-56], text of critical study of Parsons by Hovey; end paper.
[Note: The first line of each page of the poem has an ornate initial letter in orange.]

BINDING: Green or gray mesh cloth. Front cover gilt-stamped:

SEAWARD | [*within a gilt-stamped, single-rule box:*] An elegy on | the death of | [*ornament ranging the height of the foregoing two lines*] Thomas William Parsons   Spine gilt-stamped with a decorative design containing the word: SEAWARD [*reads down*].   Back cover blank.
[Note: Three binding states have been noted within the Dartmouth collection, differentiated by the color of cloth: dark green, dark gray, and light green.   It seems probable that no priority exists among these variants and that they were all issued concurrently.   The Library of Congress reports that their copyright deposit copy, which was received on May 3, 1893, is in light green cloth.   Among Dartmouth's copies that are inscribed and dated by the author, the earliest is in dark green cloth (May 11, 1893), while of three copies dated May 18, two are in dark green and one in dark gray.   A copy on deposit at Dartmouth which was inscribed by Hovey for his wife and dated May 4 is in dark gray cloth.]

NOTES: Entered for copyright May 3, 1893.

1894 Songs from Vagabondia

SONGS | FROM | VAGABONDIA | BLISS CARMAN | RICH-ARD HOVEY | DESIGNS BY | TOM B METEYARD | [*large Copeland and Day publisher's device*] | BOSTON COPELAND AND DAY | LONDON | ELKIN MATHEWS AND JOHN LANE | M DCCC XCIV

COLLATION: [Unsigned: 1^6, $2-4^8$, 5^6]; 36 leaves; pp. [i-xii], 1-54, [55-60].   Leaf measures 6¾" x 4¼", all edges untrimmed.   Printed on white laid paper, no watermark.
[Note: A blank binder's leaf is present in front of the first signature, with a corresponding one at the end of the book following the final signature.]

PAGINATION: Decorative end paper; binder's leaf; pp. [i-ii], blank; p. [iii], false title; p. [iv], blank; p. [v], statement of limitation: *This edition is limited to 750 copies.*; p. [vi], blank; p. [vii], title; p. [viii], copyright notice; p. [ix], dedication to H.F.H.; p. [x], blank; p. [xi], table of contents; p. [xii], blank; pp. 1-[55], text; p. [56], blank; p. [57], colophon, indicating the book was printed by John Wilson and Son at the University Press, Cambridge, [Mass.] during the summer of 1894; pp. [58-60], blank; binder's leaf; decorative end paper.
[Note: Front end paper is decorated with a design depicting ships and

a wharf, with a panel containing five lines of text. Back end paper decorated with design depicting trees and water, with a panel containing ten lines of text.]

BINDING: Tan boards. Front cover printed in black: SONGS FROM | VAGABONDIA | [*circular design featuring the heads of Meteyard, Carman, and Hovey*] | BLISS CARMAN | RICHARD HOVEY Spine printed in black: SONGS FROM VAGABONDIA [*reads up*]. Back cover blank.

CONTENTS: Of the thirty-three poems included, Bliss Carman has indicated in one of the first-edition copies in the Dartmouth collection, and as is substantiated by printed identifications in later editions, that fourteen are his and nineteen are by Hovey. The following are ascribed to Hovey's authorship: Vagabondia, Evening on the Potomac, The Faun, Down the Songo, The Wander-Lovers, Discovery, A Song by the Shore, A Hill Song, At Sea, Isabel, Contemporaries, A Toast, The Kavanagh, The Buccaneers, The Outlaw, The King's Son, Laurana's Song, Launa Dee, Comrades.

NOTES: Entered for copyright July 28, 1894; copies received at Copyright Office September 17, 1894. Edition statements in subsequent editions also indicate that the first edition was published in September.

A limited edition was also issued, differing from the regular one in the size of its pages, in its collation which is [Unsigned: 1^6, 2-8^4, 9^2] with blank binder's leaves present as noted above, and in the substitution of the following statement of limitation for that quoted above: THIS EDITION OF SONGS FROM VAGABONDIA, ON | ENGLISH HAND-MADE PAPER, IS LIMITED TO | SIXTY COPIES, OF WHICH FIFTY ONLY ARE | FOR SALE. THIS IS NUMBER............ Dartmouth has an unbound set of the sheets for this form of the book.

The title page of the first English edition differs from that of the American edition only in that the names of the two publishers appear in reverse order in the imprint and U.S.A. has been rubber-stamped in front of the date. The same rubber-stamping has been added following the colophon on p. [57]. Dartmouth's copy also has a label printed in red and tipped in on the initial leaf of the first signature (following the blank binder's leaf) reading: This book is now supplied by | ELKIN MATHEWS | VIGO ST., LONDON. | *October,* 1894. [*all of the foregoing within a single-rule border*].

The book went into a number of editions or printings. The last one in the Dartmouth collection is the "Thirteenth edition (750 copies) May, 1916". It also lists the dates and sizes of each of the preceding editions, showing that in all, over the twenty-two year period, 9,550 copies had been published. During the course of time Small, Maynard and Company succeeded Copeland and Day as publisher of the work.

Also present is a boxed set of the three *Vagabondia* books, issued by Small, Maynard in 1903 in limp suede. The copy of *Songs* in this set is the "Seventh edition (750 copies) November, 1903".

In 1935 Dodd, Mead & Company published *Songs from Vagabondia and More Songs from Vagabondia*, the two collections being together in a one-volume edition, completely reset.

1894 The Plays of Maurice Maeterlinck

THE PLAYS | OF | Maurice Maeterlinck | PRINCESS MALEINE · THE INTRUDER | THE BLIND · THE SEVEN | PRINCESSES | TRANSLATED BY | RICHARD HOVEY | CHICAGO | STONE & KIMBALL | MDCCCXCIV [*the foregoing overprinted in black on a tree design printed in green*]

COLLATION: [*]⁴, [1]⁸, 2-23⁸, 24²; 190 leaves; pp. [i-viii], [1-3], 4-369, [370-372]. Leaf measures 6¾" x 4¼", top edge gilt, other edges untrimmed. Printed on white laid paper, watermarked: Stone & Kimball | Chicago.
[Note: In all copies examined there is a blank leaf before the first signature, but without a corresponding binder's leaf after the final signature. The final signature is tipped in.]

PAGINATION: End paper; binder's leaf; p. [i], false title; p. [ii], blank; p. [iii], title; p. [iv], copyright notice; p. [v], statement of limitation: THIS FIRST EDITION ON SMALL | PAPER IS LIMITED TO SIX HUN- | DRED COPIES | *Stone & Kimball;* p. [vi], blank; p. [vii], table of contents; p. [viii], blank; p. [1], divisional fly title for introduction by Hovey: Modern Symbolism | and | Maurice Maeterlinck.; p. [2], blank; pp. [3]-11, text of introduction; p. [12], blank; p. [13], divisional fly title for first play; p. [14], blank; p. [15], list of characters; p. [16], blank; pp. [17]-369, text; p. [370], blank; p. [371], colophon, indicating the book was printed by John Wilson and Son at the University Press in Cambridge, [Mass.]

during September, 1894; p. [372], blank; end paper.
[Note: Divisional fly titles with versos blank also appear on pp. [209], [261], and [321], and lists of characters with versos blank on pp. [211], [263], and [323]. The false title, in addition to bearing the title of the book, identifies the volume as part of The Green Tree Library.]

BINDING: Light green mesh cloth. Front cover, spine, and back cover stamped in green with over-all tree design and overprinted with vertical lines stamped in purple. Front and back covers have series title stamped in gilt within a panel formed by a purple-stamped border on three sides: THE | GREEN | TREE | LIBRARY | [*ornament*]. Spine gilt-stamped, within a panel formed by purple-stamped horizontal rules at top and bottom: THE | PLAYS | OF | MAURICE | MAETERLINCK | [*horizontal rule*] | RICHARD | HOVEY

CONTENTS: In addition to the introduction, the volume is comprised of four plays: Princess Maleine, The Intruder, The Blind, The Seven Princesses.

NOTES: Entered for copyright February 22, 1895; copies received at Copyright Office December 10, 1894.

It is possible, judging by the publisher's statement on p. [v], that a large paper edition or issue was also published, but no copy is found within the Dartmouth collection.

Dartmouth's first edition copy contains a manuscript note in the hand of Prof. Harold Goddard Rugg reading: "A second edition of 500 copies issued in 1895".

Copies are present of the 1906 Duffield & Company edition and reissue of 1908, evidently published at the same time as new editions of *Plays . . . Second Series*. These appear to have been printed from the same type setting or plates as the first edition, but with the substitution of new title pages and the incorporation of some changes in the front matter. There are also some differences in features of the bindings as contrasted with those of the first edition.

Dartmouth's holdings also include volumes of the Dodd, Mead and Company editions of the works of Maeterlinck. One volume is composed of Hovey's translations of "The Intruder," "The Blind," and "The Seven Princesses" from *Plays . . .* and "The Death of Tintagiles" from *Plays . . . Second Series*. Another volume is devoted to his translation of "Princess Maleine." Both were published in 1911.

Sidney Kramer in *A History of Stone and Kimball* (Chicago, 1940) indicates that *Plays* . . . and *Plays* . . . *Second Series* (Kramer #32 and #70) were both reissued by Herbert S. Stone & Co. before being transferred to Duffield.

1895 The Marriage of Guenevere

THE MARRIAGE OF GUENEVERE | A TRAGEDY BY RICHARD HOVEY | [*publisher's device*] | CHICAGO | STONE & KIMBALL | MDCCCXCV

COLLATION: [1]², 2-12⁸ (signed on seventh leaf), [13]²; 92 leaves; pp. [1-9], 10-179, [180-184]. Leaf measures 7⅜" x 4¾", top edge gilt, other edges untrimmed. Printed on white laid paper, watermarked: Stone & Kimball | Chicago.
[Note: The first and last signatures are tipped in.]

PAGINATION: End paper; p. [1], false title; p. [2], blank; p. [3], title; p. [4], copyright notice; p. [5], half title; p. [6], blank; p. [7], list of characters; p. [8], blank; pp. [9]-179, text; p. [180], blank; p. [181], colophon; pp. [182-184], blank; end paper.
[Note: The book is identified on the false title as a component part of *"Launcelot and Guenevere: A Poem in Dramas."*]

BINDING: Light green mesh cloth. Front and back covers stamped in purple with the same design: over-all pattern formed by two dragons intertwined, a sword pointing downward dividing the design vertically into two identical halves; with a rectangular, single-line bordered panel in the top center of the covers, containing the text: THE · MARRIAGE · OF | GUENEVERE [*followed by two lines ranging in combined height approximately equal to the preceding word:*] BY RICHARD | [*ornament*] HOVEY [*ornament*]. Spine purple-stamped: THE | MARRIAGE | OF | GUENEVERE | [*typographic leaf*] | RICHARD HOVEY | STONE | AND | KIMBALL

NOTES: Entered for copyright September 5, 1895; copies received at Copyright Office on that date.

This is apparently the first separate edition of this work, it, together with "The Quest of Merlin" and the poem "Dedication," having been published in 1891 in the book entitled *Launcelot and Guenevere: A Poem in Dramas.* The text pages are printed from the same type setting or plates as in that volume, but with some changes made within the text and with different signatures and page numbers. *The*

Marriage of Guenevere was also subsequently republished making use of the same type setting or plates for the text (but with slight variations of certain typographic elements) and bound in a style to match the other volumes of this series as *Launcelot and Guenevere* came to have additional published parts. Dartmouth has copies of Small, Maynard and Company issuances of the work dated 1898 and 1900 and a Duffield and Company edition in green cloth, dated 1907.

Kramer (*op. cit.*) indicates that *The Marriage of Guenevere* (Kramer #48) was reissued by Herbert S. Stone & Co. in 1897 using sheets of the Stone & Kimball edition.

1896 The Plays of Maurice Maeterlinck — Second Series

THE PLAYS | OF | Maurice Maeterlinck | SECOND SERIES | ALLADINE AND PALOMIDES · PÉL- | LÉAS AND MÉLI-SANDE · HOME · | THE DEATH OF TINTAGILES | TRANSLATED BY | RICHARD HOVEY | CHICAGO | STONE & KIMBALL | MDCCCXCVI [*the foregoing overprinted in black on a tree design printed in green*]

COLLATION: [*]⁸ (*1 + *2.3), 1-15⁸; 128 leaves; pp. [i-ix], x-xv, [xvi], [1-5], 6-235, [236-240]. Leaf measures 6⅝" x 4¼", top edge gilt, other edges untrimmed. Printed on white laid paper, watermarked: Stone & Kimball | Chicago.
[Note: As noted in the collation formula above, the first signature is irregularly gathered in such a manner that the conjugate leaves are *1.8, 2.3, 4.7, 5.6 — *2.3 being tipped in between *1 and *4.]

PAGINATION: End paper; pp. [i-ii], blank; p. [iii], false title; p. [iv], blank; p. [v], title; p. [vi], copyright notice; p. [vii], table of contents; p. [viii], blank; pp. [ix]-xv, preface by Maeterlinck in French; p. [xvi], blank; p. [1], divisional fly title for first play; p. [2], blank; p. [3], list of characters; p. [4], blank; pp. [5]-235, text; p. [236], blank; p. [237], colophon, indicating the book was printed by John Wilson and Son at the University Press in Cambridge, [Mass.] during March, 1896; pp. [238-240], blank; end paper.
[Note: Divisional fly titles with versos blank also appear on pp. [57], [163], and [193], and lists of characters with versos blank on pp. [59], [165], and [195]. The false title, in addition to bearing the title of the book, identifies the volume as part of The Green Tree Library.]

BINDING: Binding particulars correspond precisely to those of the first edition of *The Plays of Maurice Maeterlinck,* except that following the author's name on the spine is added, stamped in gilt: [*horizontal rule*] | SECOND | SERIES Also, in the lower right-hand corner of the paste-down end paper of the back cover is stamped in black: BOSTON BOOKBINDING CO.

CONTENTS: In addition to the preface, the volume is comprised of four plays: Alladine and Palomides, Pélléas and Mélisande, Home, The Death of Tintagiles.

NOTES: Entered for copyright July 29, 1896; copies received at Copyright Office June 17, 1896.

Earliest author's inscription in the Dartmouth collection is in the Edmund Clarence Stedman copy, dated 23 June 1896.

As indicated in the notes for the first edition of *The Plays of Maurice Maeterlinck,* Duffield & Company published editions of *Plays . . .* and *Plays . . . Second Series* in 1906 and reissues of both 1908, according to the evidence of existing copies at Dartmouth. (See notes under *Plays . . . ,* 1894.)

1896 More Songs from Vagabondia

MORE SONGS | FROM | VAGABONDIA | BLISS CARMAN | RICHARD HOVEY | DESIGNS BY | TOM B METEYARD | [*large Copeland and Day publisher's device*] | BOSTON COPELAND AND DAY | LONDON ELKIN MATHEWS | M DCCC XCVI

COLLATION: [Unsigned: 1^4, $2\text{-}5^8$, 6^4, 7^2]; 42 leaves; pp. [i-vi], vii-viii, 1-72, [73-76]. Leaf measures 6¾" x 4¼", all edges untrimmed. Printed on white laid paper, no watermark.

[Note: A gathering of four blank binder's leaves is present in front of the first signature, with a corresponding one at the end of the book following the final signature.]

PAGINATION: Decorative end paper; four binder's leaves, as described above; p. [i], false title; p. [ii], blank; p. [iii], title; p. [iv], copyright notice; p. [v], dedication to M.G.M.; p. [vi], blank; pp. vii-viii, table of contents; pp. 1-72, text; p. [73], colophon, indicating the book was printed by John Wilson and Son at the University Press, Cambridge, Massachusetts, during October, 1896; pp. [74-76], blank; four binder's leaves, as described above; decorative end paper.

[Note: Front end paper is decorated with a design depicting a man in a canoe floating in a stream, with a panel containing ten lines of text. Back end paper decorated with design depicting sky, hills, and a man in the foreground on either side, with a panel containing nine lines of text.]

BINDING: Tan boards. Front cover printed in black: MORE SONGS | FROM | VAGABONDIA | [*circular design featuring the heads of Meteyard, Carman, and Hovey; the whole within a thick-thin-rule border*] | BLISS CARMAN | RICHARD HOVEY Spine printed in black: MORE SONGS FROM VAGABONDIA [*reads up*]. Back cover blank.

CONTENTS: According to printed identifications in later editions, twenty-nine of the book's fifty-four poems are by Hovey. Those ascribed to him are Jongleurs, The Wood-God, A Faun's Song, The Mocking-Bird, Karlene [that appearing on pp. 14-16; Carman also has a poem by the same title which is printed on pp. 16-20], Kavin Again, Across the Table, Barney McGee, The Sea Gypsy, Speech and Silence, Secrets, A Stein Song, In a Silence, The Bather, Nocturne: In Anjou, Nocturne: In Provence, June Night in Washington, A Song for Marna, September Woodlands, Three of a Kind, Shakespeare Himself, Verlaine, Distillation, A Friend's Wish, Hunting-Song, Mary of Marka, Premonition, Accident in Art, At the End of the Day. [Note: Although, as indicated above, "A Friend's Wish" is among the poems ascribed to Hovey in later editions, evidence existing within the Dartmouth collection suggests that the poem was not by Hovey but by Bliss Carman. Carman's authorship is substantiated by items contained within the Lorne Pierce Collection at Queen's University, Kingston, Ontario. The poem is there present in the last of four volumes of typewritten "fair copies" of poems written by Carman in Washington, D. C., from late in 1892 through early 1895. It appears, however, with the title "To C.W.S.," which at the time of book publication was used as a dedicatory sub-title. The Pierce Collection also includes a copy of *More Songs* . . . which bears on its false-title page the text of this poem in Carman's hand, followed by his signature.]

NOTES: Copies received at Copyright Office November 27, 1896; but no copyright entry made until three years later at the time of a subsequent deposit.

Edition notices in subsequent editions indicate that the first edition consisted of 750 copies.

A limited edition was also issued, differing from the regular one in the size of its pages, its collation which is [Unsigned: 1-10⁴, 11²] with blank binder's leaves present as noted above, the deletion from the imprint of the line identifying the English publisher, and the fact that a statement of limitation reading as follows replaces the colophon referred to above: THIS LARGE PAPER EDITION OF MORE SONGS | FROM VAGABONDIA IS LIMITED TO SIXTY | COPIES, OF WHICH FIFTY ONLY ARE FOR SALE

The book went into a number of editions or printings. The last one in the Dartmouth collection is the "Tenth Edition (750 copies) May, 1916." It also lists the dates and sizes of each of the preceding editions, showing that in the twenty year period 7,550 copies had been published. With the third edition (November, 1899), Small, Maynard and Company succeeded Copeland and Day as publisher of the work. The Library of Congress has a copy of a twelfth edition, published by Dodd, Mead & Company, which indicates that both the eleventh and twelfth editions (issued in January, 1924, and June, 1928, respectively) consisted of 500 copies each.

Also present is a boxed set of the three *Vagabondia* books, issued in 1903 in limp suede. The copy of *More Songs . . .* in this set is of the "Fifth edition (750 copies) November, 1903."

In 1935 Dodd, Mead & Company published *Songs from Vagabondia and More Songs from Vagabondia,* the two collections being together in a one-volume edition, completely reset.

1898 The Birth of Galahad

THE | BIRTH · OF | GALAHAD | RICHARD · HOVEY | [*large publisher's device*] | BOSTON | SMALL · MAYNARD · AND · COMPANY | MDCCCXCVIII

COLLATION: [*]², (plus one inserted leaf), [1]⁸, 2-7⁸, 8⁶; 65 leaves; pp. [i-vi], [1], 2-124. Leaf measures 6¾" x 4⅜", all edges trimmed and stained tan. Printed on white laid paper, no watermark. [Note: Copies are present in which the first signature ([*]) and the inserted leaf are side-stitched together before being tipped in. In other copies these elements are tipped in without being stitched together. From the dates of inscriptions in certain of the Dartmouth copies, as well as from the nature of the copyright copy in the Library of Congress collections, it appears that copies of the former class may have priority of issue.]

PAGINATION: End paper; pp. [i-ii], blank; p. [iii], false title; p. [iv], publisher's advertisement in box listing three books; p. [v], *insert,* title; p. [vi], *verso of insert,* copyright notice; p. [1], half title; p. 2, list of characters; pp. 3-124, text; end paper.
[Note: The book is identified on the false title as part three of *"Launce-lot and Guenevere: A Poem in Dramas."*]

BINDING: Tan boards with white vellum shelfback. Front and back covers blank. Spine heavily stamped in gilt: [*a border around the entire spine and divided by crossbars into panels for ornamental designs and text; the chief feature of the decoration is a sword pointing down-ward; the text reads:*] THE | BIR | TH | OF | GAL- | AHAD | Richard | Hovey | 1898·Small | Maynard | & Company

NOTES: Entered for copyright May 31, 1898; copies received at Copyright Office June 11 and 13, 1898.
Dartmouth also has copies of the book as reissued in 1900 by Small, Maynard and in 1907 by Duffield & Company. The latter is in green cloth. In both, the text is printed from the same type setting or plates as the first edition, with some variations of typographic elements.

1898 The Quest of Merlin

THE | QUEST · OF | MERLIN | RICHARD · HOVEY | [*large publisher's device*] | BOSTON | SMALL · MAYNARD · AND · COMPANY | MDCCCXCVIII

COLLATION: [Unsigned: 1^2, (plus one inserted leaf), 2-6^8]; 43 leaves; pp. [i-vi], [1-2], 3-80. Leaf measures 6¾" x 4⅜", all edges trimmed and stained tan. Printed on white laid paper, no water-mark.
[Note: The first signature is side-stitched to the inserted leaf, and the gathering is tipped in. The final signature is followed by two gather-ings of blank binder's leaves; the first consists of two leaves (tipped in), the other of four leaves (sewn in), the final leaf of the latter being pasted down as the lining paper for the back cover.]

PAGINATION: End paper; pp. [i-ii], blank; p. [iii], false title; p. [iv], publisher's advertisement in box listing three books; p. [v], *insert,* title; p. [vi], *verso of insert,* copyright notice; p. [1], half title; p. [2], list of characters; pp. 3-80, text; binder's leaves, as described above.

[Note: The book is identified on the false title as part one of "*Launce-lot and Guenevere: A Poem in Dramas.*"]

BINDING: Binding particulars correspond precisely to those of *The Birth of Galahad*, except that the text of the spine reads as follows: THE | Q [*this is an ornamental letter ranging in height equal to that of the three lines formed by the syllables of the remainder of this word and the word following*] VE | ST | OF | MER- | LIN | Richard Hovey | 1898 · Small | Maynard | & Company

NOTES: Copies received at Copyright Office June 11, 1898. This is apparently the first separate edition of this work, it, together with *The Marriage of Guenevere* and the poem "Dedication," having been published in 1891 in the book entitled *Launcelot and Guenevere: A Poem in Dramas*. The text pages are printed from the same type setting or plates as in that work, but with some changes made within the text and different page numbers supplied, and without the running heads and signatures.

A copy is present within the Dartmouth collection which corresponds to the first edition as described above except that it does not have the gatherings of binder's leaves at the end. It is apparently of a subsequent issue.

Dartmouth also has copies of the book as reissued in 1901 by Small, Maynard and in 1907 by Duffield & Company. The latter is in green cloth.

1898 Along the Trail

ALONG | THE TRAIL | A BOOK OF LYRICS | BY RICH-ARD HOVEY | [*large publisher's device in brown*] | BOSTON | SMALL, MAYNARD | AND COMPANY | 1898

COLLATION: [*]², [**]⁴, [1]⁸, 2-7⁸, 8²; 64 leaves; pp. [2], [i-viii], ix-x, [1-2], 3-115, [116]. Leaf measures 6¾" x 4¼", all edges trimmed and stained tan. Printed on white laid paper, no water-mark.
[Note: The first and last signatures are tipped in.]

PAGINATION: End paper; false title, with publisher's advertisement in box listing three books on verso; p. [i], title; p. [ii], copyright notice; p. [iii], acknowledgments; p. [iv], blank; p. [v], dedication: TO MY MOTHER; p. [vi], blank; p. [vii], half title; p. [viii],

blank; pp. ix-x, table of contents; p. [1], divisional fly title, identifying
first section of poetry: I; p. [2], blank; pp. 3-115, text; p. [116],
blank; end paper.
[Note: Divisional fly titles with versos blank also appear on pp. 19, 45,
81, and 105.]

BINDING: Brown grained cloth. Front cover gilt-stamped: [*within
the middle of three panels:*] ALONG · THE | TRAIL [*author's
name on two lines which together range in height equal to the word
preceding:*] RICHARD | HOVEY [*panels above and below the title
panel contain design of continuing trumpets; lower panel bearing the
initials B and G in the left and right bottom corners; the three panels
are inclosed within a double-rule border; maple leaf ornaments oppo-
site each corner, outside of border; all the foregoing within a single-
rule border*]. Spine gilt-stamped: [*within a single-rule border divided
into panels by cross-rules, and containing the continuing design of a
single trumpet pointing upward*] ALONG | THE [*leaf ornament*] |
TRAIL | HOVEY | 1898 · SMALL | MAYNARD | & COM-
PANY Back cover blank.

CONTENTS: Fifty-nine poems are included: Part I: The Word of
the Lord from Havana, The Call of the Bugles, Unmanifest Destiny,
America. Part II: Dead, Forgiven, Love and Change, Launcelot and
Gawaine, My Lady's Soul, After Business Hours, The Thought of
Her, Love in the Winds, Two and Fate, Faith and Fate, Chansons
de Rosemonde, A Wanderer, The Love of a Boy—Yesterday, The
Love of a Boy—To-day, An Off-Shore Villanelle, To Lesbia, Noc-
turne, The Two Lovers, Apparition, Summer Sadness, "Sprung from
the Vase's Bulge and Leap", "Balmy with Years, what Silken Ply",
Herodias. Part III: Comrades, One Leaf More, Spring, Men of
Dartmouth, The Old Pine, In Memoriam. (A.H.Q.), Dartmouth
Ode, A Winter Thought of Dartmouth in Manhattan, Our Liege
Lady—Dartmouth, Hanover Winter-Song. Part IV: The Faun, Swal-
low Song, A Health. To E.C.S., The Dramatist. To M.K., Del-
sarte, World and Poet, The South, A Caprice of Ogarow. To M.P.,
Thomas William Parsons, Beethoven's Third Symphony, August, A
Ballade of Mysteries, The Shadows, Angro-mainyus, Immanence,
Transcendence, Visitation, In Excelsis, The Veiled Lady, The Mes-
senger, Henry George. Part V: Benzaquen: A Fragment.

NOTES: Entered for copyright December 12, 1898; copies received at Copyright Office on that date. Subsequent editions also carry notes indicating that the first edition was published in December, 1898.

Dartmouth has a second edition published in March, 1899, also issued by Small, Maynard; and a fourth edition published by Duffield and Company. The latter carries 1907 on the title page, but the edition notice indicates that the fourth edition was in August, 1908, and that it was preceded by a third edition in October, 1903.

[1899] Taliesin

TALIESIN | A · MASQUE | RICHARD · HOVEY | [*large publisher's device*] | BOSTON | SMALL · MAYNARD · AND · COMPANY | MDCCCC

COLLATION: [1]⁴, (plus one inserted leaf following 11), [2-8]⁴; 33 leaves; pp. [i-iv], [1], 2-58, [59-62]. Leaf measures 6¾" x 4¼", all edges trimmed and stained tan. Printed on white wove paper, no watermark.
[Note: Signed for gatherings of eight leaves, rather than four, on what would be the second leaf of such signatures, except for the second, which is unsigned.]

PAGINATION: End paper; p. [i], false title; p. [ii], publisher's advertisement in a box listing seven books; p. [iii], *insert*, title; p. [iv], *verso of insert*, copyright notice; p. [1], half title; p. 2, list of characters; pp. 3-58, text; pp. [59-62], blank; end paper.
[Note: The book is identified on the false title as part four of *"Launcelot and Guenevere: A Poem in Dramas."*]

BINDING: Binding particulars correspond precisely to those of *The Birth of Galahad* except that the text of the spine reads as follows: TA- | LIE- | SIN | Richard | Hovey | 1900 · Small | Maynard | & Company

NOTES: Although the imprint on the title page carries the year 1900, the Copyright Office has record of four copyright entries for the work (May 18 and 23 and October 23 and 25) all in 1899. No record exists of the receipt of copies for any but the October 23, entry, which unlike the other entries is specifically identified as volume four of *Launcelot and Guenevere.* Deposit copies for this entry were received December 19, 1899. One of Dartmouth's copies bears an author's presentation inscription dated 21 December 1899.

The Dartmouth collection includes a subsequent printing of the first edition the gathering scheme of which is different and which carries a note on p. [59]: *Your attention is invited to | the notices of Mr. Hovey's | books on the following pages* This is followed by seven pages of advertising matter.

Dartmouth also has a copy in green cloth published by Duffield and Company in 1914.

BOOKS POSTHUMOUSLY PUBLISHED

[1900] Last Songs From Vagabondia

LAST SONGS | FROM | VAGABONDIA | BLISS CARMAN | RICHARD HOVEY | DESIGNS BY | TOM B METEYARD | [*publisher's device*] | BOSTON | SMALL, MAYNARD AND COMPANY | M DCCCC I

COLLATION: [Unsigned: 1⁴, 2-6⁸]; 44 leaves; pp. [i-iv], v-vi, 1-79, [80-82]. Leaf measures 6¾" x 4¼", all edges untrimmed. Printed on white wove paper, no watermark.

PAGINATION: Decorative end paper; p. [i], false title; p. [ii], publisher's advertisement in box listing a total of fifteen books; p. [iii], title; p. [iv], copyright notice; pp. v-vi, table of contents; pp. 1-79, text; p. [80], blank; p. [81], colophon, indicating the book was printed by John Wilson and Son at the University Press, Cambridge, [Mass.] during the autumn of 1900; p. [82], blank; decorative end paper. [Note: Front end paper is decorated with a design depicting sky, an expanse of land, and a building in the foreground, with a panel containing nine lines of text. Back end paper decorated with design depicting ocean waves, with a panel containing eight lines of text.]

BINDING: Tan boards. Front cover printed in black: LAST SONGS | FROM | VAGABONDIA | [*circular design featuring the heads of Meteyard, Carman, and Hovey*] | BLISS CARMAN | RICHARD HOVEY Spine printed in black: LAST SONGS FROM VAGABONDIA [*reads up*]. Back cover blank.

CONTENTS: The table of contents supplies the initials of the author of each poem after each title listed, ascribing twenty-five of the fifty-one poems to Hovey, twenty-five to Carman, with "The Adventurers" written jointly. Hovey's poems are: At the Crossroads, "At Last, O Death!", Day and Night, The Battle of Manila, The Open Door,

Japanese Love Song, "How Should Love Know?", Unforeseen, Child's Song, Harmonics, Ornithology, From the Cliff, Sea Sonnets, At a Summer Resort, New York, A Grotesque, When the Priest Left, The Gift of Art, To James Whitcomb Riley, To Rudyard Kipling, Her Valentine, Peace, A Lyric, Ten Commandments, Quatrains.

NOTES: Although the imprint on the title page carries the year 1901, the book was entered for copyright October 13, 1900, and copies were received at the Copyright Office December 10, 1900. A copy in the Dartmouth collection bears a note in the hand of the original owner stating that it was "bought on publication," December 24, 1900. Edition notices in subsequent editions also indicate that the first edition was published in December and that it consisted of 1,000 copies.

It is recorded that a limited, large paper edition of sixty copies was also issued, but no copy is present among Dartmouth's holdings.

The book went into a number of editions or printings. The last one in the Dartmouth collection is the "Seventh Edition (500 copies), May, 1916." It also lists the dates and sizes of each of the preceding editions, showing that in all 5,300 copies had been published.

Also present is a boxed set of the three *Vagabondia* books, issued in 1903 in limp suede. The copy of *Last Songs . . .* in this set is of the "Third Edition (750), November, 1903."

1907 The Holy Graal

THE | HOLY GRAAL | AND OTHER FRAGMENTS BY | RICHARD HOVEY | BEING THE UNCOMPLETED PARTS | OF THE ARTHURIAN DRAMAS | *Edited with Introduction and Notes by* | MRS. RICHARD HOVEY | *And a Preface by* | BLISS CARMAN | [*publisher's device*] | New York | DUFFIELD & COMPANY | 1907

COLLATION: [Unsigned: 1-8^8]; 64 leaves; pp. [1-4], 5, [6], 7-128. Leaf measures 6⅝" x 4⅛", all edges trimmed. Printed on white laid paper, no watermark.
[Note: The final signature is followed by a gathering of two leaves (tipped in) of publisher's advertisements.]

PAGINATION: End paper; p. [1], false title; p. [2], publisher's advertisement in box listing six books; p. [3], title; p. [4], copyright notice with statement: Published September, 1907; p. 5, table of contents; p. [6], blank; pp. 7-10, preface; pp. 11-20, introduction; p. 21, divisional fly title for first section of text; pp. 22-128, text; publisher's advertisements, as described above; end paper.

[Note: Divisional fly titles also appear on pp. [27], 67, 79, 89, and [117]. Most sections include lists of characters and pages of notes and digests. The book is identified on the false title as part five of "*Launcelot and Guenevere: A Poem in Dramas.*"]

BINDING: Green grained cloth. Front cover stamped in gilt: THE | HOLY · GRAAL | RICHARD · HOVEY Spine gilt-stamped: THE | HOLY | GRAAL | [*horizontal rule*] | HOVEY | DUFFIELD Back cover blank.

CONTENTS: In addition to the preface and introduction, the table of contents has entries for the following: Schema, The Holy Graal, Notes on the Holy Graal, Digest of the Holy Graal, Astolat, Notes on Astolat, Fata Morgana, Notes on Fata Morgana, King Arthur, Notes on King Arthur, Digest of King Arthur, Avalon, Notes on Avalon.

NOTES: Entered for copyright October 2, 1907; copies received at Copyright Office October 3, 1907.

1908 To the End of the Trail

TO THE | END OF THE TRAIL | RICHARD · HOVEY | *EDITED WITH NOTES BY* | *MRS. RICHARD HOVEY* | [*publisher's device*] | *NEW YORK* | DUFFIELD & COMPANY | *1908*

COLLATION: [Unsigned: 1^{10}, $2\text{-}10^{8}$]; 82 leaves; pp. [2], [i-vi], vii-ix, [x], [1-2], 3-148, [149-152]. Leaf measures 6⅞″ x 4⅛″, all edges trimmed. Printed on white laid paper, no watermark.

PAGINATION: End paper; false title, with publisher's advertisement in box listing six books on verso; frontispiece portrait of Hovey, *inserted*; p. [i] title; p. [ii], copyright notice; p. [iii], acknowledgments; p. [iv], blank; p. [v], editor's note; p. [vi], blank; pp. vii-ix, table of contents; p. [x], blank; p. [1], half title; p. [2], blank; pp. 3-148, text; pp. [149-152], publisher's advertisements; end paper. [Note: Divisional fly titles, bearing the number of each succeeding section of text, appear on pp. 41, 69, 93, 109, 131, and 141, with versos blank or carrying brief notes.]

BINDING: Green grained cloth, corresponding in style to the binding

of *The Holy Graal.* Front cover stamped in gilt: TO·THE·END |
OF·THE·TRAIL | RICHARD·HOVEY   Spine gilt-stamped: TO
THE | END | OF THE | TRAIL | [*horizontal rule*] | HOVEY |
DUFFIELD   Back cover blank.

CONTENTS: The table of contents lists the following: Part I: The
Laurel—an Ode, Seaward, A Vision of Parnassus.   Part II: Short
Beach, The Gypsy, The Orient, Mallarmé, Discovery, Père Am-
broise, A Lyric.   Part III: The Song of the Wind, Shakespeare, Mer-
En-Mut, The Lady of the Cape, Two Poets, Rebellion, A Patrician
Poet, Hymn for the Holy Day of St. Catherine of Alexandria.   Part
IV: (Translations from Maeterlinck:) Elle l'enchaîna dans une grotte,
Et s'il revenait un jour, Ils ont tué trois petites filles, Les filles aux
yeux bandés, Les trois sœurs aveugles, On est venu dire, Les sept filles
d'Orlamonde, Quand il est sorti, Vous avez allumé les lampes, J'ai
cherché trente ans—mes sœurs.   (Translations from Stephane Mall-
armé:) The Sigh, The Flowers, The Windows.   (Translations from
Paul Verlaine:) The Faun.   Part V: Don Juan—Canto XVII.   Part
VI: Parting, Kronos, To Prof. C. F. Richardson, A Youthful Poet
and His Critics, Dante Gabriel Rossetti, To Swinburne—I, To Swinburne—II, Per Aspera ad Astra, A Remnant Remaineth, Matthew
Arnold.   Part VII: Man and Craftsman, Models, The Last Love of
Gawaine, What Though You Love Me, Hurt Me, False Truth, Love
and Pity, Love's Silence, Au Seuil.

NOTES: Entered for copyright April 13, 1908; copies received at
Copyright Office on that date.

[1924] Dartmouth Lyrics

DARTMOUTH | LYRICS | BY | RICHARD HOVEY |
EDITED BY | EDWIN OSGOOD GROVER | [*publisher's de-
vice*] | BOSTON | SMALL, MAYNARD & COMPANY | PUB-
LISHERS

COLLATION: [Unsigned: 1-4⁸, 5⁶, 6-7⁸]; 54 leaves; pp. [i-vi],
vii-xiv, [1-2], 3-94. Leaf measures 7⅜″ x 4¹⁵⁄₁₆″, top edge stained
green, all edges trimmed.   Printed on white laid paper, no watermark.

PAGINATION: End paper; p. [i], false title; p. [ii], blank; p. [iii],
title; p. [iv], copyright notice; p. [v], dedication: TO | MEN OF
DARTMOUTH; p. [vi], blank; pp. vii-viii, foreword; pp. ix-x,
table of contents; pp. xi-xiv, introduction by Grover: RICHARD

HOVEY; p. [1], half title; p. [2], blank; pp. 3-81, text; pp. 82-87, autobiographical sketch by Hovey; pp. 88-94, notes on the poems: HISTORICAL NOTES; end paper.

BINDING: Green grained cloth. Front cover gilt-stamped: [*below a cloud and mountain design stamped in gilt and white:*] DART-MOUTH LYRICS | [*horizontal rule with blunted ends*] | RICH-ARD HOVEY Spine gilt-stamped: [*horizontal rule across top of spine*] | DARTMOUTH | LYRICS | HOVEY | SMALL | MAY-NARD | & COMPANY | [*horizontal rule across bottom of spine*]. Back cover blank.

CONTENTS: In addition to the foreword, introduction, autobiography, and notes, the table of contents lists the following poems; Men of Dartmouth, Comrades, Spring, Vagabondia, Hanover Winter Song, Eleazar Wheelock, Dartmouth Ode, To Prof. C. F. Richardson, One Leaf More, The Love of a Boy—Today, A Winter Thought of Dartmouth in Manhattan, The Old Pine, Day and Night, Our Liege Lady —Dartmouth, In Memoriam (A. H. Quint), Here's a Health to Thee—Roberts!, You Remind Me—Sweeting, Barney McGee, Hunting Song, World and Poet, My Love's Waitin', On the Hill, Dead, Wedded, Bohemia, Squab Flights, A Ballade of Mysteries, At the Club, Winter Beauty, Vita Nuova, Kronos, A Rose, Sonnets to Swinburne, College Days, Dante Gabriel Rossetti, The South, Lalage, Translation from The Anacreontea, John Keats, Sonnet (When We Are Dead), To a Friend, Philosophy.

NOTES: Entered for copyright February 25, 1924; copies received at Copyright Office April 4, 1924.

In 1938 a new edition of *Dartmouth Lyrics,* with an introduction by Prof. Francis Lane Childs, was published by Dartmouth College Publications. Only fifteen of the forty-two poems of the original edition were included, plus a new selection, a poem entitled "The Spirit of Dartmouth." The "Historical Notes" of the earlier work were not republished, nor was its other biographical or critical matter.

Works Consulted

A. BOOKS

ARCHER, WILLIAM. *Poets of the Younger Generation.* J. Lane: London and New York, 1902.

BRYAN, W. B. *A History of the National Capital.* 2 vols. New York: Macmillan, 1916.

CRAM, RALPH ADAMS. *My Life in Architecture.* Boston: Little, Brown and Co., 1936.

FORD, W. C., ed. *The Letters of Henry Adams.* Boston and New York: Houghton Mifflin, 1930.

GROVER, E. O., ed. *Dartmouth Lyrics.* Boston: Small, Maynard & Co., 1924.

[HOVEY.] DANIEL HOVEY ASSOCIATION. *The Hovy Book, Describing the English Ancestry and American Descendants of Daniel Hovey of Ipswich, Massachusetts.* . . . Haverhill, Mass.: L. R. Hovey, 1913.

HOVEY, RICHARD, *see* "A Bibliography of the First Editions of Books by Richard Hovey," pp. 229-250.

MACKAYE, PERCY. *Epoch: The Life of Steele MacKaye.* 2 vols. New York: Boni and Liveright, 1927.

MAETERLINCK, MAURICE. *The Blind, The Intruder,* trans. Mary Vielé. Washington, 1891.

————. *The Princess Maleine, The Intruder,* trans. Gerard Harry, preface by Hall Caine. London: Turner, 1892.

————. *Plays of,* trans. Richard Hovey. Chicago: Stone and Kimball, 1895.

POMEROY, E. M. *Sir Charles G. D. Roberts.* Toronto: The Ryerson Press, 1943.

PRATT, JULIUS W. *Expansionists of 1898*. Baltimore: Johns Hopkins Press, 1936.

REID, MARGARET J. C. *The Arthurian Legend*. Edinburgh: Oliver and Boyd, 1938.

SPOFFORD, JEREMIAH. *Spofford, Spafford—A Genealogical Record*. Boston: A. Mudge and Son, 1888.

STEDMAN, LAURA, and GEORGE M. GOULD. *Life and Letters of Edmund Clarence Stedman*. 2 vols. New York: Yard and Co., 1910.

TAUPIN, RENÉ. *L'Influence du symbolisme français sur la poésie Americaine de 1910 a 1920*. Paris: Champion, 1929.

WELLS, CAROLYN. *The Rest of My Life*. Philadelphia and New York: J. B. Lippincott, 1937.

B. ARTICLES

BAYLEY, EDWIN A. "Abstracts from the Address of E. A. Bayley at Memorial Service," *DAM*, XXXI (June, 1939), 16.

CARMAN, BLISS. "Richard Hovey, My Friend," *Criterion*, XXIII (April, 1900), 527.

———. "The Modern Athenian," Boston *Transcript*, August 29, 1896.

CLEAVES, F. P. "Richard Hovey,—Barnstormer!" *DAM*, XXI (March, 1929), 294-298.

HOVEY, RICHARD. At the Crossroads," *The Dartmouth Magazine*, XIX (May, 1905), 298-299.

Hovey, Richard. "Decadence or Renascence," *Time and the Hour*, Dec. 4, 1897.

———. "Delsarte and Poetry," *Independent*, XLIII (August 27, 1891), 1267.

———. "The Dying Century," *Dartmouth Literary Magazine*, II (Feb., 1888), 208-211.

———. "The Elements of Poetic Technique," I and II, *Independent*, XLVI (Sept. 27 and Oct. 4, 1894), 1241, 1275.

———. "Eleutheria. An Essay on the Growth of Democratic Ideas in English Poetry," *The Dartmouth Magazine*, XX (Jan., 1906), 95-140.

———. "Maeterlinck as a Prophet of Joy," *Bookman*, IX (March, 1899), 64.

———. "On the Threshold," *Independent*, XLIV (Nov. 3, 1892), 1546-1547.

———. "The Passing of Realism," *Independent*, XLVII (Aug. 22, 1895), 1125.

———. "Sub Jove Frigido," *Dartmouth Literary Monthly*, II (Feb., 1888), 218.

———. "The Technique of Poetry," I and II, *Independent*, XLIV (April 7 and 21, 1892), 473, 544.

———. "The Technique of Rhyme," *Independent*, XLV (Oct. 19, 1893), 1399.

McCallum, J. D. "The Apostle of Culture Meets America," *New England Quarterly*, II (July, 1929), 351-381.

Macdonald, Allan. "Charles Edward Hovey . . . " *DAM*, XXXIX (April, 1947), 21-23.

Marchand, Ernest. "Hovey's First Flight," *DAM*, XXXI (June, 1939), 15-16.

Matulka, Barbara. "Letters of Mallarmé and Maeterlinck to Richard Hovey, *Romantic Review*, XVIII (July-September, 1927), 232-237.

Page, Curtis Hidden. "The Plays and Poems of Richard Hovey," *Bookman*, VIII (Jan., 1899), 449.

Patterson, Walter B. "Reminiscences of Richard Hovey," *Dartmouth Literary Magazine*, XXIV (May, 1910), 223-225.

Quint, Wilder. "Richard Hovey in College," *The Dartmouth Magazine*, XIX (May, 1905), 293-297.

Stedman, E. C. "Just a Word about Hovey, and Several from Hovey," *The Dartmouth Magazine*, XIX (May, 1905), 300-307.

C. Magazines and Newspapers

Atlantic Monthly
Boston *Evening Record*
Boston *Home Journal*
Boston *Sunday Herald*
Boston *Traveller*
Chap Book
Cleveland *Plain Dealer*
Conservator
Criterion
Daily Tatler
Dalhousie Review
Dartmouth Literary Magazine
Dartmouth Literary Monthly
Harper's Magazine
Independent
Literary World

Nation
National Single Taxer
New York *Journal*
New York *Mail and Express*
New York *Morning Advertiser*
New York *World*
Philadelphia *Times*
Poet-Lore
Springfield *Republican*
The Dartmouth
Time and the Hour
To-Day
Town Topics
Washington *Post*
Worcester *Daily Spy*

D. UNPUBLISHED MATERIAL

Chronicles from the "Exercises of Class-Day of the Senior Class of Dartmouth College—Tuesday, June 23, 1885," DCA.

HOVEY, RICHARD. Letters in Davidson Collection, Yale University Library; and in DCA.

LEFFERT, HENRY. "Richard Hovey" (unpublished Ph. D. dissertation, New York University, 1929).

Index

in hotels, 46 f.; employed by Boston *Advertiser*, 47; super in Boston theater, 47 f.; attracted by Kenyon College post, 48; interest in Smithsonian job, 48; prepares "Songs and Monologues" volume, 48; pursued by King, 50; engaged to lecture by T. Davidson, 50; resemblance to Giotto's Dante, 50; brought to Concord by Kavanagh, 51; lectures on "Devil," 51; lectures on Goethe, 51; attracted to Milton's treatment of Satan, 51; defends Marlowe, 51; invited to Chicago by Mrs. Keene, 52; costume, 52; crowned by Lanier's widow, 52, 55; writes for *Independent*, 53, 74, 102; decides to write poetry, 56 f.; resolves on story of *Launcelot and Guenevere*, 56; attracted by consular position, 59 f.; describes self to Lindsay Smith, 60; meets Mrs. Russell, 61, 69-71; stage career, 66 f.; hangs Meteyard paintings, 68; poems accepted for *Independent* by Carman, 68; interviewed by Gilder, 69; writes to Swift on Mrs. Russell, 71; dislike of Newport, 72; sailings for England, 74, 100, 132, 219; sailings for America, 181 f., 223; protests Howells' review of Riley, 78; attracted by Arthurian legend, 81-84; plans Arthurian dramas, 84 f.; irritated by reception of Arthurian dramas, 96 f.; views Rossetti's painting, 100; an American abroad, 101; visits Stratford, 101; friendship with Perrys, 102, 113; anticipates Whittier's criticism, 103; aided by family, 103 f.; engaged by Fullerton, 104; his child born, 105; affair with Mrs. Russell concealed, 105 f.; characterizes France, 107; comments on England, 107, 155; introduced to Roberts, 108; dines with Wright, 113; request for paper on Parsons for *Atlantic*, 113; sought as literary editor by Ward, 113; visits Harte, Norton, Stedman, 113; joins Theatre of Arts and Letters, 115 f.; revises Clemmens' play, 116; poem commissioned by Psi Upsilon, 117 f., 181 f.; tells Mrs. Hovey of Mrs. Russell, 120; undertakes Nova Scotia outing, 120 f.; money

problems, 121 f., 164, 181, 209; upset by General Hovey's disapproval of Mrs. Russell, 122 f.; marriage, 124; desire for teaching position, 126 f.; lectures at Boston University, 127; reads *Vagabondia* at Alumni dinner, 127; asked to act part of Poe, 127; sends "Dartmouth Ode" to Tucker, 129 f.; talents commanded by Dartmouth College, 127 f., 131 n.; finds Boston distasteful, 131 f.; relationship with Sigurd, 151 f.; obscures birth of Julian Hovey, 152; writes *Seaward* circulars, 153; introduced to London society by Aïdé, 153; invited to visit Moschelles, 153; meets Leighton, Watts, 153; reworks "Temptation" for Aïdé, 153 f.; befriended by Lady Brooke, 154; entertained by Russell, 154; meets Beardsley, Blunt, John Davidson, Gosse, Meredith, Sharp, 155; translates Maeterlinck, 155, 156 f., 160, 162 f.; attends Maeterlinck, Ibsen plays, 159; praises Lugné-Poe's acting, 159; meets Maeterlinck, 159 f.; admires *Treasure of the Humble*, 160; visits Giverny, 164; reunited with Julian Hovey, 166 f.; attracted to Symbolism, 167; translates Mallarmé, 170, 172-175; characterizes Mme Mallarmé, 170 f.; friendship with Vielé-Griffin, 171 f., 176; poems published by *Magazin International*, 172, 172 n.; translates *Faun*, 178 n.; visits Bois, 180; meets Mrs. Vielé-Griffin, 180; meets Mme Dorien, 180; pays Baudy, 181; praises America, 183 f.; delivers "Spring," 186 f.; seeks position at Adelbert College, 187; in Nova Scotia with Carman, 188; contributes to *Daily Tatler*, 190 f.; seeks Central High School post, 192; studies Merrymount experiment, 193; plans comedy, 193 f.; friendship with Sandham, 193 f.; visits Meteyard, 194; visits Small, 194; relationship with wife, 194-197; nationalism of, 197 f.; espouses Henry George's program, 200; literary weekly suggested by Stedman, 209; attempts purchase of *Literary World*, 209 f.; honored by "Pewter Mugs," 210; at Barnard,